Lecture Notes of the Institute for Computer Sciences, Social Informatics and Telecommunications Engineering　421

More information about this series at https://link.springer.com/bookseries/8197

Walayat Hussain · Mian Ahmad Jan (Eds.)

IoT as a Service

7th EAI International Conference, IoTaaS 2021
Sydney, Australia, December 13–14, 2021
Proceedings

Editors
Walayat Hussain ⓘ
University of Technology Sydney
Sydney, NSW, Australia

Mian Ahmad Jan ⓘ
Abdul Wali Khan University
Mardan, Pakistan

ISSN 1867-8211   ISSN 1867-822X (electronic)
Lecture Notes of the Institute for Computer Sciences, Social Informatics
and Telecommunications Engineering
ISBN 978-3-030-95986-9   ISBN 978-3-030-95987-6 (eBook)
https://doi.org/10.1007/978-3-030-95987-6

This Springer imprint is published by the registered company Springer Nature Switzerland AG
The registered company address is: Gewerbestrasse 11, 6330 Cham, Switzerland

Preface

It is my great pleasure to introduce the proceedings of the seventh edition of the European Alliance for Innovation (EAI) International Conference on the Internet of Things (IoT) as a Service (IoTaaS 2021).

The Internet of Things (IoT) plays a vital role in the existing and future generation of information, communication, and applications. IoT is typically employed to improve the efficiency of computing and sensing and can be used in many scenarios. IoT combines with other leading technologies such as cloud, edge, AI, and Big Data analytics to make human lives and society comfortable. Hybrid technologies are attracting immense research interest and have found their presence in numerous applications such as healthcare, transportation, manufacturing, energy, automation, and many others.

EAI organised this international conference in collaboration with the University of Technology Sydney, Australia. IoTaaS 2021 aimed to bring together researchers, academicians, students, practitioners, and professionals from academia and industry interested in creating IoT-based services. The objective of the event was to provide an international forum where researchers could present existing, evolving, or novel ideas and share their views, fostering discussions and future collaborations among different stakeholders. The conference received 129 papers, and after a rigorous peer-review process, only 42% of the papers were accepted. The research contributors of this event came from across the globe, including Australia, China, New Zealand, the UK, Germany, Turkey, Egypt, Saudi Arabia, Pakistan, Kenya, and Iraq. These authors shared their original research and exchanged their ideas, including key research findings, and future research directions.

The technical program of IoTaaS 2021 consisted of 17 full papers in oral presentation sessions at the main conference tracks: Track 1 – Intelligent IoT Communication Solutions; Track 2 – Social Internet of Things: Security, and management; and Track 3 – Machine Learning Prediction and Recommendation in IoT. Aside from the high-quality technical paper presentations, the technical program also featured two keynote speeches given by Fethi Rabhi from the University of New South Wales, Australia, and Halit Hami OZ from Istanbul Gedik University, Turkey.

I want to thank Imrich Chlamtac for his continuous support and guidance. I want to thank all presenters and participants of this event who submitted their research work. We would like to express our sincere gratitude to the inspirational keynote speakers, Program Committee members, and anonymous reviewers for their time and energy to critically reviewed papers. I also want to thank all EAI staff members, particularly the conference manager, Lucia Sladeckova, who made this event possible.

I strongly believe that the IoTaaS conference provides a good forum for all researchers, developers, and practitioners to discuss all science and technology aspects relevant to smart communications.

June 2022   Walayat Hussain
                                                                            Mian Ahmad Jan

Organization

Steering Committee

Imrich Chlamtac   University of Trento, Italy

Organizing Committee

General Chair

Walayat Hussain   Victoria University, Melbourne, Australia & University of Technology Sydney, Sydney, Australia

General Co-chairs

Mian Ahmad Jan   Abdul Wali Khan University, Pakistan
Saqib Ali   Sultan Qaboos University, Oman
Honghao Gao   Shanghai University, China

TPC Chair and Co-chairs

José Maria Merigó   University of Technology Sydney, Australia
Asma Musabah Alkalbani   University of Technology and Applied Sciences, Oman
Asaf Varol   Maltepe University, Turkey

Sponsorship and Exhibit Chair

Honghao Gao   Shanghai University, China

Publicity and Social Media Chairs

Nausheen Saeed   Dalarna University, Sweden
Raheel Raza   Firat University, Turkey

Publications Chairs

Walayat Hussain   University of Technology Sydney, Australia
Raheel Raza   Firat University, Turkey

Web Chair

Fazlullah Khan   Abdul Wali Khan University, Pakistan

Technical Program Committee

Junaid Babar   University of Balochistan, Pakistan
Muhammad Raheel Raza   Firat University, Turkey
Walayat Hussain   University of Technology Sydney, Australia
Mian Ahmad Jan   Abdul Wali Khan University, Pakistan
Fethi Rabhi   University of New South Wales, Australia
Muhammad Akram   BUITEMS, Pakistan
Abdul Khalique Shaikh   Sultan Qaboos University, Oman
Mahmoud Bekhit   University of Technology Sydney, Australia
Paria Sadeghian   Dalarna University, Sweden
Muhammad Irshad Nazeer   IBA University, Pakistan
Ernesto Leon-Castro   Universidad Católica de la Santísima Concepción,
                                     Chile
Hafsa Usmani   Hamdard University, Pakistan
Arif Ali   Wellington Institute of Technology, New Zealand
Antonino Galletta   University of Messina, Italy
Alessandro Ruggiero   University of Salerno, Italy
Marta Chinnici   ENEA, Italy
Lela Mirtskhulava   San Diego State University Georgia, USA
Amara Atif   University of Technology Sydney, Australia
Nadir Zia   Sultan Qaboos University, Oman
Nausheen Saeed   Dalarna University, Sweden
Aqdas Malik   Sultan Qaboos University, Oman
Adil Hammadi   Curtin University, Australia
Raja Waseem Anwar   Arab Open University, Oman
Fan Zhang   Dalarna University, Sweden
Muhammad Saqib   Data61, CSIRO, Australia
Mounim A. El Yacoubi   Institut Polytechnique de Paris, France
Nestor Velasco Bermeo   University College Dublin, Ireland
Mohamed Firdhous   University of Moratuwa, Sri Lanka
Srdjan Skrbic   University of Novi Sad, Serbia
Marcin Paprzycki   Systems Research Institute, Polish Academy of
                                     Sciences, Poland

Contents

Machine Learning Predictions and Recommendations in IoT

Intelligent IoT Communication Solutions

Stochastic Security Ephemeral Generation Protocol for 5G Enabled Internet of Things

Mustafa A. Al Sibahee[1,2], Vincent Omollo Nyangaresi[3], Junchao Ma[1(✉)], and Zaid Ameen Abduljabbar[4,5]

[1] College of Big Data and Internet, Shenzhen Technology University, Shenzhen 518118, China
{mustafa,majunchao}@sztu.edu.cn
[2] Computer Technology Engineering Department, Iraq University College, Basrah, Iraq
mustafa.alsibahee@iuc.edu.iq
[3] Faculty of Biological and Physical Sciences, Tom Mboya University College, Homabay, Kenya
vnyangaresi@tmuc.ac.ke
[4] Department of Computer Science, College of Education for Pure Sciences, University of Basrah, Basrah, Iraq
zaid.ameen@uobasrah.edu.iq
[5] Shenzhen Institute, Huazhong University of Science and Technology, Shenzhen, China

Abstract. To ensure secure access to the data held in internet of things, many lightweight authentication schemes have been developed using approaches such as symmetric cryptography or hashing operations. Although these schemes achieve forward key secrecy and user anonymity, de-synchronization is a major problem in these protocols. As such, many other schemes have been presented to address this pertinent security challenge. However, some of these schemes are still susceptible to smart card loss attacks among others. In this paper, stochastic security ephemeral generation protocol for 5G enabled internet of things is presented. It is demonstrated to offer mutual authentication and session key agreement. It is also robust against packet replays, eavesdropping and man-in-the-middle attacks. In terms of performance, it has the lowest computation and communication overheads.

Keywords: 5G · Authentication · Ephemeral · IoT · Key agreement · Stochastic

1 Introduction

The Internet of Things (IoT) is a fairly recent technology that executes remote sensing and control in heterogeneous networks. To achieve this, Radio Frequency Identification (RFID) and Wireless Sensor Networks (WSNs) are deployed [1]. It basically consists of sensors, home appliances and smart devices such as smart-phones that users deploy to interact with the controlled devices [2]. In this scenario, the home appliances owners exchange packets with the controlled devices over the internet. According to [3], WSNs play critical roles in industrial internet of things (IIoT). As explained in [1], the incorporation of cloud computing with IoT can realize various smart environments such as smart

W. Hussain and M. A. Jan (Eds.): IoTaaS 2021, LNICST 421, pp. 3–18, 2022.
https://doi.org/10.1007/978-3-030-95987-6_1

transport system, smart healthcare and smart grid [4]. Here, the smartness crops from the usage of smart sensors to perceive and collect information from the environment.

According to [5], the WSN is composed of miniature low powered sensors that act as nodes and have found applications in agriculture, military, disaster management, surveillance systems, environmental monitoring and safety. As explained in [6], the sensors perceive their environment and transmit the collected data to the base stations (sink nodes). Unfortunately, these sensor nodes are resource limited in terms of computation power and storage [7, 8]. In addition, WSN have coverage, energy, security and connectivity constraints [9]. Due to its support for device ultra-densification and high bandwidths, 5G networks form the backbone for most of the IoT applications such as smart homes [10], smart cities [11], smart health and smart grids [12].

Despite the many application domains of IoT and the attained convenience, industrial WSN (IWSN) face numerous privacy and security challenges owing to their internet connectivity from unattended environments [9]. The need to access real-time data from the sensor nodes calls for strong user authentication protocols. Since smart-phones are increasing being used to access and control IoT devices [2] over cellular networks or Wi-Fi networks, there is need to protect malware in these devices. According to [13], the usage of broadcast messages in WSN can lead to various attacks and vulnerabilities. As such, there is need for sensor nodes to execute authentication and key agreement before accepting packets from each other. Authors in [14] explain that IoT sensors collect private and sensitive data such as personal health information emanating from wearable medical devices. In addition, home sensors and vehicular ad hoc networks (VANETs) also collect and transmit private data that must be properly protected.

Authors in [5] have identified smart card loss, offline guessing, sensor node capture as being serious challenges in WSN, due to the open wireless transmission medium and operation in unattended environment. Consequently, the provision of privacy and security in WSN is a challenging task. The results of any data leakages or successful attack in WSNs are catastrophic due to their sensitivity, for instance in the military [13]. There is therefore need for secure transmission of the exchanged packets to the end devices. Authors in [15] have identified the openness of the deployed communication medium as being a major challenge in WSN. Proper authentication between the user and the sensor node has therefore been recommended. On the other hand, the integration of 5G and IoT has been identified in [16] as having increased the attack surfaces in an IoT environment.

As explained in [17], the resource limitation of sensor nodes, coupled with the transfer of data over open wireless channels render security the biggest challenge during deployment of WSNs. Since users can access the sensor node data anytime and from any location, authentication is key before this access is granted. On the other hand, authors in [7] have identified bogus message insertion, packet interception, malicious deletion and packet re-routing as being major issues in WSNs. Similarly, active and passive attacks have been identified in [18] as being critical challenges. In addition, authors in [9] have cited physical and cloning attacks as serious threats in IWSNs. Enforcing session key agreement and user authentication is tricky due to the difficulty in replacing or recharging battery of deployed sensors [7]. As such, reduction of energy consumption at the sensor node is crucial. Unfortunately, the conventional internet protocols are inapplicable in

IoT due to the low computation power of the supported devices [5]. Consequently, the design of efficient security protocols for IoT devices is still challenging due to their resource constrained nature [3].

To boost privacy in these networks, anonymity and untraceability need to be implemented [19]. Here, anonymity hides participants' identity so that there is no knowledge of who accesses data at particular instant. On the other hand, untraceability prevents tracking of particular user's different sessions based on the exchanged packets. In addition, authorization and access control are essential in securing IoT messages.

Based on the above mentioned challenges, secure communication is vital for the protection of packets exchanged over IoT environment. To achieve this, user authentication should be executed, followed by key agreement [20, 21]. As such, many lightweight authentication and key agreement protocols have been designed based on symmetric encryption and decryption algorithms. However, most of these schemes still face de-synchronization threats as they pursue forward key secrecy and anonymity [22]. Consequently, upholding secure access to private and sensitive data in an IoT environment is still an open challenge, owing to the large attack vectors [7]. The major contributions of this paper include the following:

- A trusted authority based authentication scheme is developed to offer stochastic generation of security tokens needed for secure packet exchanges in an IoT environment.
- Message source authentication is executed to protect against session hijacking and de-synchronization attacks.
- Security analysis is carried out to demonstrate that the proposed protocol offers key agreement and mutual authentication, in addition to thwarting attacks such as man-in-the-middle.
- The performance of the proposed protocol, is executed using communication and computation costs as metrics, which shows that the proposed protocol has the least values of these two metrics.

The rest of this research paper is organized as follows: Sect. 2 presents related work in this research domain while Sect. 3 discusses the system model of the proposed protocol. On the other hand, Sect. 4 presents and discusses comparative evaluation of the proposed protocol while Sect. 5 concludes the paper and offers some future directions.

2 Related Work

Security and privacy challenges in IoT devices have seen the development of a myriad of authentication protocols. However, none of these schemes effectively satisfies IoT security issues at low performance costs. For instance, an authentication and key agreement (AKA) protocol presented in [23] has a number of security flaws [24, 25]. On the other hand, the schemes in [26, 27] cannot uphold forward key secrecy and user anonymity [28]. Similarly, the protocol in [29] has some security vulnerabilities [30]. Although the scheme in [31] upholds authentication, confidentiality, integrity and non-repudiation, the deployed bilinear pairing operations lead to high computational complexities [32].

Authors in [33] introduce a temporal key based user authentication scheme that is shown to have high efficiency. However, this approach is susceptible to impersonation, offline guessing and injection attacks [34].

A novel three-factor authentication approach is developed in [35], but authors in [36] point out that this scheme has security flaws. Similarly, a bio-hashing protocol is presented in [37], but which is vulnerable to privileged insider and node capture attacks. In addition, this scheme fails to offer user anonymity [27]. On the other hand, the scheme in [38] offers protection against traceability, offline-guessing, impersonation, packet replays and side-channel attacks, but at the expense of slightly high communication and computation overheads. Although the protocol in [34] addresses some of the security weakness of the scheme in [33], it is susceptible to traceability, impersonation and smart card loss attacks. Similarly, the two-factor authentication scheme in [39] is not robust against some attacks [30]. The biometrics-based scheme in [40] is vulnerable to collusion and de-synchronization attacks, and cannot offer sensor node anonymity [39]. On the other hand, the elliptic curve cryptography (ECC) based technique in [41], just like the schemes in [33, 34], is susceptible to de-synchronization and ephemeral leakage attacks.

The protocol presented in [28] is unable to detect invalid passwords during logins while the scheme in [42] is susceptible to de-synchronization and physical capture attacks [40], and does not offer sensor node anonymity [22]. Similarly, the protocol in [43] is vulnerable to smart card loss, offline password guessing and traceability attacks. In addition, the biometric authentication scheme in [2] is susceptible to smart card loss attacks. On the other hand, the two-factor protocol in [44] is vulnerable to session key disclosure, impersonation and smart card loss attacks [45]. Similarly, the fuzzy verifier based scheme in [46] is susceptible to replay attacks. Although the protocol in [47] can prevent de-synchronization attacks, it has high communication and computation overheads.

The anonymous three-factor authentication scheme in [24] prevents offline guessing attacks, but is susceptible to privileged insider attacks. On the other hand, the protocol in [45] is vulnerable to offline password guessing, smart card loss and impersonation attacks [35]. Although the authors in [48] claim that their scheme prevents known attacks, this scheme is not robust against known secret attacks and has high computation costs. On the other hand, the scheme in [49] is vulnerable to forgery and offline password guessing attacks [28].

3   System Model

The entities involved in the proposed protocol include the sensor device (SD), trusted authority (TA) and the gateway node (GWN) as shown in Fig. 1. In this network model, the sensor node gathers relevant data upon request by its operators.

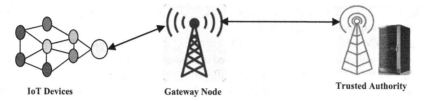

Fig. 1. Network model

It then processes the collected data before transmitting it to the target entity such as a GWN. Table 1 presents the symbols used in this paper, including their brief descriptions.

Table 1. Symbols and their descriptions

Symbol	Description
SID_i	Smart device identity
$\breve{g}$	TA secret key
$E_Ҡ$	Encryption using key Ҡ
$D_Ҡ$	Decryption using key Ҡ
U_{ID}	User identity
$\hat{p}$	User secret key
$\check{Z}$	User's authentication token
T_e	Expiration time for $\check{Z}$
T_i	Timestamp
ID_{GWN}	Gateway node identity
$\hat{p}^*$	Session key
$\mathbb{N}_i$	Random nonce

The proposed protocol then executes system parameter setting, which is followed by mutual authentication and key agreement. These two major phases are discussed below.

3.1 System Parameter Setting Phase

The activities carried out during this phase involves the generation of security parameters by the TA, which are then assigned to both the gateway node and the sensor device as explained in steps 1 to 4.

Step 1: The trusted authority (TA) derives secret key pair (A_i, B_i) for each IoT sensor device SD_i, which is then buffered in its memory before being transmitted to these devices through some secure channels.

Step 2: Each SDi generates random challenge C_i at timestamp T_i before storing them in its tamper proof device (TPD). This is followed by the TPD's computation of

$Ł_1 = h(A_i, SID_i, C_i, T_i)$. Next, SD_i composes $M_1 = \{Ł_1, SID_i, C_i, T_i\}$ and sends it together with registration request Reg_{Req} to the TA.

Step 3: On receipt of M_1, the TA executes integrity validation followed by data source authentication on the received message. To achieve this, it computes $Ł_1^* = h(A_i, SID_i, C_i, T_i)$ from its locally buffered A_i and the received $\{SID_i, C_i, T_i\}$. If $Ł_1^* \neq Ł_1$, registration is aborted, otherwise the TA derives $Ł_2 = h(A_i, B_i + C_i)$. Next, it randomly selects secret key $\breve{g}$ before computing parameter $Ł_3 = h(\breve{g}, SID_i, C_i)$. This is followed by the construction of registration response Reg_{Res} together with $M_2 = \{Ł_3, SID_i\}$ that is then conveyed to the SD_i through a secure channel.

Step 4: Upon receiving M_2, the SD_i derives $Ł_2^* = (A_i, B_i + C_i)$ at the TPD. Next, it calculates $Ł_3^* = h(\breve{g}, SID_i, C_i)$ and checks whether $Ł_3^* = Ł_3$. If this condition does not hold, M_2 is flagged as malicious, otherwise the SD_i trusts that M_2 was from a genuine TA.

3.2 Authentication and Key Agreement Phase

In this phase, the parameters that were assigned to the sensor nodes and gateway node during the previous phase are deployed to verify the messages exchanged among the communicating entities. After successful mutual authentication, a session key is derived to protect the exchanged packets as explained in step 1 to 6 below.

Step 1: The TA generates temporary key $Ķ_1 = h(\breve{g})$ followed by the derivation of security parameter $\check{Z} = E_{Ķ_1}(U_{ID}, \beta, T_e)$. It then forwards $\check{Z}$ to the user's SD_i, which stores it in its memory.

Step 2: The SD_i selects random number $\mathbb{N}_1$ and generates the message authentication code (MAC) $\phi_{M1} = h(\beta, U_{ID}, \mathbb{N}_1, \check{Z}, T_1)$. Afterwards, the SD_i composes authentication request $Auth_{Req}$ together with $M_3 = \{U_{ID}, ID_{GWN}, \mathbb{N}_1, \check{Z}, T_1, \phi_{M1}\}$ that are then sent to the GWN.

Step 3: On receiving M_3, the GWN verifies whether the timestamp in this message is within the permitted range, and if this is not the case, the authentication request is rejected. However, if it is, the GWN derives temporary key $Ķ_1^* = h(\breve{g})$ that is utilized to decrypt the received $\check{Z}$. This decryption yields security parameters β and T_e. Next, the validity of T_e is confirmed such that if it is incorrect, the authentication session is terminated. However, if it is legitimate, the GWN utilizes the obtained β to validate the received ϕ_{M1}. If ϕ_{M1} is invalid, the GWN rejects the authentication request from the SD_i, otherwise it believes that ϕ_{M1} is from a legitimate SD_i.

Step 4: The GWN selects random number $\mathbb{N}_2$ and computes message authentication code $\phi_{M2} = h(\beta, ID_{GWN}, \mathbb{N}_2, T_2)$. It then updates secret key $\beta^* = h(\beta, U_{ID}, ID_{GWN}, \mathbb{N}_2, \mathbb{N}_1)$. Finally, it composes authentication response $Auth_{Res}$ together with $M_4 = \{U_{ID}, ID_{GWN}, \mathbb{N}_2, T_2, \phi_{M2}\}$ that are sent over to the SD_i.

Step 5: On receiving M_4, freshness check is executed on this message using timestamp T_2 such that if it is invalid, the authentication session is terminated. However, if it is valid, it proceeds to confirm whether ϕ_{M2} is legitimate or not. On condition that the verification of T_2 and ϕ_{M2} flops, the session is terminated, otherwise the SD_i computes secret key $\beta^* = h(\beta, U_{ID}, ID_{GWN}, \mathbb{N}_2, \mathbb{N}_1)$. Next, it derives $\phi_{M3} = h(\beta^*, U_{ID}, ID_{GWN}, \mathbb{N}_2, T_3)$ before composing $M_5 = \{ID_{GWN}, \mathbb{N}_2, T_3, \phi_{M3}\}$ and delivering it to the GWN.

Step 6: After getting ϕ_{M3}, the GWN validates it such that if the verification is unsuccessful, the session is terminated, otherwise the GWN trusts the SD_i. Afterwards, the new secret key β^* is shared between the GWN and SD_i.

4   Comparative Analysis and Evaluation

In this section, the proposed protocol is evaluated using the various attack models as well as performance metrics as discussed in Sect. 4.1 and Sect. 4.2 below.

4.1   Security Evaluation

Both formal security analysis and informal analysis are carried out in this section to show the robustness of the proposed protocol. This is elaborated in Sects. 4.1.1 and Sect. 4.1.2 that follow.

Formal Security Analysis. In this section, the Burrows-Abadi-Needham (BAN) logic is employed as a formal model to proof that the proposed protocol attains the formulated security goals. To achieve this, the BAN logic rules and notations in [10, 19] are deployed. Based on the BAN logic analytical procedures, the following two goals are formulated:

Goal 1: $GWN|\equiv SD_i \xleftrightarrow{\beta} GWN$

Goal 2: $GWN|\equiv SD_i |\equiv SD_i \xleftrightarrow{\beta^*} GWN$

For the successful execution of the logical analysis of the proposed protocol, initial state assumptions (IAs) are critical. As such, the initial assumptions in Table 2 are made.

Table 2. Initial state assumptions

IA_1	$SD_i |\equiv SD_i \xleftrightarrow{\beta} GWN$
IA_2	$SD_i |\equiv TA \xleftrightarrow{\breve{g}} GWN$
IA_3	$GWN|\equiv TA \xleftrightarrow{\breve{g}} GWN$
IA_4	$GWN|\equiv \#(T_e)$
IA_5	$GWN|\equiv (SD_i/TA)| \Rightarrow SD_i \xleftrightarrow{\beta} GWN$
IA_6	$SD_i|\equiv \#(T_2)$
IA_7	$GWN|\equiv \#(T_1)$
IA_8	$GWN|\equiv \#(T_3)$
IA_9	$SD_i|\equiv \#(\mathbb{N}_1)$
IA_{10}	$GWN|\equiv \#(\mathbb{N}_2)$

During the mutual authentication and key agreement phase, messages $M_3 = \{U_{ID}, ID_{GWN}, \mathbb{N}_1, \check{Z}, T, \phi_{M1}\}$, $M_4 = \{U_{ID}, ID_{GWN}, \mathbb{N}_2, T_2, \phi_{M2}\}$ and $M_5 = \{ID_{GWN}, \mathbb{N}_2, T_3, \phi_{M3}\}$ are exchanged between the SD_i and GWN. For easier analysis during the BAN logic proofs, these three messages are transformed into idealized format as shown below.

$$\textbf{M}_3\text{: GWN} \triangleleft \{U_{ID}, ID_{GWN}, \mathbb{N}_1, \check{Z}, T_1\{U_{ID}, SD_i \overset{\beta}{\longleftrightarrow} GWN, T_3\}_{K_1},$$

$$\{U_{ID}, \mathbb{N}_1, T_1, \{ U_{ID}, SD_i \overset{\beta}{\longleftrightarrow} GWN, T_e\}_{K_1}\}_{\beta}\}$$

$$\textbf{M}_4\text{: SD}_i \triangleleft \{U_{ID}, ID_{GWN}, \mathbb{N}_2, T_2\{U_{GWN}, \mathbb{N}_2, T_2, SD_i \overset{\beta^*}{\longleftrightarrow} GWN\}_{\beta}$$

$$\textbf{M}_5\text{: GWN} \triangleleft \{ID_{GWN}, \mathbb{N}_2, T_3, SD_i \overset{\beta^*}{\longleftrightarrow} GWN\}_{\beta^*}.$$

Afterwards, based on the BAN logic rules, initial state assumptions and idealized message exchanges, the BAN logic proof proceeds as follows.

Based on M_3 and IA_3, the message meaning rule (MMR) is applied to yield B_1:

B_1: GWN $| \equiv SD_i/TA|\sim\{U_{ID}, \mathbb{N}_1 T_1, ID_{GWN}, \ SD_i \overset{\beta}{\longleftrightarrow} GWN, T_e\}$.
On the other hand, according to B_1, nonce verification rule (NVR) is applied in both IA_4 and IA_7 to obtain B_2:

B_2: GWN $| \equiv SD_i| \equiv SD_i \overset{\beta}{\longleftrightarrow} GWN$.
Based on B_2 and IA_5, jurisdiction rule (JR) is applied to get B_3:

B_3: GWN $| \equiv SD_i \overset{\beta}{\longleftrightarrow} GWN$, hence achieving **Goal 1**.
According to M_4 and IA_1, the MMR is applied to obtain B_4:

B_4: $SD_i | \equiv GWN|\sim \{ID_{GWN}, \mathbb{N}_2, T_2, SD_i \overset{\beta}{\longleftrightarrow} GWN\}$.
On the other hand, based on B_4, IA_6 and IA_9 the application of NVR results in B_5:

B_5: $SD_i| \equiv GWN | \equiv SD_i \overset{\beta}{\longleftrightarrow} GWN$.
Afterwards, MMR is used in M_5 and B_3 to yield B_6:

B_6: GWN $| \equiv SD_i|\sim\{ID_{GWN}, \mathbb{N}_2, T_3, SD_i \overset{\beta^*}{\longleftrightarrow} GWN\}$.
Based on IA_8, IA_{10} and B_6, the application of NVR results in B_7:

B_7: GWN$|\equiv SD_i |\equiv SD_i \overset{\beta^*}{\longleftrightarrow} GWN$, attaining **Goal 2**.
The attainment of both Goal 1 and Goal 2 demonstrates that the proposed protocol executes mutual authentication between the GWN and the SD_i before the onset of data exchanges between these two entities.

Informal Security Analysis. In this section, it is shown that the proposed protocol is resilient against some of the most common attack vectors in the internet of things environment. These attack vectors include man-in-the-middle, eavesdropping and packet replays. It is also shown that it offers mutual authentication and session key agreement.

Man-in-the-Middle Attacks. Suppose that an attacker is interested in deriving the new session key β^*. To accomplish this, public parameters exchanged over the wireless channels must be eavesdropped. However, this new session key $\beta^* = h(\beta, U_{ID}, ID_{GWN}, \mathbb{N}_2, \mathbb{N}_1)$ is computed from secret values β after every successful mutual authentication. As such, without proper authentication to the GWN or SD_i, this attack is infeasible. Now, suppose that the attacker is interested in deriving valid MAC $\{\phi_{M1} = h(\beta, U_{ID}, \mathbb{N}_1, \check{Z}, T_1), \phi_{M2} = h(\beta, ID_{GWN}, \mathbb{N}_2, T_2)$ and $\phi_{M3} = h(\beta^*, U_{ID}, ID_{GWN}, \mathbb{N}_2, T_3)\}$ that may be utilized to fool the network entities. However, derivation of any valid MAC requires secret key β and hence MitM attack fails.

Mutual Authentication. The proposed protocol attains mutual authentication between the SD_i and GWN. Here, the GWN authenticates the SD_i by checking whether the received $\phi_{M1} = h(\beta, U_{ID}, \mathbb{N}_1, \check{Z}, T_1)$, where $\beta = D_{K_1}(\check{Z})$. Clearly, it is only legitimate SD_i that can derive secret key β needed to generate valid ϕ_{M1}. To authenticate the GWN, the SD_i confirms whether the received $\phi_{M2} = h(\beta, ID_{GWN}, \mathbb{N}_2, T_2)$. It is only the legitimate GWN that can derive $K_1 = h(\breve{g})$ that is deployed to decrypt $\check{Z}$, thus obtaining secret key β. As such, there is a strong mutual authentication between SD_i and GWN.

Eavesdropping Attacks. In the proposed scheme, the GWN enciphers and encapsulates secret key β in $\check{Z} = E_{K_1}(U_{ID}, \beta, T_e)$ using ephemeral key $K_1 = h(\breve{g})$. As such, even if an attacker intercepts authentication token $\check{Z}$ over the communication channel, secret key β cannot be derived since K_1 is unknown. In addition, the sensitive data protection encryption keys are never sent over the transmission channels. Consequently, adversaries cannot eavesdrop these keys and hence cannot access the sensitive messages being transmitted between the GWN and SD_i.

Session Key Agreement. In the proposed scheme, the SD_i negotiates some session key $\beta^* = h(\beta, U_{ID}, ID_{GWN}, \mathbb{N}_2, \mathbb{N}_1)$ with the GWN. This session key is derived from secret key β, and random numbers $\mathbb{N}_1$ and $\mathbb{N}_2$ that are dynamically derived by the SD_i and GWN respectively. Here, only the legitimate SD_i has knowledge of secret key β. Similarly, only the legitimate GWN can compute ephemeral $K_1 = h(\breve{g})$ required to retrieve secret key β through the decryption of $\check{Z}$. The adversary is unable to derive the stochastic ephemeral keying parameters and hence cannot derive the established session key between the SD_i and GWN.

Packet Replay Attacks. Suppose that an attacker attempts to intercept the messages exchanged between the GWN and SD_i. Afterwards, bogus authetication message is constructed to fool the network entities. However, in the proposed protocol, timestamps are used to carry out the freshness checks of all received messages. Due to the limited permissible transmission delays, the intercepted and replayed message will have elongated transmission delay and hence will be easily detected at the end devices. Since these timestamps are hashed to obtain the message authentication codes $\phi_{M1} = h(\beta, U_{ID}, \mathbb{N}_1, \check{Z}, T_1)$, $\phi_{M2} = h(\beta, ID_{GWN}, \mathbb{N}_2, T_2)$ and $\phi_{M3} = h(\beta^*, U_{ID}, ID_{GWN}, \mathbb{N}_2, T_3)$, they cannot be modified and substituted with bogus ones. Consequently, the replayed packets are easily detected through verification of the message authentication codes, coupled with freshness checks. Table 3 presents the comparison of the security features provided by the proposed protocol and those of other related schemes.

It is evident that the proposed protocol has more security features compared with the rest of the schemes.

Table 3. Security features comparisons

Attack model	[29]	[39]	[48]	[28]	[38]	[24]	[3]	[46]	Proposed
Key agreement	√	√	√	√	√	√	√	√	√
Man-in-the-middle	√	√	√	√	-	√	x	√	√
Replay	x	x	√	x	√	√	x	x	√
Eavesdropping	-	-	-	-	-	-	-	-	√
Mutual authentication	√	√	√	√	√	√	√	√	√

Legend
√ Effective
x Ineffective
- Not considered

4.2 Performance Evaluation

During the performance evaluation of authentication protocols, computation overheads as well as communication costs are the most utilized metrics. As such, in this section, it is shown that the proposed protocol has the lowest computation and communication costs when compared with other related approaches.

Computation Overheads. The proposed protocol executed a single one-way hashing (T_H) operation and one symmetric key encryption (T_E) during the system parameter setting phase. However, during the authentication and key agreement phase, $7T_H$, $1T_E$ and one symmetric decryption (T_D) operation are executed. Using the cryptographic execution times in [28] shown in Table 4, the computation overheads of the proposed protocol is derived.

Table 4. Cryptographic operations execution time

Cryptographic operation	Time (ms)
ECC point multiplication	7.3529
One-way hashing	0.0004
Symmetric encryption or decryption	0.1303
Bio-deterministic reproduction	7.3529

Based on the values in Table 4, the computation overhead of the proposed protocol is derived as follows:

$$7T_H\{7 * 0.0004 = 0.0028\}$$
$$1T_E\{1 * 0.1303 = 0.1303\}$$
$$1T_D\{1 * 0.1303 = 0.1303\}$$

As such, the total execution time of the proposed protocol during AKA procedures is 0.2634 ms. Table 5 presents the comparisons results of the obtained execution time with other related schemes.

Table 5. Computation overheads

Protocol	Overheads (ms)
[29]	29.94
[39]	29.42
[48]	51.99
[28]	36.77
[38]	1.04
[24]	51.48
[3]	29.42
[46]	44.13
Proposed	0.2634

Based on the values in Table 5, the scheme in [48] has the highest computation costs of 51.99 ms followed by the scheme in [24] with execution time of 51.48 ms. On the other hand, the proposed protocol has the least computation costs of 0.2634 ms. Consequently, it is the most applicable in an IoT environment where resources are limited in terms of computation power.

Communication Overheads. In this evaluation, a consideration is given to the size of the messages exchanged during the mutual authentication and key agreement phase. During this phase, messages $M_3 = \{U_{ID}, ID_{GWN}, \mathbb{N}_1, \check{Z}, T_1, \phi_{M1}\}$, $M_4 = \{U_{ID}, ID_{GWN}, \mathbb{N}_2, T_2, \phi_{M2}\}$ and $M_5 = \{ID_{GWN}, \mathbb{N}_2, T_3, \phi_{M3}\}$ are exchanged between the SD_i and GWN. Using the parameter sizes in Table 6, the communication overhead in the proposed protocol is derived.

Table 6. Parameter size

Parameter	Size (bits)
Identity	32
One-way hashing	160
Random nonce	128
AES symmetric encryption/decryption	128
Timestamp	32

Based on the values in Table 6, the communication overhead of the proposed protocol is computed as follows:

$$M_3 = \{U_{ID} = ID_{GWN} = T_1 = 32, N_1 = \cancel{Z} = 128, \Phi_{M1} = 160\} = 384 \text{ bits}$$
$$M_4 = \{U_{ID} = ID_{GWN} = T_2 = 32, N_2 = 128, \Phi_{M2} = 160\} = 384 \text{ bits}$$
$$M_5 = \{ID_{GWN} = T_3 = 32, N_2 = 128, \Phi_{M3} = 160\} = 352 \text{ bits}$$

As such, the cumulative communication overhead in the proposed protocol is 1120 bits, which is equivalent to 140 bytes. Table 7 presents the communication costs comparison results of the proposed protocol with other related schemes.

Table 7. Communication overheads

Protocol	Overheads (bits)
[29]	3208
[39]	3424
[48]	2880
[28]	3072
[38]	1920
[24]	2368
[3]	2496
[46]	2880
Proposed	1120

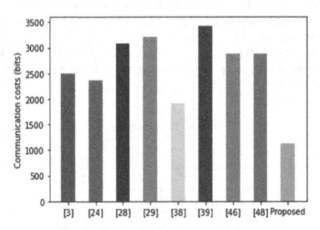

Fig. 2. Communication costs comparisons

Based on the values in Table 7, the graphs in Fig. 2 are plotted. It is clear from Fig. 2 that the protocol in [39] had the largest communication costs followed by the scheme in

[29]. On the other hand, the proposed protocol had the least number of bits exchanged during the authentication and key agreement phase. As such, the proposed protocol makes the most efficient usage of the network bandwidth. Consequently, it is ideal for deployment in an internet of things environment where devices are energy constrained. Since the number of bits transmitted is directly proportional to the energy consumed, the proposed protocol is the most energy efficient among all these other schemes.

Based on these analyses, the proposed scheme exhibits the lowest computation and communication overheads, and has most security features. As such, it has superior security features and best performance among all the other schemes.

5 Conclusion and Future Work

IoT devices have become ubiquitous to an extent that they potentially enhance convenience in people's day to day activities. These devices exchange massive amount of data that are private and sensitive. As such, any leakage of these data items can have devastating effects on the privacy of the parties involved in the communication process. Although many schemes have been developed to address these issues, they still face numerous security and performance issues. On the other hand, the presented protocol is shown to have the least communication and computation costs. As such, it is the most suitable for deployment in resource-constrained IoT devices. Moreover, the scheme offers admirable security features such as mutual authentication and key agreement, in addition to being resilient against a number of attacks such as packet replays. Future work in this research domain lies in the practical implementation of the proposed protocol in a real-world IoT scenario so that the attained performance and security issues can be verified.

Acknowledgements. This work is supported by Natural Science Foundation of Top Talent of SZTU (Grant number: 20211061010016).

References

1. Fu, Z., Huang, F., Ren, K., Weng, J., Wang, C.: Privacy-preserving smart semantic search based on conceptual graphs over encrypted outsourced data. IEEE Trans. Inf. Forensics Secur. **12**, 1874–1884 (2017)
2. Shin, S., Kwon, T.: A privacy-preserving authentication, authorization, and key agreement scheme for wireless sensor networks in 5G-integrated Internet of Things. IEEE Access **8**, 67555–67571 (2020)
3. Li, X., Niu, J., Kumari, S., Wu, F., Sangaiah, A.K., Choo, K.K.: A three-factor anonymous authentication scheme for wireless sensor networks in internet of things environments. J. Netw. Comput. Appl. **103**, 194–204 (2018)
4. Nyangaresi, V.O., Affane Moundounga, A.R.: Secure data exchange scheme for smart grids. In: 2021 IEEE 6th International Forum on Research and Technology for Society and Industry (RTSI), pp. 312–316. IEEE, Naples (2021)
5. Kumar, D., Singh, H.K., Ahlawat, C.: A secure three-factor authentication scheme for wireless sensor networks using ECC. J. Discrete Math. Sci. Cryptogr. **23**(4), 879–900 (2020)

6. Pundir, S., Wazid, M., Singh, D.P., Das, A.K., Rodrigues, J.J., Park, Y.: Intrusion detection protocols in wireless sensor networks integrated to Internet of Things deployment: survey and future challenges. IEEE Access **8**, 3343–3363 (2019)

7. Amin, R., Islam, S.H., Kumar, N., Choo, K.K.R.: An untraceable and anonymous password authentication protocol for heterogeneous wireless sensor networks. J. Netw. Comput. Appl. **104**, 133–144 (2018)

8. Nyangaresi, V.O., Ogundoyin, S.O.: Certificate based authentication scheme for smart homes. In: 2021 3rd Global Power, Energy and Communication Conference (GPECOM), pp. 202–207. IEEE, Antalya (2021)

9. Gope, P., Das, A.K., Kumar, N., Cheng, Y.: Lightweight and physically secure anonymous mutual authentication protocol for real-time data access in industrial wireless sensor networks. IEEE Trans. Industr. Inf. **15**(9), 4957–4968 (2019)

10. Nyangaresi, V.O.: Lightweight key agreement and authentication protocol for smart homes. In: 2021 IEEE AFRICON, pp. 1–6. IEEE, Arusha (2021)

11. Zhu, H., Tan, Y.A., Zhu, L., Wang, X., Zhang, Q., Li, Y.: An identity-based anti-quantum privacy-preserving blind authentication in wireless sensor networks. Sensors **18**(5), 1–15 (2018)

12. Nyangaresi, V.O., Alsamhi, S.H.: Towards secure traffic signaling in smart grids. In: 2021 3rd Global Power, Energy and Communication Conference (GPECOM), pp. 196–201. IEEE, Antalya (2021)

13. Karakaya, A., Akleylek, S.: A survey on security threats and authentication approaches in wireless sensor networks. In: 2018 6th International Symposium on Digital Forensic and Security (ISDFS), pp. 1–4. IEEE, Antalya (2018)

14. Nyangaresi, V.: Hardware assisted protocol for attacks prevention in ad hoc networks. In: Miraz, M.H., Southall, G., Ali, M., Ware, A., Soomro, S. (eds.) iCETiC 2021. LNICSSITE, vol. 395, pp. 3–20. Springer, Cham (2021). https://doi.org/10.1007/978-3-030-90016-8_1

15. Ferrag, M.A., Maglaras, L.A., Janicke, H., Jiang, J., Shu, L.: Authentication protocols for Internet of Things: a comprehensive survey. Secur. Commun. Network **2017**, 1–41 (2017)

16. Nyangaresi, V., Rodrigues, A., Taha, N.: Mutual authentication protocol for secure VANET data exchanges. In: Perakovic, D., Knapcikova, L. (eds.) FABULOUS 2021. LNICSSITE, vol. 382, pp. 58–76. Springer, Cham (2021). https://doi.org/10.1007/978-3-030-78459-1_5

17. Shen, J., Chang, S., Shen, J., Liu, Q., Sun, X.: A lightweight multi-layer authentication protocol for wireless body area networks. Futur. Gener. Comput. Syst. **78**, 956–963 (2018)

18. Sureshkumar, C., Sabena, S.: Fuzzy-based secure authentication and clustering algorithm for improving the energy efficiency in wireless sensor networks. Wireless Pers. Commun. **112**(3), 1517–1536 (2020)

19. Nyangaresi, V.O., Petrovic, N.: Efficient PUF based authentication protocol for internet of drones. In: 2021 International Telecommunications Conference (ITC-Egypt), pp. 1–4. IEEE, Alexandria (2021)

20. Choo, K.K.R., Nam, J., Won, D.: A mechanical approach to derive identity-based protocols from Diffie-Hellman-based protocols. Inf. Sci. **281**, 182–200 (2014)

21. Nyangaresi, V.O., Mohammad, Z.: Privacy preservation protocol for smart grid networks. In: 2021 International Telecommunications Conference (ITC-Egypt), pp. 1–4. IEEE, Alexandria (2021)

22. Xiong, L., Xiong, N., Wang, C., Yu, X., Shuai, M.: An efficient lightweight authentication scheme with adaptive resilience of asynchronization attacks for wireless sensor networks. IEEE Trans. Syst. Man Cybern. Syst. **51**(9), 5626–5638 (2019)

23. Park, Y., Park, Y.: Three-factor user authentication and key agreement using elliptic curve cryptosystem in wireless sensor networks. Sensors **16**(12), 2123 (2016)

24. Wang, C., Xu, G., Sun, J.: An enhanced three-factor user authentication scheme using elliptic curve cryptosystem for wireless sensor networks. Sensors **17**(12), 2946 (2017)

25. Maurya, A., Sastry, V.N.: Fuzzy extractor and elliptic curve based efficient user authentication protocol for wireless sensor networks and Internet of Things. Information **8**(4), 136 (2017)
26. Das, A.K.: A secure and robust temporal credential-based three-factor user authentication scheme for wireless sensor networks. Peer-Peer Network. Appl. **9**(1), 223–244 (2016)
27. Das, A.K.: A secure and effective biometric-based user authentication scheme for wireless sensor networks using smart card and fuzzy extractor. Int. J. Commun. Syst. **30**(1), e2933 (2017)
28. Wu, F., Xu, L., Kumari, S., Li, X.: An improved and provably secure three-factor user authentication scheme for wireless sensor networks. Peer-Peer Network. Appl. **11**(1), 1–20 (2018)
29. Wu, F., Xu, L., Kumari, S., Li, X.: A new and secure authentication scheme for wireless sensor networks with formal proof. Peer-Peer Network. Appl. **10**(1), 16–30 (2017)
30. Wang, D., Li, W., Wang, P.: Measuring two-factor authentication schemes for real-time data access in industrial wireless sensor networks. IEEE Trans. Industr. Inf. **14**(9), 4081–4092 (2018)
31. Li, F., Xiong, P.: Practical secure communication for integrating wireless sensor networks into the internet of things. IEEE Sens. J. **13**(10), 3677–3684 (2013)
32. Nyangaresi, V.O., Rodrigues, A.J., Abeka, S.O.: Efficient group authentication protocol for secure 5G enabled vehicular communications. In: 2020 16th International Computer Engineering Conference (ICENCO), pp. 25–30. IEEE, Giza (2020)
33. Xue, K., Ma, C., Hong, P., Ding, R.: A temporal-credential-based mutual authentication and key agreement scheme for wireless sensor networks. J. Netw. Comput. Appl. **36**, 316–323 (2013)
34. He, D., Kumar, N., Chilamkurti, N.: A secure temporal-credential-based mutual authentication and key agreement scheme with pseudo identity for wireless sensor networks. Inf. Sci. **321**, 263–277 (2015)
35. Amin, R., Islam, S.H., Biswas, G.P., Khan, M.K., Leng, L., Kumar, N.: Design of an anonymity-preserving three-factor authenticated key exchange protocol for wireless sensor networks. Comput. Netw. **101**, 42–62 (2016)
36. Jiang, Q., Zeadally, S., Ma, J., He, D.: Lightweight three-factor authentication and key agreement protocol for Internet-integrated wireless sensor networks. IEEE Access **5**, 3376–3392 (2017)
37. Li, X., Niu, J., Kumari, S., Liao, J., Liang, W., Khan, M.K.: A new authentication protocol for healthcare applications using wireless medical sensor networks with user anonymity. Secur. Commun. Networks **9**(15), 2643–2655 (2016)
38. Peter, S.N., Vincent, O.N., Solomon, O.O.: Efficient authentication algorithm for secure remote access in wireless sensor networks. J. Comput. Sci. Res. **3**(4), 43–50 (2021)
39. Wu, F., Xu, L., Kumari, S., Li, X.: A privacy-preserving and provable user authentication scheme for wireless sensor networks based on Internet of things security. J. Ambient. Intell. Humaniz. Comput. **8**(1), 101–116 (2017)
40. Adavoudi-Jolfaei, A., Ashouri-Talouki, M., Aghili, S.F.: Lightweight and anonymous three-factor authentication and access control scheme for real-time applications in wireless sensor networks. Peer-Peer Netw. Appl. **12**(1), 43–59 (2019)
41. Jiang, Q., Ma, J., Wei, F., Tian, Y., Shen, J., Yang, Y.: An untraceable temporal-credential-based two-factor authentication scheme using ECC for wireless sensor networks. J. Netw. Comput. Appl. **76**, 37–48 (2016)
42. Gope, P., Hwang, T.: A realistic lightweight anonymous authentication protocol for securing real-time application data access in wireless sensor networks. IEEE Trans. Ind. Electron. **63**(11), 7124–7132 (2016)
43. Chang, C.C., Le, H.D.: A provably secure, efficient, and flexible authentication scheme for ad hoc wireless sensor networks. IEEE Trans. Wireless Commun. **15**(1), 357–366 (2016)

44. Turkanović, M., Brumen, B., Hölbl, M.: A novel user authentication and key agreement scheme for heterogeneous ad hoc wireless sensor networks, based on the internet of things notion. Ad Hoc Networks **20**, 96–112 (2014)
45. Farash, M.S., Turkanović, M., Kumari, S., Hölbl, M.: An efficient user authentication and key agreement scheme for heterogeneous wireless sensor network tailored for the internet of things environment. Ad Hoc Networks **36**, 152–176 (2016)
46. Li, X., Peng, J., Obaidat, M.S., Wu, F., Khan, M.K., Chen, C.: A secure three-factor user authentication protocol with forward secrecy for wireless medical sensor network systems. IEEE Syst. J. **14**(1), 39–50 (2019)
47. Xiong, L., Peng, D., Peng, T., Liang, H., Liu, Z.: A lightweight anonymous authentication protocol with perfect forward secrecy for wireless sensor networks. Sensors **17**(11), 2681 (2017)
48. Lu, Y., Xu, G., Li, L., Yang, Y.: Anonymous three-factor authenticated key agreement for wireless sensor networks. Wireless Netw. **25**(4), 1461–1475 (2019)
49. Das, A.K.: A secure and efficient user anonymity-preserving three-factor authentication protocol for large-scale distributed wireless sensor networks. Wireless Pers. Commun. **82**(3), 1377–1404 (2015)

An Enhancement to Channel Access Mechanism for the IEEE 802.15.3C MillimeterWave (5G) Standard to Support Stringent QoS Requirements of IoT

Muhammad Sajjad Akbar[✉], Zawar Hussain, Quan Z. Sheng, and Subhas Mukhopadhyay

Macquarie University University, Sydney, Australia
muhammadsajjad.akbar@mq.edu.au

Abstract. The ubiquitous nature of the Internet of Things (IoT) constitutes a set of stringent quality of service (QoS) requirements from the underlying 5G network. To address the issues, this paper proposes an enhancement for the channel access period (CAP) of the widely used IEEE 802.15.3C (millimeter wave (mmW)) standard using a priority mechanism that fulfills the requirement of prioritized channel access for the IoT based applications. According to the hybrid medium access control (MAC) protocol of the IEEE 802.15.3C, to reserve time-division multiple access (TDMA) based slot in channel time allocation period (CTAP), a node will first send a channel time allocation (CTA) request to piconet controller (PNC) by using carrier-sense multiple access with collision avoidance (CSMA/CA) mechanism in the contention-access period (CAP). After successful delivery of CTA's request, PNC will reserve a CTA for a specific node. However, there is no guarantee that a node will get a channel in the contention process in the existing standard. Hence, the existing CAP mechanism could demonstrate a bottleneck for a data sending device in terms of less delay and high throughput. To solve this issue, we first design a numerical model of CAP using the IEEE 802.15.3C standard's specification, and then we propose a priority-based mechanism with three priority classes: high priority (HP), medium priority (MP), and low priority (LP) with each class having different contention windows (CW) range that makes the value of backoff period shorter. To evaluate the performance of the proposed mechanism, modifications are applied to the proposed numerical model. The performance comparison is conducted among prioritized classes devices in terms of transmission delay, channel access delay, and throughput. The conducted evaluations include two types of data rates i.e., 1.5 Gbps and 3 Gbps. The proposed scheme shows promising results for a node that requires high priority in an IoT environment.

© ICST Institute for Computer Sciences, Social Informatics and Telecommunications Engineering 2022
Published by Springer Nature Switzerland AG 2022. All Rights Reserved
W. Hussain and M. A. Jan (Eds.): IoTaaS 2021, LNICST 421, pp. 19–38, 2022.
https://doi.org/10.1007/978-3-030-95987-6_2

Keywords: IoT · 5G · MilimeterWave · IEEE 802.15.3C · User priority · Personal area networks

1 Introduction

IoT is considered as a system of interrelated computing devices [1]. IoT uses standard communication protocols and various access technologies depending on the application. Machine to Machine (M2M) communication is one of the promising areas for future IoT. It is estimated that more than 30 billion IoT devices in 2025 [2]. Such a high volume of devices will generate massive data and require time bounded and reliable data delivery services so that it could be useful for the application layer at the destination. The standards IEEE 802.15.4 [10], IEEE 802.15.6 (WBAN) [11], ZigBee [12], 6lowPAN [13] and 6tisch are widely used as IoT networks.

Concurrently, 5G has evolved and promises to provide higher throughput and less delay for a huge number of inter-connected devices [3]. Mostly, 5G is associated with cellular networks; however, it is important to understand that 5G is expected to employ stand-alone in personal and local area networks as well as cellular networks. The FP7 Project METIS for 5G, discussed the machine-type communications (MTC) with its issues and challenges to incorporate 5G with IoT [4]. Both academia and industry are enthusiastically working on the integration of 5G with IoT-based networks so that IoT could take advantage of this gigabit networks [5].

In recent years, millimeter wave (mmW) appeared as one of the potential candidates for 5G by providing data rates up to gigabits/sec. It uses the spectrum between 30 and 300 GHz and corresponds to wavelengths between 10 mm to 1 mm. The characteristics of mmW include high bandwidth, short-wavelength/high frequency, and high attenuation [18]. Huge path loss is expected in mmW communications, to overcome these high power levels are required. Due to high attenuation from solid material (bricks and buildings), mmW requires line of sight (LoS) for efficient and reliable communication. The interference levels in mmW communication are much lower than the 2.4 GHz and 5 GHz. Multiple-antennas solutions in mmW allow the transmission to use narrow beams which help to reduce the attenuation and the interference [19]. There have been several standardization activities for mmW MAC in the 60 GHz band. Most of these standardization efforts are for personal and local area networks under IEEE 802.15.3c and IEEE 802.11ad. IEEE 802.15.3c standard also known as piconet specifies the mmW by supporting a high data rate over 2 Gbps in the 60 GHz band. Among a cluster of IEEE 802.15.3c based devices, one will be selected as the piconet coordinator (PNC) and it manages the synchronization among devices by broadcasting beacon messages. The devices content for the time slots using carrier sense multiple access/collision avoidance (CSMA/CA) and send data using time division multiple access (TDMA) [16]. The IEEE 802.11ad introduced several modifications at MAC and physical layer of existing IEEE 802.11 standard to enable mmW support. It claims to provide a 6.75 Gbps data rate.

The coordinator uses a superframe structure to manage the channel access of the connected stations which is composed of beacons, contention access period (CAP) and contention-free period (CFP) [17].

There are several pre-standardization activities for mmW in cellular networks such as in the FP-7 EU project (METIS); however, more efforts are still.

1.1   Required Level of Integration

Before jumping to the integration's discussion between 5G and IoT, it is important to revisit the IoT applications with a communication requirements perspective. Figure 1 describes some of the popular IoT applications with their delay and data rate requirements. Further, it also identifies that either 5G or legacy networks can fulfill these requirements. It can be seen that most of these applications which are in the white area have bandwidth requirements up to 100 Mbps maximum. Further, delay values for these applications are between 10 ms and 1000 ms. These applications (white area) are performing well under various existing standards and technologies for low power wireless sensor and body area networks i.e., IEEE 802.15.4 (WSN) [10], IEEE 802.15.6 (WBAN) [11], ZigBee [12], 6lowPAN [13] and 6tisch [14].

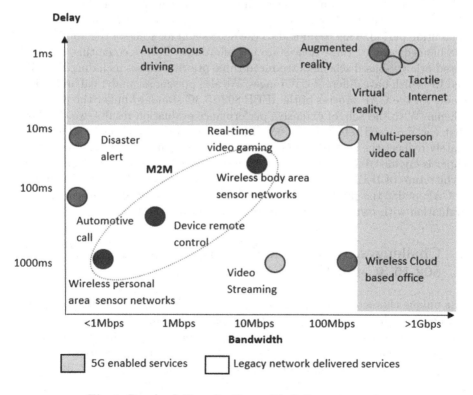

Fig. 1. Popular IoT applications with QoS requirements

The grey area in Fig. 1 represents the IoT application for which we need 5G technologies. These applications demand high bandwidth (greater than 1 Gbps) and a lower delay i.e., between 1 ms and 10 ms. mmW [15] is considered as one of the promising key enabler band for 5G, and IEEE 802.15.3c [16] and IEEE 802.11ad [17] provide support for mmW. The sensors sense the environment and send data frequently to the controller to an IEEE 802.15.4 or IEEE 802.15.6 based network. The controller requires high data rate links to transmit the huge data received with a very short delay. For this, we need to link these networks to the IEEE 802.15.3C-mmW based devices to take advantage of advanced technologies like mmW. A dual-frequency enabled device (2.4 GHz and 60 GHz) can create this link. However, it is also important for mmW based devices to provide the required quality of service (QoS) for the application data received from these devices after integration. In this regard, the main objective of this paper is to propose an enhancement for the hybrid MAC scheme of the IEEE 802.15.3C standard in terms of a channel access priority mechanism at CAP. Similar enhancement with different parameters was also proposed in IEEE 802.11; however, IEEE 802.11 deals with high spectrum with long range and takes WiFi into consideration. Our proposed enhancement is particularly for IoT devices under IEEE 802.15.3C with short range.

To reserve the slot in CTAP, a node must contend for the channel to transmit CTA requests to the piconet. A node that wins the contention process would be able to reserve the time slot in CTAP, the other nodes need to wait for the next contention period. This could add to the delays and for some of the applications like biomedical etc., these delays are not affordable. To overcome this, our proposed priority-based scheme introduced three priority classes including HP, MP, and LP which have different CW ranges. We also present an analytical/numerical model for the CAP process of the IEEE 802.15.3C standard under the proposed scheme. With the help of extensive performance evaluation results, we establish that the proposed scheme provides the priority to a specific node which ultimately reduces the transmission delay and increases throughput. The rest of the paper is organized as follows: Sect. 2 discusses the challenges, requirements, and architecture of IEEE 802.15.3C standard, Sect. 3 presents the analytical model of CAP under the proposed priority scheme, Sect. 4 provides the performance evaluation with results, and the paper is concluded in Sect. 5.

2   Challenges, Requirements and Architecture of IEEE 802.15.3C-mmW

The unique characteristics of mmW pose various challenges including blockage, deafness, synchronization, concurrent transmissions, multiple access, and user association and mobility relay. Optimal association of mmW devices with wireless access points is a challenging task. The recent mmW standards are using receive signal strength indicator (RSSI) as a link quality to select an access point as coordinator; however, higher RSSI values do not always mean a good link [20]. Therefore, it is critical for mmW devices to select a reliable access point as a coordinator to accommodate delay-sensitive and bandwidth-hungry applications.

IEEE 802.15 is a working group for the specification of WPAN communications. The IEEE 802.15.3x working group specifies the physical (PHY) and medium access control (MAC) layer for high data rate WPAN. The IEEE 802.15.3C standard amends the PHY and MAC layer for the existing IEEE 802.15.3 to support the operation of the 60 GHz mmW band. This standard proposed a piconet wireless network that permits a number of independent devices (DEVs) to communicate using a piconet controller (PNC).

2.1 Architecture and Channel Access Mechanism in CAP

IEEE 802.15.3c standard specifies that multiple DEVs can autonomously connect in form of a piconet. The standard defines four radio channels as stated in Table 1. A PNC is selected among DEVs and PNC has the responsibility of registering the DEVs, broadcasting timing allocations, coordinating, scheduling, and synchronizing devices with the channel by transmitting beacons. The standard proposes a hybrid MAC protocol having contention-based and scheduled channel access schemes. The timing in IEEE 802.15.3C WPAN is based on a superframe structure that consists of three parts: beacons, contention access period (CAP), and channel time allocation period (CTAP). Figure 2 shows the superframe structure of the omnidirectional mode of IEEE 802.15.3C.

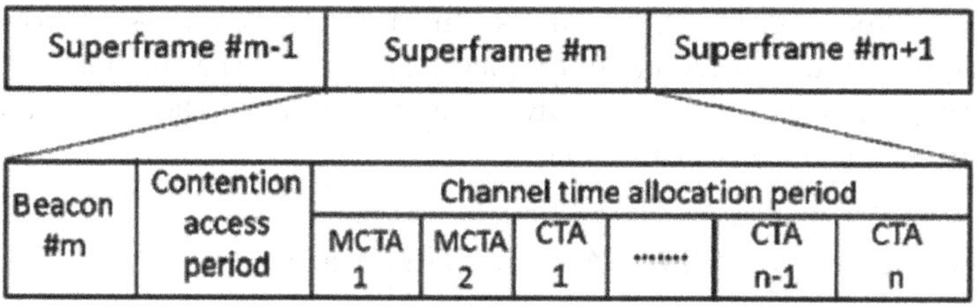

Fig. 2. IEEE superframe structure of omni-directional mode [16]

Beacon. The PNC broadcast beacons at the start of each superframe. The beacons consist of timing allocations for DEVs and the management information for a piconet.

Contention Access Period. During the CAP period, DEVs contend for channel access using CSMA/CA. CAP uses binary exponential backoff (BEB) algorithm to manage the channel access. The DEV first waits for a backoff interframe spacing (BIFS) duration, as described in the standard. After the BIFS wait, DEV calculates backoff_count (BC) = bw_random(retry_count) and maintains this counter for BC that is decreased when the medium is idle for the duration of pBackoffSlot. *BC* is calculated based on random function taking range zero to backoff window (BW) (A BW table is provided by the standard that has predefined values). The retry_count (RC) shall be set to zero for the first transmission attempt of a frame. If the channel is sensed as busy, the BC should be suspended. The channel shall remain idle for the duration of a BIFS period before it is resumed. When the BC reaches zero, the DEV may transmit a data frame.

If a collision occurs while sending data, the DEV needs to retransmit the data/request frame by initiating a new backoff stage with a doubled CW size. DEV is capable of dropping a frame from its queue after a few retransmission attempts (suggested by the standard). If the CAP period is not sufficient then DEV has to defer the frame and may try in the next CAP. CAP is designed for small asynchronous data transmission.

An Imm-ACK is expected when sending a CTA request to PNC, before that the DEV shall check whether there is enough time remaining in the time slot to accommodate the current frame that is 2 SIFS periods, and the Imm-ACK frame at the same PHY rate as the transmitted frame. If there is not enough time remaining for this entire frame exchange sequence, then the DEV shall abort the transmission and not use the remainder of the CTA. Figure 3 shows the flow chart of the CAP mechanism used in 802.15.3C.

Channel Time Allocation Period (CTAP). In CTAP, scheduled-based frame transmissions occur. CTAP is further divided into CTA and management channel time allocation (MCTA). DEVs send their CTA requests during CAP to their PNC. The information about allocated CTAs for the current superframe is sent to the DEVs using beacons. MCTA is used to send the command where CTA is utilized for data transmission.

2.2 Aggregation and Block Acknowledgement

The aggregation process is introduced to handle the QoS requirements of high-speed and delay-sensitive applications. In the aggregation process, multiple data frames are combined to transmit in a single superframe. When the data is received in the form of MAC service data unit (MSDUs) from the upper layer, the MAC headers are applied, and then it is called MAC protocol data unit (MPDU) and is ready for the physical layer. The combination of multiple MPDUs creates aggregated MPDU (A-MPDU). A-MPDU is generated before passing to the PHY layer for final transmission. The MAC does not wait for a certain number of MPDUs to create A-MPDU, so if a node gets channel access, the MAC takes available MPDUs to make A-MPDU for transmission. The destination of all MPDUs must be the same. Further, for reliable data transmission of five different types of acknowledgments (ACKs) are defined in Piconet: block ACK (Blk-ACK), immediate ACK (Imm-ACK), delayed ACK (Dly-ACK), implied ACK (Imp-ACK), and no ACK (no-ACK). Mostly Blk-ACK is used to acknowledge the sender for an A-MSDU frame.

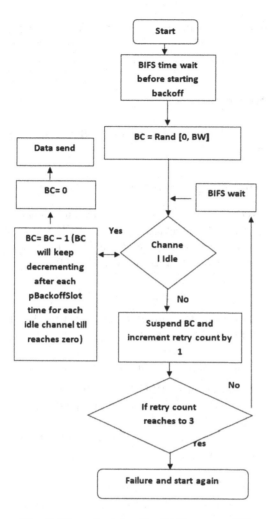

Fig. 3. Flow chart for the CAP process [16]

2.3 Communication Procedure of Piconet

The communication procedure in IEEE 802.15.3C can be sub-divided into five. When a DEV is turned on it starts scanning for the channel and if it finds the beacon of an existing Piconet network, it joins the Piconet as a slave device. In case, the DEV receives a beacon and doesn't find the desired Piconet then it starts operating like a PNC and waits for DEVs to join by periodically broadcasting beacon frames. In the second step, if the DEV receives a beacon from desired PNC then it sends an association request to PNC. When the PNC receives an association request, it sends back the response. The PNC may request for encryption key from the sender. After this, access is given to the requesting node. A DEV needs to make a request for a time slot if it wants to send data in CTA. Once the DEV sends the data, it waits to receive the ACK in the allocated period. Finally, if the communication finishes, then PNC sends a beacon announcing the end of the piconet and turns its power off.

3   Proposed System

In this section, we provide the analytical modelling to evaluate the CAP and our proposed mechanism.

3.1   Analytical Modelling of the CAP

We present an analytical model to evaluate the end-to-end delay (ED) and throughput (TP) for the CAP mechanism of the IEEE 802.15.3C. The purpose is to understand how much time it takes for a CTA request in the worst-case scenario. The ED can be calculated as given in Eq. (1):

$$ED = T_{frame} + T_{ACK} + T_{CH} \tag{1}$$

where T_{frame} represents frame transmission time for a CTA request frame. Further, T_{frame} can be computed as given in Eq. (2):

$$T_{frame} = T_{Preamble(PHY)} + T_{Header(MAC+PHY)} + T_{Payload} \tag{2}$$

where T_{Preamble} is the duration of PLCP preamble, T_{Header} is the duration of PLCP header and T_{Payload} is the duration of the payload. These duration are given in the IEEE 802.15.3C standard.

T_{ACK} represents the time duration of the ACK, in this case, ACK duration computed as given in Eq. (3):

$$T_{ACK} = T_{ImmACK} + 2SIFS \tag{3}$$

Figure 4 describes the Imm-ACK procedure given by the standard.

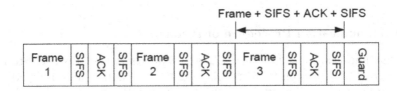

Fig. 4. Immediate ACK [16]

Where T_{ImmACK} is time duration of the immediate ACK and can be computed as given in Eq. (4):

$$T_{ImmACK} = T_{Preamble} + T_{Header} \tag{4}$$

The ACK of the ImmACK has only MAC header and not a payload as each packet is expected to be acknowledged immediately.

T_{CH} represents the time to access the channel, it is computed as given in Eq. (5):

$$T_{CH} = (RC * BIFS) + (BC * pBackoffSlot) \qquad (5)$$

where RC is the retry counter in the backoff process and its value will be 3 in the worst case, BIFS is the backoff IFS and it is calculated by Eq. (6):

$$BIFS = pSifsTime + pCcaDetectTime \qquad (6)$$

The values of pSifsTime and pCcaDetectTime are given in the Table 1 mentioned by the in the IEEE 802.15.3C standard.

BC is the backoff counter calculated as given in Eq. (7):

$$BC = Rand(0, BW) \qquad (7)$$

BC is computed using a random function that finds a random integer value between zero and BW (backoff window). The value of BW is given in Table 1.

Table 1. Timing and space parameters mentioned by IEEE 802.15.3C standard [16]

PHY parameter	Duration HSI (μs)
pSIFSTime	2.5
pCcaDetectTime	2.5
pBackoffSlot	5
T_Preamble	1.31
T_Header	0.44
Backoff Windows	[7, 15, 31, 63]
Retry Count	0 to 3
CAP duration (μs)	0 to 65,535
Superframe duration (μs)	0 to 65,535
MAC header (bytes)	10
PHY header (bytes)	48
Acknowledgement (bytes)	10
Beacon packet (bytes)	100
Data frame (bytes)	512 to 8,388,608
Channel data rate (Gbps)	1.5, 3, 5

3.2   Proposed Priority Mechanism

We consider an independent piconet having a PNC and N number of DEVs. According to IEEE 802.15.3C specifications, for the transmission of data frame during the CTAP, a DEV have to send a CTA request in CAP. For that, it will first use CSMA/CA mechanism specified in the standard. After successful delivery of the CTA request, the PNC will reserve a CTA for a specific node. Therefore, the CAP mechanism could become a bottleneck for a DEV that needs to send data with less delay and high throughput.

We propose to use a priority mechanism for IEEE 802.15.3C DEVs. This mechanism uses CAP to provide a priority to a certain DEV by sending its CTA request to PNC at a low, high, or medium priority.

We apply this scheme to the HSI and AV PHY mode of IEEE 802.15.3C with NLOS. It is suited for applications that require bidirectional, high speed, and low latency NLOS communications. The purpose of NLOS with HSI/AV is to organize an ad hoc network that can provide connectivity to computers and other nearby devices.

We define three levels of priorities: low, medium, and high as given in Table 2. In the proposed scheme, the priority is assigned to low, high, and medium DEVs using multiple sizes of the contention windows (CW) ranges under a user priority level. A node with a minimum CW value gets the higher priority and vice versa. Similarly, when a node tries to access the channel and finds it busy then the BC computed based on the prioritized level of CW will be freeze and the priority for the next retry will remain the same. The ranges of CW levels are selected in a way that each level has a different range to obtain a specific priority.

3.3   Analysis of Proposed Priority Mechanism

A DEV that uses high priority will select the CW range of high priority. The value of CW will be used when calculating the BC value which actually produces an integer as waiting for factor for channel access. Higher the BC, lower will be the priority and vice versa. BC can be computed using Eq. (8):

$$BC = Rand(0, CW) \tag{8}$$

In case of highest priority, the equation will be:

$$BC = Rand(1, 8)$$

For lower priority

$$BC = Rand(25, 50)$$

Figure 5 describes the updated flowchart under the proposed scheme.

The probability that a node can successfully get the channel access by considering n number of maximum backoff periods is given by Eq. (9) [21–23]:

Table 2. Timing and Space parameters mentioned by IEEE 802.15.3C standard [16]

DEV priority	CW range
Low (1)	25–50
Medium (2)	12–20
High (3)	1–8

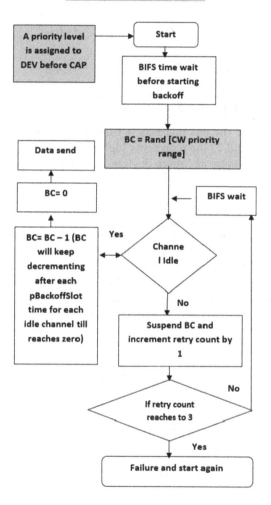

Fig. 5. Flowchart of CAP under proposed priority scheme

$$P_s = \sum_{i=1}^{n} p_a (1 - p_a)^{(i-1)} \tag{9}$$

where P_a represents the success probability that a node accesses the channel at the end of backoff period. For k number of DEVs in the network, P_a is given by Eq. (10)

$$P_a = (1 - q)^{(k-1)} \tag{10}$$

The ED value for each priority can be computed as:

$$ED_{AL} = T_{frame} + T_{ACK} + T_{CHL}$$

$$ED_{AM} = T_{frame} + T_{ACK} + T_{CHM}$$

$$ED_{AH} = T_{frame} + T_{ACK} + T_{CHH}$$

where T_{CHL} represents the channel access time for low priority, T_{CHM} denotes the medium priority and T_{CHH} represents high priority.

Average delay of a network where devices have low, medium and high priorities is given by Eq. (11):

$$EDA = 1/ED_{T_{CHH}} + 1/ED_{T_{CHL}} + 1/EDT_{CHM} \tag{11}$$

The presented numerical needs to be validated, which is conducted by comparing the maximum throughput (MT) values of the analytical/numerical model (values through statistical equations described above) with MT theoretical values mentioned by the IEEE 802.15.3C. The MT is defined as a ratio of transmitted information in bits to the transmission duration. Throughput is defined as the ratio of payload size (x) to total time required to transmit payload, in the case when there is no priority set the maximum network throughput (MT) can be computed as given in Eq. (12):

$$MT = X/ED \tag{12}$$

The MT for prioritized network can be computed as given by Eq. (13):

$$MT = X/EDA \tag{13}$$

4   Experiments and Discussion

The performance of the proposed priority scheme is evaluated based on analytical and numerical models. We explored various simulators including network simulator version 2 (NS2), NS3, OMNet++, and MATLAB but could not find any implementation regarding the channel access mechanism (i.e., CSMA/CA in our case) defined by the IEEE 802.15.3C standard for mmW. The performance of the proposed priority scheme is evaluated in terms of delay, throughput, and bandwidth efficiency (BE). We assume that a PNC initially managing a network for 4 nodes, out of 4, 3 nodes require a specific priority class i.e., HP, MP, LP.

The remaining one node will operate on no priority (NP) mode. We are assuming that each node is trying to transmit a CTA request packet to the PNC so that it could reserve a TDMA slot in CTAP. The performance is evaluated for two different data rates: 1.5 Gbps and 3 Gbps.

Figure 6 shows a comparative analysis of the channel access delay among 4 nodes having different priorities. Further, the scenario also considers the number of retries to access the channel. There is a total of three retries. It can be seen from Fig. 6 that a node having HP shows the minimum delay i.e., 25 μs if it gets access in the first retry. The reason for such a low value of the delay is less BC values which are obtained from the average CW range for HP which is [1–8]. The maximum value of delay for HP goes to 35 μs which is in the third retry. Similarly, the node using MP shows the delay starting from 70 μs (1st retry) and goes to 85 μs in the third retry. The node with NP shows the highest delay values in all retries i.e., 170 μs, 175 μs, and 180 μs. The reason for the high delay is the high value of BC obtained from the average CW range [15–67]. Due to the high value of BC, a node needs to wait longer.

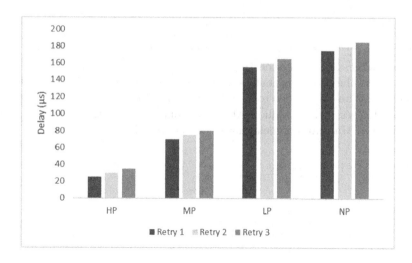

Fig. 6. Delay involve in channel access for priority classes

Figures 7, 8 and 9 show the comparative analysis of the total delay with different values of packet sizes. The minimum value of the packet is considered as 32 bytes and it goes up to 138 bytes. We selected the maximum value of packet size 138 bytes because the maximum size of CTAP packet is 138 bytes and we are assuming that nodes are trying to send a CTA request to reserve a TDMA based slot in CTAP. The CTA request packet can vary from 32 to 138 bytes. The considered data rate is 1.5 Gbps for these scenarios.

Figure 7 shows the delay comparison in the first retry case. It can be seen that the node with HP performs better than the other nodes. The transmission delay keeps increasing with the packet size. The minimum delay value for HP is

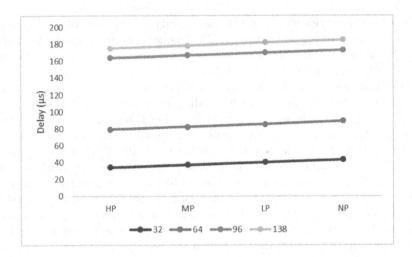

Fig. 7. Total transmission delay comparison among prioritized and non prioritized classes in 1st retry

35 μs for the 32 bytes packet and the maximum delay for HP is 55 μs for the 138-byte packet. It can be seen that the delay values of LP and NP are close to each other, the reason is that both nodes attained higher CW values in the backoff process and they need to spend more waiting time. It is also noticed that the channel access delay's value is the main contributor to the total delay. The data and ACK transmission delay have very short values.

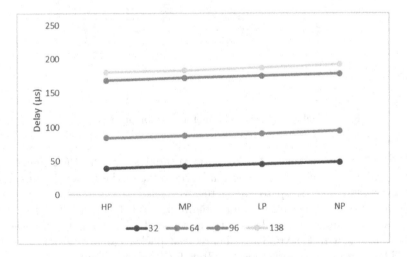

Fig. 8. Total transmission delay comparison among prioritized and non prioritized classes in the second retry

Figures 8 and 9 show the delay comparison for the 2nd and 3rd backoff retry case. It can be seen that the node with HP performs better than the other nodes in the 2nd and 3rd retry. The 3rd retry in Fig. 9 shows the worst case for HP, MP, LP, and NP in terms of delay. The HP shows a delay of 60 μs for 138 bytes of CTA request; whereas this delay is 110 μs, 170 μs, and 210 μs for MP, LP, and NP respectively. The reason for higher delay values in this scenario is that channel remains busy in two retries and a node gets a chance to transmit in the third retry.

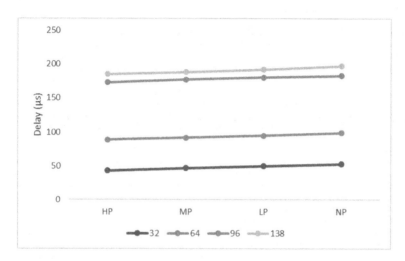

Fig. 9. Total transmission delay comparison among prioritized and non prioritized classes in third retry

Figures 10, 11 and 12 show the comparative analysis of throughput with different values of packet sizes in with various retries. The minimum value of the packet is considered as 32 bytes and it goes up to 138 bytes. We selected the maximum value of packet size 138 bytes because the maximum size of CTAP packet is 138 bytes and we are assuming that nodes are trying to send a CTA request to reserve a TDMA based slot in CTAP. The CTA request packet can vary from 32 to 138 bytes. The considered data rate is 1.5 Gbps for these scenarios.

Figure 10 shows the TP comparison in the first retry case. It can be seen that the node with HP performs better than the other nodes. The TP keeps increasing with the packet size. The minimum TP value for HP is 8 Mbps for the 32 bytes packet and the maximum TP for HP is 25 Mbps for the 138-byte packet. It can be seen that the TP values of LP and NP are close to each other, the reason is that both nodes attained higher CW values in the backoff process and they need to spend more waiting time. The NP gives a maximum of 6 Mbps for the 138-byte CTA request packet. The MP's TP values are also promising. It is also noticed that TP grows as a function of packet size. Figures 11 and 12 show the TP comparison for the 2nd and 3rd backoff retry case. It can be seen

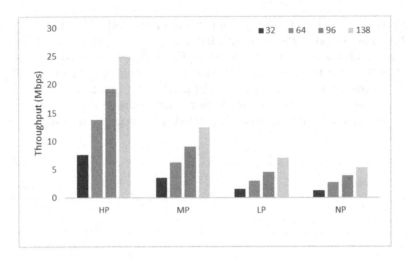

Fig. 10. Throughput comparison among prioritized and non prioritized classes in first retry

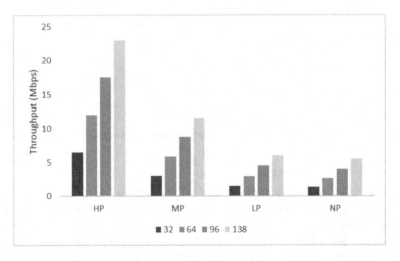

Fig. 11. Throughput comparison among prioritized and non prioritized classes in second retry

that the node with HP performs better than the other nodes in 2nd and 3rd retry.

The 3rd retry in Fig. 12 shows the TP comparison in the 3rd retry. The HP shows a minimum TP of 6.5 Mbps for 32 bytes of CTA request and for 138 bytes packet TP is 22.5 Mbps. The reason for the reduction of HP's throughput is the increased channel waiting time due to the third retry. Similarly, NP shows a degraded TP value for all the packet sizes from 32 bytes to 138 bytes.

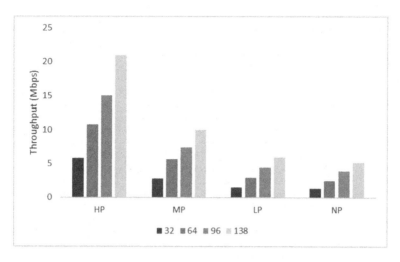

Fig. 12. Throughput comparison among prioritized and non prioritized classes in third retry

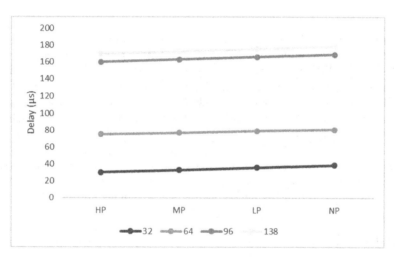

Fig. 13. delay comparison among prioritized and non prioritized classes in first retry for the 3 Gbps

Figures 13 shows the delay comparison in the first retry case where the data rate is considered as 3 Gbps. It can be seen that the node with HP performs better than the other nodes. The delay keeps increasing with the packet size. The minimum delay value for HP is 20 µs for the 32 bytes packet and the maximum delay for HP is 40 µs for the 138-byte packet. If we compare Figs. 13 and 7, it can be clearly seen that results of Fig. 13 are better due to higher data rate i.e., 3 Gbps; with 1.5 Gbps of data rate. Higher data rates help to reduce the transmission delay.

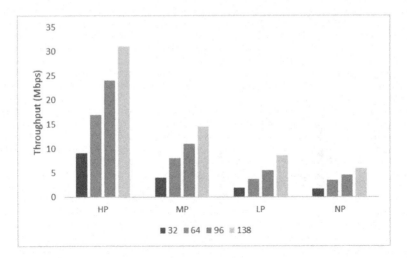

Fig. 14. Throughput comparison among prioritized and on prioritized classes in first retry for 3 Gbps

Figure 14 shows the TP comparison in the first retry case for 3 Gbps. It can be seen that the node with HP performs better than the other nodes and provides higher TP values i.e., 32 Mbps for the packet of 138 bytes. The TP keeps increasing with the packet size. The MP, LP, and NP show the TP of 15 Mbps, 10 Mbps, and 5 Mbps respectively for the packet size of 138 bytes. The reason for the lesser TP value than the HP is the channel access delay which is different for MP, LP, and NP. The delay reduces the transmission time. If we compare Fig. 14 and 10, it can be clearly seen that Fig. 14 shows better results than Fig. 10. The reason is the higher data rate value which is 3 Gbps in Fig. 14 as compared to Fig. 10 where the data rate is 1.5 Gbps. A higher data rate will transmit the payload quickly, hence results in lesser delay and high TP.

5   Conclusion

In this paper, a prioritized channel access mechanism is proposed as an enhancement to the IEEE 802.15.3C's CAP mechanism. The aim is to provide priority to a CTA request so that it could reserve a TDMA-based time slot in CTAP, otherwise, the contention process could cause more delay to the nodes which have delay-sensitive data. The priority mechanism provides three different priority classes: HP, MP, and LP. Each class has a different range of values for the CW. In this paper, initially, numerical modeling is proposed for the IEEE 802.15.3C CAP, and then the performance of the proposed priority mechanism is evaluated using our proposed model. The evaluation is performed by assessing channel access delay, transmission delay, and throughput. The comparative analysis is provided between prioritized and non-prioritized traffic by considering two levels of data rates: 1.5 Gbps and 3 Gbps. The results show that the channel access process with HP outperforms the others and it is also noticed that the delay increased as a function of packet size. The main contributor to the delay value is channel access delay. Shorter channel access delay leads towards higher priority. CW values play a key role in assigning the priority process. On the other hand, the HP provides the highest TP value compared to MP, LP, and NP, with different sizes of CTA requests, which is 138 bytes for a maximum-sized CTA request. The higher the packet size, the higher will be throughput and less delay. A comparison is also provided between delay and TP values of nodes having data rates of 1.5 Gbps and 3 Gbps. The higher data rate with HP provides the best results.

References

1. Whitmore, A., Agarwal, A., Da, X.L.: The internet of things - a survey of topics and trends. Inf. Syst. Front. **17**, 261–74 (2015)
2. Atzori, L., Lera, A., Morabito, G.: Understanding the internet of things: definition potentials and societal role of a fast evolving paradigm. Ad Hoc Netw. **56**, 122–40 (2017)
3. Agiwal, M., Roy, A., Saxena, N.: Next generation 5G wireless networks: a comprehensive survey. IEEE Commun. Surv. Tutorials **18**, 1617–55 (2017)
4. Deliverable D6.6, METIS: Final report on the METIS system concept and technology roadmap (2015)
5. Shah, S.H., Yaqoob, I.: A survey: Internet of Things (IoT) technologies applications and challenges. Smart Energy Grid Eng., 381–85 (2016)
6. Al-Fuqaha, A., Guizani, M., Mohammadi, M., Aledhari, M., Ayyash, M.: Internet of things: a survey on enabling technologies, protocols and applications. IEEE Commun. Surv. Tutorials **17**(4), 2347–76 (2015)
7. Palattella, M., et al.: Internet of things in the 5G era: enablers, architecture and business models. IEEE J. Sel. Areas Commun. **34**(3), 510–27 (2016)
8. Andrews, J.G., et al.: What will 5G be? IEEE J. Sel. Areas Commun. **32**(6), 1065–82 (2014)
9. https://www.itu.int/en/ITU-D/Projects/Pages/default.aspx
10. https://hal.archives-ouvertes.fr/hal-02161803/document
11. https://ieeexplore.ieee.org/document/6161600
12. https://zigbeealliance.org/solution/zigbee/
13. https://datatracker.ietf.org/wg/6lowpan/documents/
14. https://datatracker.ietf.org/wg/6tisch/about/,   https://datatracker.ietf.org/wg/6tisch/documents/
15. Rappaport, T., et al.: Millimeter wave mobile communications for 5G cellular: it will work! IEEE Access **1**, 335–349 (2013)
16. IEEE 802.15.3c Part 15.3: Wireless medium access control (MAC) and physical layer (PHY) specifications for high rate wireless personal area networks (WPANs) amendment 2: Millimeter-wave-based alternative physical layer extension (2009)
17. IEEE 802.11ad. Part 11: Wireless LAN medium access control (MAC) and physical layer (PHY) specifications - amendment 3: Enhancements for very high throughput in the 60 GHz band (2012)
18. Rangan, S., Rappaport, T., Erkip, E.: Millimeter wave cellular wireless networks: Potentials and challenges. Proc. IEEE **102**, 366–385 (2014)

19. Caglar, T., Korpeoglu, I.: 60 GHz wireless data center networks: a survey. Comput. Netw. **185**, 107730 (2021)
20. Bhattacharjee, A., Bhattacharjee, R., Bose, S.K.: An approach for mitigation of beam blockage in mmWave based indoor networks. IEEE Internet Things J. **8**, 14607–14622 (2021)
21. Akbar, M.S., Yu, H., Cang, S.: TMP: tele-medicine protocol for slotted 802.15. 4 with duty-cycle optimization in wireless body area sensor networks. IEEE Sens. J. **17**(6), 1925–1936 (2016)
22. Akbar, M.S., Yu, H., Cang, S.: Delay, reliability, and throughput based QoS profile: a MAC layer performance optimization mechanism for biomedical applications in wireless body area sensor networks. J. Sens. **2016** (2016)
23. Akbar, M.S., Yu, H., Cang, S.: IEEE 802.15. 4 frame aggregation enhancement to provide high performance in life-critical patient monitoring systems. Sensors **17**(2), 241 (2017)

Channel Estimation for Millimeter Wave MIMO System: A Sequential Analysis Approach

Jinduo Zhang[1(✉)], Rongfei Fan[2], and Peng Liu[3]

[1] School of Information and Electronics, Beijing Institute of Technology,
Beijing, People's Republic of China
3120190835@bit.edu.cn
[2] School of Cyberspace Science and Technology, Beijing Institute of Technology,
Beijing, People's Republic of China
fanrongfei@bit.edu.cn
[3] China Ship Research and Development Academy, Beijing, People's Republic of China

Abstract. Channel estimation is crucial for a millimeter wave MIMO system. Due to the existence of massive antenna elements, the overhead to perform channel estimation with traditional methods would be huge, which will degrade the throughput severely. Thanks to the sparsity of channel model on millimeter wave band, most existing literature make use of this feature to compress the number of signaling based on the technique of compressive sensing. In this paper, by making use of the fact that the angle of arrival (AoA) and angle of departure (AoD) vary much slower than the channel coefficients, we go one step forward on saving the number of signaling for channel measurement. Specifically, with a consideration of channel sparsity feature, we design a set of methods to detect the variation of AoA and AoD in time, which includes the case of appearance of new path and disappearance of existing path, through sequential analysis approach. Moreover, to enhance the performance of our proposed method, procoder and combiner are designed respectively to generate beam on anticipated directions, through semi-definite programming method. With the above operations, we only need to measure channel coefficients when the AoA and AoD are not detected to change, which does not require much signaling. Through this way, the overhead for channel measurement is further saved compared with the methods based on compressive sensing.

Keywords: Millimeter wave · Channel measurement · Multiple input multiple output (MIMO) system · Sequential analysis · Semi-definite programming

1 Introduction

Millimeter wave communication technology is one of the most effective technologies for the next generation of wireless communication systems. The short wavelength of millimeter wave can reduce the size of the antenna element and make the use of large-scale antenna arrays feasible [1], which can further increase the gain of the array to combat the deep fading on millimeter wave band. Therefore, a millimeter wave system

W. Hussain and M. A. Jan (Eds.): IoTaaS 2021, LNICST 421, pp. 39–53, 2022.
https://doi.org/10.1007/978-3-030-95987-6_3

generally comes up with the implementation of a massive MIMO system, which is called as millimeter wave MIMO system for the ease of presentation in the following.

For a communication system, in order to achieve high throughput, it is a prerequisite to obtain channel state information (CSI) before sending the information. Millimeter wave MIMO system is not an exception. To acquire the CSI, channel measurement is required, whose task to recover the angle of arrival (AoA) and angle of departure (AoD) and channel coefficient of every path through multiple signaling signals. Recalling traditional channel measurement methods. They mainly include the one based on channel gain's covariance matrix (CCM method) [2] and the one based on spatial basis expansion model (SBEM method) [3], both of which rely on the knowledge of channel gain's covariance matrix. However, due to the huge number of antenna elements in a millimeter wave MIMO system, a lot of signaling will be required to estimate the channel gain's covariance matrix, which is time-consuming. To reduce the signaling overhead, the sparsity of channel model for millimeter wave signal prorogation is made use of and the channel measurement methods are developed based on compressing sensing (CS) theory in literature [4–6]. On the other hand, one more feature of the millimeter wave channel model is omitted in current related research works: The coherence time of every path's AoA and AoD is much larger than the coherence time of the path's channel coefficient [7]. With such a feature, it is possible to only estimate every path's channel coefficient when the associated AoA and AoD do not change, which will surely saving signaling overhead compared with the channel measurement methods based CS theory. As a complement, one more method is required to detect the change of channel's AoA or AoD.

In this paper, we realize the above idea for the channel measurement of millimeter wave MIMO system with the aid of sequential analysis approach. Specifically, we categorize the change of channel's AoA or AoD into two cases: 1) The appearance of new path; 2) The disappearance of existing path. For each case, in order to save signaling overhead, a quickest detection problem is formulated, which targets at minimizing the delay for detecting the variation of investigated statistics, and the Cumulative Sum (CUSUM) method is proposed to serve as the solution. To enhance the performance of detection (to make the divergence between the investigated statistics before change and after change to be larger), the precoder at the transmitter and the combiner at the receiver are proposed to be designed. In response to every case of AoA/AoD variation, two types of beamforming problems are formulated, which are shown to be non-convex. With some transformations and relaxation, we change the formulated beamforming problems into two semi-definite programming (SDP) problems, which are convex. Optimal solution and a good-enough feasible solution for the original two beamforming problems can be found based on the solutions obtained by solving the transformed SDP problems, respectively.

2   System Model

Consider a millimeter wave MIMO system with one transmitter and one receiver. There are N_T antennas at the transmitter and N_R antennas at the receiver, both of which are aligned in unitary linear array (ULA). To overcome the hardware limitation, a hybrid analog and digital beamforming architecture is adopted at both the transmitter and the receiver. The hybrid analog and digital beamforming architecture is the concatenation of a low-dimensional digital beamformer and a high-dimensional analog beamformer. For the hybrid beamforming structure at the transmitter, the overall precoder $\mathbf{v} \in \mathbb{C}^{N_T \times 1}$ can be written as $\mathbf{v} = \mathbf{V}^{RF} \times \mathbf{v}^D$, where $\mathbf{V}^{RF} \in \mathbb{C}^{N_T \times N_t^{RF}}$ is the RF precoding matrix and $\mathbf{v}^D \in \mathbb{C}^{N_t^{RF} \times 1}$ is the digital precoding matrix. For the receiver, the overall precoder $\mathbf{w} \in \mathbb{C}^{N_R \times 1}$ can be written as $\mathbf{w} = \mathbf{W}^{RF} \times \mathbf{w}^D$, where $\mathbf{W}^{RF} \in \mathbb{C}^{N_R \times N_r^{RF}}$ is the RF precoding matrix and $\mathbf{w}^D \in \mathbb{C}^{N_r^{RF} \times 1}$ is the digital precoding matrix. For an analog precoder, only phase can be shifted, thus there are $|\mathbf{V}^{RF}(i,j)| = 1$ and $|\mathbf{W}^{RF}(i,j)| = 1$, where $\mathbf{V}^{RF}(i,j)$ and $\mathbf{W}^{RF}(i,j)$ indicate the element of matrix $\mathbf{W}^{RF}$ and $\mathbf{V}^{RF}$ on ith row and jth column, respectively. We assume the $N_t^{RF} \geq 2N_T$ and $N_r^{RF} \geq 2N_R$. In this case, the hybrid structure is equivalent with the full digital beamformer[8].

With such a hybrid structure, suppose the transmitted signal $s = 1$ without loss of generality, then the broadcasted signal at the N_T antennas of the transmitter, denoted as $\mathbf{x}$, can be written as

$$\mathbf{x} = \mathbf{v}s = \mathbf{V}^{RF}\mathbf{v}^D s = \mathbf{V}^{RF}\mathbf{v}^D \tag{1}$$

Suppose $\mathbf{H} \in \mathbb{C}^{N_R \times N_T}$ is the channel matrix and $\mathbf{z} \sim \mathcal{CN}(\mathbf{0}, \sigma^2 \mathbf{I}_{N_R})$, then the received signal at N_R antennas of the receiver, denoted as $\mathbf{y}_0 \in \mathbb{C}^{N_R \times 1}$, can be written as

$$\mathbf{y}_0 = \mathbf{Hx} + \mathbf{z}, \tag{2}$$

and the received signal, denoted as y, can be written as

$$\begin{aligned} y &= \mathbf{w}^H \mathbf{Hx} + \mathbf{w}^H \mathbf{z} \\ &= \mathbf{w}^H \mathbf{Hv} + \mathbf{w}^H \mathbf{z} \end{aligned} \tag{3}$$

For the channel matrix $\mathbf{H}$, suppose there are N_S scatters, denote $\mathcal{N}_S \triangleq \{1, 2, ..., N_S\}$, $\mathbf{H}$ can be written as

$$\mathbf{H} = \sum_{n=1}^{N_S} \alpha_n \boldsymbol{\alpha}_r(\phi_n^\dagger) \boldsymbol{\alpha}_t^H(\theta_n^\dagger) \tag{4}$$

where α_n is the channel coefficient, $\phi_n^\dagger$ is the AoD, and the $\theta_n^\dagger$ is the AoA, of nth path for $n \in \mathcal{N}_S$. Specifically,

$$\boldsymbol{\alpha}_t(\theta_n^\dagger) = \frac{1}{\sqrt{N_T}} \left[1, e^{j\frac{2\pi}{\lambda} d \sin(\theta_n^\dagger)}, ..., e^{j\frac{2\pi}{\lambda} d \sin(\theta_n^\dagger)(N_T-1)} \right]^T \tag{5}$$

and

$$\boldsymbol{\alpha}_r(\phi_n^\dagger) = \frac{1}{\sqrt{N_R}} \left[1, e^{j\frac{2\pi}{\lambda} d \sin(\phi_n^\dagger)}, ..., e^{j\frac{2\pi}{\lambda} d \sin(\phi_n^\dagger)(N_R-1)} \right]^T \tag{6}$$

where d is the inter-antenna spacing and λ is the wavelength of signal. According to [9], N_S is no larger than 4. Moreover, the α_n changes more frequently than $\phi_n^\dagger$ and $\theta_n^\dagger$ for $n \in \mathcal{N}_S$ [7].

Before channel estimation, we do not know the set of $\{\theta_n\}$ and $\{\phi_n\}$. Thus we need to represent the channel matrix $\mathbf{H}$ in another way. Discretize all the AoD as N_D

uniformly-spaced angles, which are denoted as θ_1, ..., θ_{N_D}, and all the AoA as N_A uniformly-spaced angles, which are denoted as ϕ_1, ..., ϕ_{N_A}. Note that both $N_D \gg N_S$ and $N_A \gg N_S$. Denote

$$\boldsymbol{\Gamma}_t = [\boldsymbol{\alpha}_t(\theta_1), \boldsymbol{\alpha}_t(\theta_2), ..., \boldsymbol{\alpha}_t(\theta_{N_D})], \tag{7}$$

$$\boldsymbol{\Gamma}_r = [\boldsymbol{\alpha}_r(\phi_1), \boldsymbol{\alpha}_r(\phi_2), ..., \boldsymbol{\alpha}_r(\phi_{N_A})], \tag{8}$$

where $\boldsymbol{\Gamma}_t \in \mathbb{C}^{N_T \times N_D}$ and $\boldsymbol{\Gamma}_r \in \mathbb{C}^{N_R \times N_A}$. Then we can write $\mathbf{H}$ as

$$\mathbf{H} = \boldsymbol{\Gamma}_r \boldsymbol{\Lambda} \boldsymbol{\Gamma}_t^H \tag{9}$$

where $\boldsymbol{\Lambda} \in \mathbb{C}^{N_A \times N_D}$ is a sparse matrix only with N_S non-zero elements. When $\theta_i = \theta_n^*$ and $\phi_j = \phi_n^*$ for $n \in \mathcal{N}_S$, the element of $\boldsymbol{\Lambda}$ on ith column and jth row is α_n for $n \in \mathcal{N}_S$. All the other elements of $\boldsymbol{\Lambda}$ are zero. For the ease of discussion in the following, we vectorize $\mathbf{H}$ as $\text{vec}(\mathbf{H}) \in \mathbb{C}^{N_T N_R \times 1}$, define $\boldsymbol{\Psi} \triangleq \boldsymbol{\Gamma}_t^* \otimes \boldsymbol{\Gamma}_r$ where $\otimes$ is the Kronecker product, and $\mathbf{h} \triangleq \text{vec}(\boldsymbol{\Lambda}) \in \mathbb{C}^{N_D N_A \times 1}$ which is a sparse vector with N_S non-zero elements, then (9) can be rewritten as

$$\text{vec}(\mathbf{H}) = \boldsymbol{\Psi}\mathbf{h}. \tag{10}$$

and (3) can be rewritten as

$$\begin{aligned} y &= (\mathbf{v}^T \otimes \mathbf{w}^H)\text{vec}(\mathbf{H}) + \mathbf{w}^H\mathbf{z} \\ &= (\mathbf{v}^T \otimes \mathbf{w}^H)\boldsymbol{\Psi}\mathbf{h} + \mathbf{w}^H\mathbf{z} \end{aligned} \tag{11}$$

Suppose at time instant k, the associated precoding vector is $\mathbf{v}_k$ and the combining vector is $\mathbf{w}_k$, the received signal is y_k, then there is

$$y_k = (\mathbf{v}_k^T \otimes \mathbf{w}_k^H)\boldsymbol{\Psi}\mathbf{h} + \mathbf{w}_k^H\mathbf{z} \tag{12}$$

Hence the channel measurement is to reconstruct $\mathbf{h}$ from a number of y_k for $k = 1, 2, ...$

3   Brief Procedure

With the above system model, we focus on two special features of the investigated millimeter wave MIMO system:

- The maximal number of scatters N_S, denoted as $N_S^{\max}$, is no larger than 4.
- The α_n changes more frequently than $\phi_n^\dagger$ and $\theta_n^\dagger$ for $n \in \mathcal{N}_S$.

These two features motives us to reconstruct $\mathbf{h}$ with less number of measurements compared with the methods based on CS, which is given as follows

- Design an algorithm to closely monitor the change of $\phi_n^\dagger$ and $\theta_n^\dagger$ for $n \in \mathcal{N}_S$.
- When $\phi_n^\dagger$ and $\theta_n^\dagger$ for $n \in \mathcal{N}_S$ change and is detected by our designed monitoring algorithm, traditional channel estimation method, such as the CS method, can be resorted to so as to estimate the newly changed $\phi_n^\dagger$ and $\theta_n^\dagger$ for $n \in \mathcal{N}_S$, and the associated α_n for $n \in \mathcal{N}_S$.

- When $\phi_n^\dagger$ and $\theta_n^\dagger$ for $n \in \mathcal{N}_S$ is detected to be unchanged, current $\phi_n^\dagger$ and $\theta_n^\dagger$ for $n \in \mathcal{N}_S$ is effective. Hence we know which element of $\mathbf{h}$ is non-zero. Additionally, since the number of scatters N_S is no larger than 4, only 4 elements of $\mathbf{h}$ is needed to be estimated. In this case, 4 samples of y_k is enough to reconstruct $\mathbf{h}$, i.e., α_n for $n \in \mathcal{N}_S$, according to [10][1].

Through this way, it can be easily found that the number of y_k can be saved since $\phi_n^\dagger$ and $\theta_n^\dagger$ for $n \in \mathcal{N}_S$ does not need to be estimated compared with the channel measurement methods based on CS theory, which estimates not only α_n but also $\phi_n^\dagger$ and $\theta_n^\dagger$ for $n \in \mathcal{N}_S$ in every instance. This type of reduction of y_k samples would be significant since α_n changes more frequently than $\phi_n^\dagger$ and $\theta_n^\dagger$ for $n \in \mathcal{N}_S$.

In the following, we focus on designing the algorithm that can realize our idea. Specifically, we design the precoder and combiner, which can enhance the performance of monitoring whether there is a change of AoA or AoD. In terms of AoA/AoD change detection, we transform it into a quickest detection problem in the area of sequential analysis and propose the CUSUM method to serve as a solution. When the angle disappearance is being detected, we amplify the monitored path and suppress other scattering paths. Detailed discussion will be expanded in the following two sections.

4 Design of Precoder and Combiner

On the change of $\phi_n^\dagger$ and $\theta_n^\dagger$ for $n \in \mathcal{N}_S$, one of the following two cases may happen:

- Case I: Disappearance of one or more existing path.
- Case II: Appearance of one or more path, which does exist currently.

In the following two subsections, how to design precoder and combiner for Case I and Case II will be discussed, respectively.

4.1 Design of Precoder and Combiner for Case I

For the ease of discussion, the following notations are made. Since one path can be composed of one combination of ϕ_n and θ_n, denote the set of all the possible paths as $\mathcal{P} \triangleq \{1, 2, ..., N_A N_D\}$ and the set of currently existing paths as $\mathcal{P}_S$, where $\mathcal{P}_S \subset \mathcal{P}$ and $|\mathcal{P}_S| = |\mathcal{N}_S| = N_S$. For $p \in \mathcal{P}$, the associated path gain, AoA, and AoD are written as $\alpha_{n(p)}$, $\phi_{n(p)}$, and $\theta_{n(p)}$, respectively. Without loss of generality, we investigate the received signal at time instant k, y_k. Then by referring to (3) and (4), y_k can be written as

$$y_k = \sum_{p \in \mathcal{P}_S} \alpha_{n(p)} \mathbf{w}_k^H \boldsymbol{\alpha}_r(\phi_{n(p)}) \cdot \boldsymbol{\alpha}_t^H(\theta_{n(p)}) \mathbf{v}_k + \mathbf{w}_k^H \mathbf{z} \tag{13}$$

When one of the existing paths, denoted as path p^*, is being observed for disappearance, the signal from the paths $\mathcal{P}_S \setminus \{p^*\}$ should be isolated, thus there should be

$$v_k^H \boldsymbol{\alpha}_t(\theta_{n(p)}) = 0, \forall p \in \mathcal{P}_S \setminus \{p^*\} \tag{14}$$

---

[1] If the number of samples y_k is more than 4, the estimation accuracy of α_n for $n \in \mathcal{N}_S$ would be higher, which depends on the selection of user in real application.

at the precoder, and

$$w_k^H \alpha_r(\phi_{n(p)}) = 0, \forall p \in \mathcal{P}_S \setminus \{p^*\} \tag{15}$$

at the combiner. The constraints (14) and (15) can be written as the following equivalent form, respectively.

$$\mathbf{v}_k^H \Lambda_t(\theta_{n(p)})\mathbf{v}_k = 0, \forall p \in \mathcal{P}_S \setminus \{p^*\} \tag{16}$$

$$\mathbf{w}_k^H \Lambda_r(\phi_{n(p)})\mathbf{w}_k = 0, \forall p \in \mathcal{P}_S \setminus \{p^*\} \tag{17}$$

where $\Lambda_t(\theta_{n(p)}) \triangleq \alpha_t(\theta_{n(p)})\alpha_t^H(\theta_{n(p)})$ and $\Lambda_r(\phi_{n(p)}) \triangleq \alpha_r(\phi_{n(p)})\alpha_r^H(\phi_{n(p)})$.

In addition, in case that there is new path $p \in \mathcal{P} \setminus \mathcal{P}_S$ appears, the signals coming from the paths in $\mathcal{P} \setminus \mathcal{P}_S$ should also be suppressed, i.e., there should be

$$\mathbf{v}_k^H \left(\sum_{p \in \mathcal{P} \setminus \mathcal{P}_S} \Lambda_t(\theta_{n(p)}) \right) \mathbf{v}_k \leq \varepsilon_t \tag{18}$$

at the precoder and

$$\mathbf{w}_k^H \left(\sum_{p \in \mathcal{P} \setminus \mathcal{P}_S} \Lambda_r(\phi_{n(p)}) \right) \mathbf{w}_k \leq \varepsilon_r \tag{19}$$

at the receiver, where ε_t and ε_r are pre-defined thresholds. At the precoder, there is a maximal transmit power constraint, which can be written as

$$\mathbf{v}_k^H \mathbf{v}_k \leq P_T \tag{20}$$

where P_T is maximal transmit power at the transmitter.

For the precoder, collecting the listed constraints (16), (18), and (20), the problem of designing $\mathbf{v}_k$ can be written as

Problem 1

$$\max_{\mathbf{v}_k} \quad \mathbf{v}_k^H \Lambda_t(\theta_{n(p^*)})\mathbf{v}_k$$

$$\text{s.t.} \quad \mathbf{v}_k^H \Lambda_t(\theta_{n(p)})\mathbf{v}_k = 0, \forall p \in \mathcal{P}_S \setminus \{p^*\}, \tag{21a}$$

$$\mathbf{v}_k^H \left(\sum_{p \in \mathcal{P} \setminus \mathcal{P}_S} \Lambda_t(\theta_{n(p)}) \right) \mathbf{v}_k \leq \varepsilon_t, \tag{21b}$$

$$\mathbf{v}_k^H \mathbf{v}_k \leq P_T. \tag{21c}$$

For the design of combiner, the problem of designing $\mathbf{w}_k$ can be given as

Problem 2

$$\min_{\mathbf{w}_k} \quad \mathbf{w}_k^H \mathbf{w}_k$$

$$\text{s.t.} \quad \mathbf{w}_k^H \Lambda_r(\phi_{n(p^*)})\mathbf{w}_k \geq \tau_r, \tag{22a}$$

$$\mathbf{w}_k^H \Lambda_r(\phi_{n(p)})\mathbf{w}_k = 0, \forall p \in \mathcal{P}_S \setminus \{p^*\}, \tag{22b}$$

$$\mathbf{w}_k^H \left(\sum_{p \in \mathcal{P} \setminus \mathcal{P}_S} \Lambda_r(\phi_{n(p)}) \right) \mathbf{w}_k \leq \varepsilon_r, \tag{22c}$$

where τ_r is the pre-define threshold for guaranteeing the received signal strength from path p^*.

Both Problem 1 and Problem 2 are non-convex. A broadly used method to solve such kind of optimization problem via SDP method [11]. Specifically, define $A \bullet B \triangleq \mathrm{tr}(AB)$. Then $\mathbf{x}^H A \mathbf{x} = A \bullet \mathbf{xx}^H$. Define $\mathbf{W}_k = \mathbf{w}_k^H \mathbf{w}_k$ and $\mathbf{V}_k = \mathbf{v}_k^H \mathbf{v}_k$, Problem 1 and Problem 2 can be relaxed to be

Problem 3

$$\max_{V_k} \qquad V_k \bullet \Lambda_t(\theta_{n(p^*)})$$

$$\text{s.t. } V_k \bullet \Lambda_t(\theta_{n(p)}) = 0, \forall p \in \mathcal{P}_S \setminus \{p^*\}, \tag{23a}$$

$$V_k \bullet \left(\sum_{p \in \mathcal{P} \setminus \mathcal{P}_S} \Lambda_t(\theta_{n(p)}) \right) \leq \varepsilon_t, \tag{23b}$$

$$V_k \bullet I \leq P_T, \tag{23c}$$

$$V_k \succeq 0, \tag{23d}$$

and

Problem 4

$$\min_{W_k} \qquad W_k \bullet I$$

$$\text{s.t.} \qquad W_k \bullet \Lambda_r(\phi_{n(p^*)}) \geq \tau_r, \tag{24a}$$

$$W_k \bullet \Lambda_r(\phi_{n(p)}) = 0, \forall p \in \mathcal{P}_S \setminus \{p^*\}, \tag{24b}$$

$$W_k \bullet \left(\sum_{p \in \mathcal{P} \setminus \mathcal{P}_S} \Lambda_r(\phi_{n(p)}) \right) \leq \varepsilon_r, \tag{24c}$$

respectively.

It can be noticed that by adding the constraint $\mathrm{rank}(\mathbf{V}_k) = 1$ and $\mathrm{rank}(\mathbf{W}_k) = 1$ into Problem 3 and Problem 4, they would turn to be equivalent with Problem 1 and Problem 2, respectively. Thus if the optimal solution of Problem 3 or Problem 4 is rank-one, it is also the optimal solution of Problem 1 or Problem 2.

According to Corollary 4.6 of [12], there is rank-one optimal solution for Problem 3 and Problem 4, which can be found by following Algorithm 2 of [12]. Hence by following Algorithm 2 of [12], we can find the optimal solution of Problem 1 and Problem 2, respectively.

4.2 Design of Precoder and Combiner for Case II

For Case II, we do not know which path will appear. To detect the appearance of some path, we need to scan over all the possible AoDs ($\{\theta_n | n = 1, 2, ..., N_A\}$) while keeping the combiner to be omnidirectional, and scan over all the possible AoAs ($\{\phi_n | n = 1, 2, ..., N_D\}$) while keeping the precoder to be omnidirectional, respectively. In the following, we will show how to generate beamforming vectors for scanning over all the possible AoDs while keeping the combiner to be omnidirectional. How to generate beamforming vectors to scan all the possible AoAs can be realized in a similar way and is omitted for brevity.

To speed up the scanning process, we divide N_D angles of AoD into multiple clusters, each one of which has equal number of AoD angles. Then we can scan AoD angles cluster by cluster. At the precoder, suppose the ith cluster is being investigated, i.e., the set of AoD angles being investigated is $\mathcal{N}_{D_i} \subset \mathcal{N}_D \triangleq \{1, 2, ..., N_D\}$. Note that $\mathcal{N}_{D_i} \cap \mathcal{N}_{D_j} = \emptyset$, $\bigcup_i \mathcal{N}_{D_i} = \mathcal{N}_D$, and $|\mathcal{N}_{D_i}| = |\mathcal{N}_{D_j}|$. Then the problem of designing $\mathbf{v}_k$ can be written as

Problem 5

$$\max_{\mathbf{v}_k, t_T} \quad t_T$$

$$\text{s.t.} \quad \mathbf{v}_k^H \boldsymbol{\Lambda}_t(\theta_n)\mathbf{v}_k \geq t_T, \forall n \in \mathcal{N}_{D_i}, \tag{25a}$$

$$\mathbf{v}_k^H \left(\sum_{n \in \mathcal{N}_D \backslash \mathcal{N}_{D_i}} \boldsymbol{\Lambda}_t(\theta_n) \right) \mathbf{v}_k \leq \varepsilon_{ts}, \tag{25b}$$

$$\mathbf{v}_k^H \mathbf{v}_k \leq P_T, \tag{25c}$$

where ε_{ts} is the pre-defined threshold.

For the combiner, the omnidirectional beamforming problem of designing $\mathbf{w}_k$ can be given as

Problem 6

$$\max_{\mathbf{w}_k, t_R} \quad t_R$$

$$\text{s.t.} \quad \mathbf{w}_k^H \boldsymbol{\Lambda}_r(\phi_n)\mathbf{w}_k \geq t_R, \forall n \in \mathcal{N}_A, \tag{26a}$$

$$\mathbf{w}_k^H \mathbf{w}_k \leq \varepsilon_{rs}, \tag{26b}$$

where ε_{rs} is the pre-defined value for the purpose of suppressing the noise power of received signal.

By following the SDP relaxation method in Sect. 4.1, Problem 5 and Problem 6 can be relaxed to be

Problem 7

$$\max_{V_k, t_T} \quad t_T$$

$$\text{s.t.} \quad V_k \bullet \boldsymbol{\Lambda}_t(\theta_n) \geq t_T, \forall n \in \mathcal{N}_{D_i}, \tag{27a}$$

$$V_k \bullet \left(\sum_{n \in \mathcal{N}_D \backslash \mathcal{N}_{D_i}} \boldsymbol{\Lambda}_t(\theta_n) \right) \leq \varepsilon_{ts}, \tag{27b}$$

$$V_k \bullet I \leq P_T, \tag{27c}$$

$$V_k \succeq 0, \tag{27d}$$

and

Problem 8

$$\max_{\boldsymbol{W}_k, t_R} \quad t_R$$

$$\text{s.t. } \boldsymbol{W}_k \bullet \Lambda_r(\phi_n) \geq t_R, \forall n \in \mathcal{N}_A, \tag{28a}$$

$$\boldsymbol{W}_k \bullet \boldsymbol{I} \leq \varepsilon_{rs}, \tag{28b}$$

$$\boldsymbol{W}_k \succeq 0, \tag{28c}$$

respectively.

Problem 7 and Problem 8 can be solved by bisection searching the maximal t_T or t_R such that the constraints in (27) and (28) are feasible respectively, which involves SDP for every given t_T or t_R.

Since the vector $\boldsymbol{\alpha}_t(\theta_{n(p)})$ and $\boldsymbol{\alpha}_r(\theta_{n(p)})$ for $p \in \mathcal{P}$ are Vandermonde, then according to [13], there is rank-one optimal solution for Problem 7 and Problem 8. Unfortunately, how to generate the rank-one optimal solution for the type of problem like Problem 7 and Problem 8 is not characterized in [13]. Here we resort to Gaussian sampling method to generate the rank-one solution [14].

5 AoA/AoD Change Detection

5.1 Problem Formulation for Case I: Disappearance of Path

In this case, with the precoder and combiner implemented as the way in Sect. 4.1, we get a sequence of received signal $y_k, k = 1, 2, \ldots$ for watching the p^*th path. There is a time Γ_1, before which the path p^* is still active and after which the path p^* disappears. Before Γ_1, the sequence of $y_k, k = 1, 2, \ldots$ are subject to one distribution, denoted as $f_0^I(x)$, independently. For $f_0^I(x)$, since $\mathbf{z} \sim \mathcal{CN}(\mathbf{0}, \sigma^2 \mathbf{I}_{N_R})$ and combining the fact in (13), $f_0^I(x)$ is a Gaussian distribution conditioned on $\alpha_{n(p^*)}$, which can be also denoted as $f_0^I(x|\alpha_{n(p^*)})$, with mean being $\left(\alpha_{n(p^*)} \mathbf{w}_k^H \boldsymbol{\alpha}_r(\phi_{n(p^*)}) \cdot \boldsymbol{\alpha}_t^H(\theta_{n(p^*)}) \mathbf{v}_k\right)$ and variance being $\sigma^2 \mathbf{w}_k^H \mathbf{w}_k$. As previously assumed, $\alpha_{n(p^*)}$ is a complex Gaussian random variable with mean being zero and variance being P_{att}. After time Γ_1, the sequence of $y_k, k = 1, 2, \ldots$ are subject to distribution $f_1^I(x)$ independently, which is a Gaussian distribution with mean being 0 and variance being $\sigma^2 \mathbf{w}_k^H \mathbf{w}_k$.

Define $\mathbb{P}_t$ and $\mathbb{E}_t$ as the probability measure and corresponding expectation under the event $\{\Gamma^I = t\}$. Hence $\mathbb{P}_\infty$ and $\mathbb{E}_\infty$ denote the case $t = \infty$. Our target is to find a stopping time T^I, such that the disappearance of the path p^* is declared once it happens. By following the problem formulation of Lorden's quickest change detection, define

$$d_t(T^I) = \text{ess sup } \mathbb{E}_t\left[\left(T^I - t + 1\right)^+ | \mathcal{F}_{t-1}\right] \tag{29}$$

and

$$d(T^I) = \sup_{t \geq 1} d_t(T^I), \tag{30}$$

where $(x)^+ = \max(x, 0)$ and $\mathcal{F}_t = \sigma(y_1, y_2, \ldots, y_t)$. The function $d(T^I)$ is actually a measure of detection delay. Our target is to solve the following optimization problem

Problem 9

$$\min_{T^I \in \mathcal{T}} \quad d(T^I)$$

$$s.t. \ \mathbb{E}_\infty[T^I] \geq \eta \tag{31a}$$

where $\mathcal{T} \triangleq \{T | \mathbb{E}_t[T] < \infty\}$. This is a change-point detection problem in the field of sequential analysis.

5.2 Problem Formulation for Case II: Appearance of Path

In this case, the AoA or AoD of a new appearing path will be disjoint from the ones in existing paths. Thus we need to detect the appearance of a new AoA or AoD angle separately so as to catch the appearance of a new path. With the precoder and combiner implemented as the way in Sect. 4.2 and suppose the cluster being watched is i, we get a sequence of received signal y_k^i, $k = 1, 2, \dots$. To study the case in a more convenient way, we turn to investigate the signal $|y_k^i|$, $k = 1, 2, \dots$. The sequence of $\{|y_k^i|\}$ falls into one of the falling two hypothesis

$$\mathcal{H}_0 : |y_k^i| \overset{i.i.d.}{\sim} f_0^{II}(x), k = 1, 2, \dots$$
$$\mathcal{H}_1 : |y_k^i| \overset{i.i.d.}{\sim} f_1^{II}(x), k = 1, 2, \dots$$

For ith sector under hypothesis $\mathcal{H}_0$, $f_0^{II}(x)$ may be uncertain.

– When there is no path appearing in all the other sectors, $f_0^{II}(x)$ would be a Rice distribution with ν_0 being 0 and σ_0 being $\sqrt{\sigma^2 \mathbf{w}_k^H \mathbf{w}_k}$, where ν_0 and σ_0 are parameters in the PDF of Rice distribution. The PDF of Rice distribution can be written as

$$f(x|\nu_0, \sigma_0) = \frac{x}{\sigma_0^2} e^{\frac{-(x^2 + \nu_0^2)}{2\sigma_0^2}} I_0 \left(\frac{x\nu_0}{\sigma_0^2} \right)$$

where $I_0(y)$ is the first kind modified Bessel function with order zero.
– When there are $(N_S^{\max} - N_S)$ paths appearing in every other sector rather than ith sector, $f_0^{II}(x)$ would be a Rice distribution with ν_0 being $|\alpha_n| (N_S^{\max} - N_S) \sqrt{\varepsilon_{ts} t_R^{\max}}$ at most and σ_0 being $\sqrt{\sigma^2 \mathbf{w}_k^H \mathbf{w}_k}$. Note that α_n represents the random channel coefficient, which is complex Gaussian random variable with mean being 0 and variance being P_{att}, and

$$t_R^{\max} \triangleq \max_{n \in \mathcal{N}_A} |\mathbf{w}_k^H \boldsymbol{\alpha}_r(\phi_n)|.$$

For ith sector under hypothesis $\mathcal{H}_1$, $f_1^{II}(x)$ may be uncertain either.

– When there is only one path appearing in ith sector and there is no path appearing in all the other sectors, $f_1^{II}(x)$ would be a Rice distribution with ν_0 being $|\alpha_n| \sqrt{t_T t_R}$ and σ_0 being $\sqrt{\sigma^2 \mathbf{w}_k^H \mathbf{w}_k}$.

– Where there are $(N_S^{\max} - N_S)$ paths in ith sector, $f_1^{\mathrm{II}}(x)$ would be a Rice distribution with ν_0 being $|\alpha_n| (N_S^{\max} - N_S) \sqrt{t_T^{\max} t_R^{\max}}$ where

$$t_T^{\max} \triangleq \max_{n \in \mathcal{N}_D} |\mathbf{v}_k^H \boldsymbol{\alpha}_t(\theta_n)|,$$

and σ_0 being $\sqrt{\sigma^2 \mathbf{w}_k^H \mathbf{w}_k}$.

Denote the index of cluster we are observing at time k is s_k. Then the observed sequence can be written as $\{y_k^{s_k}; k = 1, 2, ...\}$, which generates a filtration $\{\mathcal{G}_k, k = 1, 2, ...\}$ where $\mathcal{G}_k = \sigma(y_1^{s_1}, y_2^{s_2}, ..., y_k^{s_k})$. Define $\varpi_k(\mathcal{G}_k)$ as the $\mathcal{G}_k$-measurable switching function at time k. $\varpi_k(\mathcal{G}_k) = 0$ indicates that we decide to continue to watch on s_kth sequence, i.e., $s_{k+1} = s_k$; $\varpi_k(\mathcal{G}_k) = 1$ means that we switch to observe the next sequence, i.e., $s_{k+1} = s_k + 1$. Denote Υ as the set of stopping time associated with the filtration $\mathcal{G}_k$ [15]. There should be also one stopping time $\tau \in \Upsilon$ indicating that when we should stop sampling and claim the current observed sequence is subject to $\mathcal{H}_1$, i.e., sequence s_k is subject to $\mathcal{H}_1$ when $\tau = k$.

Our purpose is to optimize the stopping time τ and the switching rule $\varpi = \{\varpi_1, \varpi_2, ...\}$ to minimize the a mixed measure of false alarm probability and average sampling number, $\Pr(\mathcal{H}^{s_\tau} = \mathcal{H}_0) + c\mathbb{E}[\tau]$, where c is positive constant. Suppose the stopping time is no larger than T^{II}, i.e., we have to stop by time T^{II}. The T^{II} can be the maximal number of samples in one fading block or a fraction of it for the purpose of suppressing the overhead of channel sensing. Summarizing all the constraints and the objective function, the specific optimization problem can be formulated as follows

Problem 10

$$\inf_{\tau, \varpi} \Pr(\mathcal{H}^{s_\tau} = \mathcal{H}_0) + c\mathbb{E}[\tau]$$
$$s.t. \ 0 \leq \tau \leq T^{II}, \tag{32}$$
$$\tau \in \Upsilon.$$

5.3   Solution for Case I and Case II

To detect the disappearance and appearance of a path, according to [16], the CUSUM algorithm can serve as a solution, which is usually asymptotic optimal for change point detection problems like the form of Problem 9 or Problem 10. In essence, it can detect the change point of distribution for the observed random time series with low delay. Assume the investigated sequential signal is o_k, $k = 1, 2, ...$, with a change point of distribution at n. The sequences o_k before and after n are supposed to be independent and identically distributed. The distribution before n is $f_0(x)$, and the distribution after n is $f_1(x)$. Then the statistic of CUSUM method can be given as $Z_k = \max\left\{0, Z_{k-1} + \log \frac{f_1(o_k)}{f_0(o_k)}\right\}$ for $k \geq 1$ and $Z_k = 0$ for $k = 0$.

Set a threshold h, if $Z_t \geq h$, we can claim that the distribution of the observed sequence has changed. The threshold h can be selected to satisfy the required constraint of formulated optimization problem through Mont Carlo simulation.

6 Numerical Results

In this section, numerical results are presented to verify the effectiveness of our proposed method. The major system parameters are set as follows. $N_T = 128$ and $N_R = 128$. $N_D = N_A = 20$. The total transmit power $P_T = 1$. $N_S = 4$. The AoA and AoD of every path are randomly generated between $[0, 2\pi]$. The wavelength is $\lambda = 0.001$ m, and the distance between adjacent antenna elements is $\frac{\lambda}{2}$. In terms of SDP problem, CVX toolbox is utilized with default setting. All the ε (including ε_t, ε_r, ε_{ts}, and ε_{rs}) when solving a SDP problem is 0.001.

First, in order to prove the effectiveness of the CUSUM algorithm, we compared it with the traditional binary detection algorithm. We are investigating a sequential sequence with 1000 samples, the change-point of which happens at 501. We set different thresholds for the CUSUM algorithm and the traditional binary detection algorithm, and obtained the detection delay and false alarm probability of the two algorithms under these thresholds, and compared the performance of the two algorithms. In Fig. 1 and Fig. 2, the time delay and false alarm probability under various selection of h is plotted. These two figures can help to characterize the relationship between detection time delay and false alarm probability.

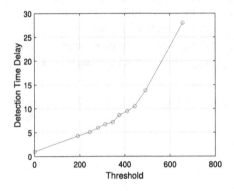

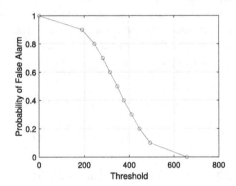

Fig. 1. Time delay of CUSUM   **Fig. 2.** False alarm of CUSUM

In Fig. 3, the performance of CUSUM is compared with the performance of traditional binary detection method, which is respective of the detection delay. It can be seen from Fig. 3 that the CUSUM method can always outperform the binary detection method, which proves the effectiveness of the CUSUM method.

And most importantly, we compared our algorithm with the traditional OMP algorithm. We assume that the channel coefficient changes 10 times in a fading block of the angles, so for the traditional algorithm, in an angle fading block, we use 10 times of OMP algorithm for channel estimation. On the other hand, for our algorithm, we use the CUSUM algorithm in the detection process and the least squares estimation algorithm in estimating the channel coefficients.

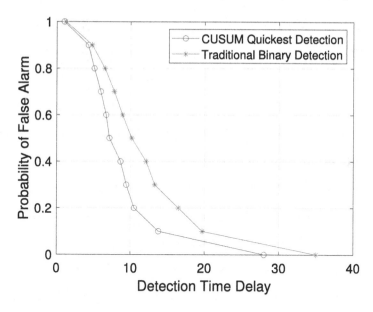

Fig. 3. Comparison of CUSUM and binary detection

In our algorithm, we first detect whether the angle disappears, and then detect whether the angle appears, if a change is detected, we use the OMP algorithm to re-estimate the channel, otherwise we only estimate the channel coefficient. In the process of detecting the disappearance of the angle, we check each current path in turn. On the other hand, in the process of detecting angle generation, we inspect all sectors in turn. In addition, we discretize the angle into 20 parts, and when detecting whether the angle is generated, divide the angle into 5 sectors, where each sector contains 4 discrete angles. The longest number of observation points in a detection is 20, which means that if the number of observation points exceeds 20 and no change is detected, then we determine that the channel angle remains unchanged We compare the relationship between the number of observation points of the two algorithms and the NMSE under three different SNR (3.2 dB, 0 dB, −2.6 dB).

It can be seen from Fig. 4 that under different Signal-to-Noise Ratios(SNR), when the same observation points are used, the NMSE of the current algorithm is smaller than that of the OMP algorithm, which means that when the same NMSE is reached, the number of observation points used by our algorithm is less than that of the traditional OMP algorithm.

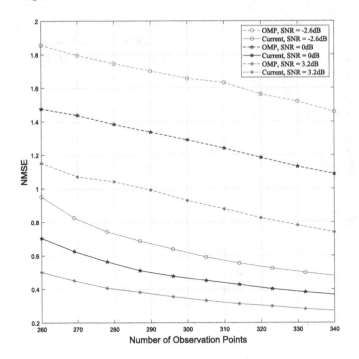

Fig. 4. Comparison of current method and OMP method

7 Conclusion

In this paper, we propose a method of channel measurement for millimeter MIMO system based on the fact that the AoA/AoD coherence time is much longer than the one of channel coefficient. To realize our idea, we utilize the CUSUM method to detect the variation of AoA/AoD with low delay, which falls into the area of sequential analysis. To enhance the performance of CUSUM, we design beamforming for both the precoder and combiner. Through SDP, optimal or sub-optimal solution can be achieved for the formulated beamforming problems. The simulation results show that when the same effect is achieved, our algorithm reduces the time overhead compared with the traditional OMP algorithm. Our proposed method can help to save the signaling overhead for the channel measurement.

References

1. Hu, C., Wang, X., Dai, L., Ma, J.: Partially coherent compressive phase retrieval for millimeter-wave massive MIMO channel estimation. IEEE Trans. Sig. Process. **68**, 1673–1687 (2020)
2. Yin, H., Gesbert, D., Filippou, M., Liu, Y.: A coordinated approach to channel estimation in large-scale multiple-antenna systems. IEEE J. Sel. Areas Commun. **31**(2), 264–273 (2013)
3. Xie, H., Gao, F., Zhang, S., Jin, S.: A unified transmission strategy for TDD/FDD massive MIMO systems with spatial basis expansion model. IEEE Trans. Veh. Technol. **66**(4), 3170–3184 (2017)

4. Xie, H., González-Prelcic, N.: Dictionary learning for channel estimation in hybrid frequency-selective mmWave MIMO systems. IEEE Trans. Wirel. Commun. **19**(11), 7407–7422 (2020)
5. Heath, R.W., González-Prelcic, N., Rangan, S., Roh, W., Sayeed, A.M.: An overview of signal processing techniques for millimeter wave MIMO systems. IEEE J. Sel. Top. Sig. Process. **10**(3), 436–453 (2016)
6. Alkhateeb, A., Ayach, O.E., Leus, G., Heath, R.W.: Channel estimation and hybrid precoding for millimeter wave cellular systems. IEEE J. Sel. Top. Sig. Process. **8**(5), 831–846 (2014)
7. Va, V., Choi, J., Heath, R.W.: The impact of beamwidth on temporal channel variation in vehicular channels and its implications. IEEE Trans. Veh. Technol. **66**(6), 5014–5029 (2017)
8. Sohrabi, F., Yu, W.: Hybrid digital and analog beamforming design for large-scale antenna arrays. IEEE J. Sel. Top. Sig. Process. **10**(3), 501–513 (2016)
9. Akdeniz, M.R., et al.: Millimeter wave channel modeling and cellular capacity evaluation. IEEE J. Sel. Areas Commun. **32**(6), 1164–1179 (2014)
10. Cheng, P., et al.: Channel estimation for OFDM systems over doubly selective channels: a distributed compressive sensing based approach. IEEE Trans. Commun. **61**(10), 4173–4185 (2013)
11. Boyd, S.P., Vandenberghe, L.: Convex Optimization. Cambridge University Press, Cambridge (2004)
12. Huang, Y., Palomar, D.P.: Rank-constrained separable semidefinite programming with applications to optimal beamforming. IEEE Trans. Sig. Process. **58**(2), 664–678 (2010)
13. Karipidis, E., Sidiropoulos, N.D., Luo, Z.Q: Far-field multicast beamforming for uniform linear antenna arrays. IEEE Trans. Sig. Process. **55**(10), 4916–4927 (2007)
14. Palomar, D.P., Eldar, Y.C.: Convex Optimization in Signal Processing and Communications. Cambridge University Press, Cambridge (2010)
15. Zou, S., Veeravalli, V.V., Li, J., Towsley, D.: Quickest detection of dynamic events in networks. IEEE Trans. Inf. Theory **66**(4), 2280–2295 (2020)
16. Tartakovsky, A., Nikiforov, I., Basseville, M.: Sequential Analysis: Hypothesis Testing and Changepoint Detection. CRC Press, Florida (2014)

A Comprehensive Study on the Energy Efficiency of IoT from Four Angles: Clustering and Routing in WSNs, Smart Grid, Fog Computing and MQTT & CoAP Application Protocols

Ziyad Almudayni[1(✉)], Ben Soh[2], and Alice Li[2]

[1] Hail University, Hail, Saudi Arabia
20167676@students.latrobe.edu.au
[2] La Trobe University, Melbourne, Australia
{b.soh,a.li}@latrobe.edu.au

Abstract. The Internet of things (IoT) technologies have been developing since their inception. Consequently, the number of connected devices increases yearly. The development of IoT devices has to be set, taking into consideration parameters such as security, data rate and energy. In this paper, we carried out a comprehensive review on the main concern, which is the energy efficacy of IoT devices. We will target four research areas to make the searching process interesting and easier for researchers. The four research areas are related to clustering and routing in WSNs, smart grid, fog computing and MQTT & CoAP application protocols.

Keywords: Fog computing · WSNs · Routing · Clustering · Smart grid · CoAP and MQTT

1 Introduction

The Internet of things (IoT) can be described as the ability of IoT nodes to communicate with each other via the Internet to perform tasks. Establishing IoT technologies in any environment can make the work process more convenient and save time. Therefore, this technology might witness a vast evolution, and each person might need from three to four connected devices. Developers have been working to make IoT systems more secure and accurate by establishing and running complex algorithms on these systems; however, these algorithms consume power to run accurately [1]. To make IoT networks more accurate and scalable, especially with the large number of connected devices, it is vital to improve the IoT system's performance from all angles: energy, data rate, bandwidth, coverage, and more. In this study, we will target the energy performance of the IoT systems by collecting previous related studies to help developers to find gaps and target areas. Therefore, the sources of energy in IoT networks have to be clarified first, which are sensing, processing, and data transmission for instance of developing these factors,

W. Hussain and M. A. Jan (Eds.): IoTaaS 2021, LNICST 421, pp. 54–70, 2022.
https://doi.org/10.1007/978-3-030-95987-6_4

it is necessary for researchers to know how long the IoT systems execute data and aim to reduce that time to save power. Moreover, the data rate is another critical point in IoT systems that affects the energy efficacy of IoT deceives, as it is generally known that increasing the data rate means consuming more power. Thus, it is vital to know exactly the amount of data rate that each IoT application requires to avoid wasting data rate and power by giving data rate for an IoT application more than its needs. Moreover, the IoT application's range of coverage is another critical point, which is directly related to the IoT systems' power consumption, as coverage increases power increases so, knowing the exact range where each IoT application needs to cover to sense and transmit data could be considered the key to solving this issue, as there will be no more extra coverage than the needs and no power wasting [2]. However, to address the gaps in IoT systems or any system, we have to read previous studies about the point we aim to address deeply from more than one angle and analyse these previous studies that are related to the same area to find gaps and address these gaps. In this study, we review previous studies on enhancing energy efficiency in IoT systems from four angles. The first angle is related to the clustering and routing mechanisms in the WSNs. The second angle is related to scheduling, balancing and finding the best resource in fog computing to process the IoT tasks. The third concern is developing the use of IoT systems in the smart grid (SG) to save power. The last angel is related to the two most vital application protocols MQTT and CoAP and how can the modification on these protocols contribute in improving the energy efficiency of IoT networks. Figure 1 lists the four angles.

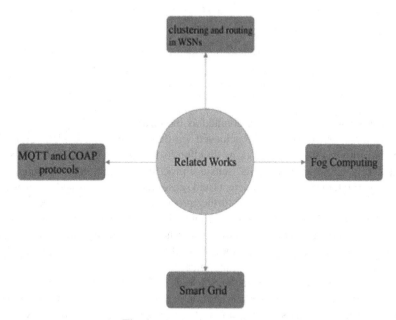

Fig. 1. Four main research areas

2   Energy Efficiency, Routing and Clustering for WSNs in IoT

In this section we review recent studies in the literature about improving IoT networks' energy efficiency through addressing the gaps and finding optimal solutions for clustering, and routing in WSNs. Figure 2 shows how these three areas are linked.

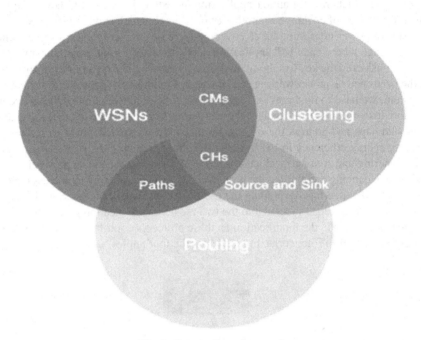

Fig. 2. Intersection of research

The IoT sensor nodes could be counted as the heart of the IoT system as most of the IoT systems' objectives can be achieved via theses sensor nodes. Therefore, it is vital to know how an IoT WSN work by dividing its function into units. The IoT sensor node generally has four main units: sensing, processing, communication and power supply units. First, the sensing unit detects and senses the movements and changes in the surrounding areas to be collected for further processing. Seconds, the processing unit analyses the collected data to perform tasks and take actions. Third, the communication unit transfers the data between IoT nodes via a network. Finally, the power unit has power restrictions to supply sensors nodes with the required power. Comparing theses four units from an energy angle, the communication unit could be counted as the highest power energy consumers due to its nature of work in sending and receiving data [3].

Xiong C et al. [4] proposed Source location privacy (SLP) to secure networks in the industrial internet of Things (IIoT), aiming to protect the networks from any attacks; however, this protection requires more power to operate as IIoT has to run more complex algorithms in the network. Therefore, the authors used distributed energy resources (DERs) to prolong the network lifetime, aiming to balance the network between security and power consumption. The reason behind proposing this approach is because in some cases in IIoT applications, attackers can track the packages by locating the nodes; so hiding the location of sensors is vital. The proposed approach is capable of hiding the locations of sensors by using phantom nodes, rings, and fake paths (PRFs). It creates fake paths and nodes to distribute attackers. The main disadvantage of the proposed approach is that it only works when nodes are constant.

Zhang X et al. [5] proposed an optimal path selection method (OPSM) based on an ant routing algorithm that can find the optimal path, aiming to improve the performance of IoT networks. The reason behind proposing this approach is to prevent the IoT networks from causing delays and prolong the network lifetime. Therefore, the network lifetime, mobile distance and node coverage are considered in OPSM. The method basically divides the network monitoring area into several fixed-size grids, and it keeps dividing until the network lifetime becomes greater than or equal to the time threshold to select the optimal path. The simulation results demonstrate that OPSM successfully makes the transmission time shorter and prolongs the network lifetime.

Pereira H et al. [6] proposed a new metric for routing protocol for the low and lossy networks (RPL) instead of the previous routing metrics expected transmission count (ETC) to enhance load balancing and increase the lifetime of WSNs. The new metric is called network interface average power (NIAP). NIAP can estimate the average power consumed in the network interface. Moreover, it can pick the best routes from multiple paths, which contributes to improving load balancing and increasing the lifetime of WSNs. After various experiments, the results prove that NIAP can be a satisfying alternative to ETX because of its simplicity regarding implementation, and it does not require any modifications for the RPL standard. However, NIAP has some limitations. It requires changing the parent node frequently to find the best path and it works on short-scale topologies.

Khan F et al. [7] proposed a new routing mechanism called modified-percentage LEACH to address gaps in the current protocol: low-energy adaptive clustering hierarchy (LEACH). The new routing protocol aims to prolong the network lifetime by decreasing communications between CHs and the sink. Therefore, the new approach divides nodes in the cluster into two groups based on the destination to the sink: near to sink (N) far from the sink (F). In the former, nodes communicate directly with the sink as they are close to the sink. In the latter, nodes require a CH to link them to the sink as they are far away from the sink. As a result, the new approach success in enhancing the energy efficacy and outperforms the energy performance of previous protocols: LEACH, V-LEACH and MOD-LEACH. However, the new protocol works only on two types of deployments: free space and multi-path schemes.

Abdullah S et al. [8] proposed an energy-scheduling algorithm to prolong the network lifetime in IoT networks. The new approach divides things/sensors into clusters, and each cluster has its private broker, whose mission is to link cluster members to the sink. Moreover, the broker schedules messages and decides which message goes first using the SPF (shortest processing time first) technique. The selection of a broker is not randomly as in LEACH; it is based on the distance of a node and its residual energy. The simulation results show that the proposed approach improves the residual energy and keeps more nodes alive compared to LEACH.

Iqbal S et al. [9] proposed a zone-based routing algorithm to change the selfish behavior as nodes try not to share energy with their neighbours to save their energy because they have limited battery power. Therefore, IoT nodes should cooperate with other nodes to boost the network lifetime rather than saving power for them only. Thus, the zone-based routing algorithm employs a game theory solution to force nodes to share energy with neighbours. The algorithm consists of four main steps: structuring zones, selecting a leader for the zone, discovering routes and selecting paths. The simulation outcomes show that the proposed approach improves the packet delivery ratio, network lifetime, and throughput compared to AODV and ZCG.

Safara F et al. [10] proposed a new routing method based on energy and security called (PriNergy), intending to enhance the energy efficiency for IoT systems. The routing method employs RPL as its routing model. Each node in the network calculates the time to send data to the destination, aiming to increase routing quality in the network. Moreover, the new approach divides nodes into high priorities and low priorities to avoid congestion on the network. NS-2 was used to evaluate the proposed approach. The PriNergy simulation results show better energy consumption, end-to-end delays, and routing overhead compared to QRPL.

Shen J et al. [11] proposed a new routeing protocol called energy-efficient centroid-based routing protocol (EECRP) for IoT wireless sensors to enhance the energy efficiency of IoT networks. The proposed method consists of three key factors to obtain its objective:

- A new distributed method to allow nodes to organise themself locally.
- New algorithms to select a cluster head in a centre position aim to divide the workload equally among all sensor nodes.
- A new mechanism to prolong the network lifetime for communication in long-distance.

Therefore, the new approach is suitable for long lifetime networks where the base station (BS) is placed in the same network. The simulation outcomes show that EECPR achieves better results than LEACH, LEACH-C, and GEEC.

XU Y et al. [12] modified the standard LEACH to improve the performance in WSNs. As known, the selections of the CHs occur randomly in the tradition LEACH. However, in the modified approach to factors are considered to select a CH. First, the residual energy of the nodes and nodes can calculate its residual energy. Second, the distance between CHs and the sink and nodes can measure this distance. The simulation results show that the proposed approach outperforms the standard LEACH in terms of energy efficiency.

Ouhab A et al. [13] proposed a new model to support the lack of efficient routing to handle device-to-device communication on a large scale in IoT. The proposed mechanism aims to satisfy the QoS requirements for the network by providing two new control mechanisms. First, a new routing protocol for RPL stands on the multi-hop clustering technique (MHC-RPL) to control and organise nodes locally. Second, the integration of (SDN) with Q-routing algorithm is implemented to control the network globally. The simulation results show that the new approach has better outcomes than the current state-of-the-art in terms of energy consumption, packet delivery ratio and end-to-end delay.

Tang L et al. [14] proposed a new routing algorithm called energy balanced routing algorithm for network lifetime enhancement (EBRA-NLE) based on a DS evidence theory in the WSNs. The new approach aims to achieve two objectives: increasing network lifetime and balancing workload among nodes. Three attribute indexes are implemented in this algorithm: Energy Balance Factor (EB), Relay Coefficient (RC), and Buffer Idleness (BI). EB to distribute workload equally among nodes, RC selects the best optimal path for a node to the base station, and BI estimates the capacity of nodes to receive data. Using MATLAB 2019, the simulation outcomes prove that the network lifetime improved by the use of the EBRA-NLE algorithm and shows better results than MCRP and DS-EERA algorithms by about 313% and 72%, respectively.

Iwendi C et al. [15] proposed a metaheuristic optimisation approach to prolong the network lifetime by reducing the power consumption in the network. The proposed method used a hybrid metaheuristic algorithm: whale optimization algorithm (WOA) to select the optimal Cluster Head CH in the IoT network. Moreover, temperature, residual energy, load, and the number of alive nodes are considered as metric performance to select an appropriate cluster head. The simulation of selecting CHs in Matlab R2015a proves that the new approach outperforms the existing algorithm: artificial bee colony algorithm, genetic algorithm and adaptive gravitational search algorithm.

Sarma S et al. [16] proposed a new routing algorithm based on search and rescue optimization algorithm (SAR) to select an appropriate Cluster head (CH), aiming to improve the performance of WSNs. Distance, delay and energy are considered to support the process of choosing CHs. The evaluation of the proposed approach was done by MATLAB. The simulation results show that SAR has better energy performance and success in keeping more nodes alive compared to existing approaches: Grey Wolf Optimization (GWO) and Firefly Cyclic Grey Wolf Optimization (FCGWO).

Reddy P et al. [17] proposed a new approach that is based on combining two algorithms called Gravitational Search Algorithm (GSA) and Artificial Bee Colony (ABC) algorithm to select the best optimal CHs for WSNs in IoT network. Moreover, distance, energy, delay, load, and temperature are considered to select a Ch. The simulation results show that the proposed approach success in prolonging the network lifetime compared to existing protocols: artificial bee colony (ABC), genetic algorithm (GA), particle swarm optimization (PSO), and GSA algorithm.

WiseMid middleware was launched as a software tool to IoT hardware devices and data to work in one environment. The WiseMid can contribute to enhancing the energy efficiency of IoT systems by introducing four mechanisms. Data aggregation: This aims to minimise the overall size of the sent message to avoid traffic in the network by removing extra data. Reply storage timeout: This prevents the system from sending messages with the same value that has been sent already. Atomic type conversion: This converts the type of messages to remove the extra bytes. Invocation asynchronous patterns: The asynchronous messaging's objective is to avoid delays when a client sends a request [18].

In healthcare systems, the Body Sensors Network (BSNs) consumes power, as these sensors have to work continuously for a long time to collect the patient's data for further monitoring. To minimise the power consumption for these sensors, in [19] the authors proposed a machine learning (ML) algorithm to classify patients' status into two categories: normal situation and emergent situation based on the collected data from the four sensors, namely, the accelerometer electrocardiogram (ECG), temperature and humidity. In normal situations, the transmission level will be low, whereas, in emergent situations, the level of transmission will be high.

3   Energy Efficiency for IoT Using Fog Computing

In this section we review recent studies in the literature about how an IoT node finds the best optimal source to compute data. Figure 3 shows how optimization algorithms can help IoT nodes to find optimal resources in fog computing are linked.

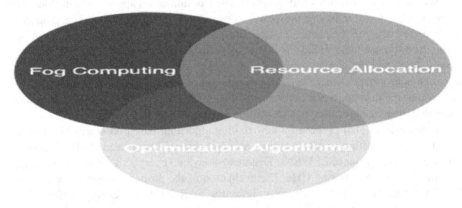

Fig. 3. Intersection of research

The linear fog-computing (LFC) model is introduced to reduce energy consumed in IoT nodes. In LFC, fog nodes are connected in one line from sensors to servers. It is designed to serve a fewer number of sensors, and it cannot be operated when there are many sensors due to the limited capacity of each fog node. Adding to the limited capacity, the processes of fog nodes to process data are not disrupted equally, which causes an unbalanced workload in fog nodes. In [20] the authors proposed a tree-based fog-computing (TBFC) model that aims to minimise the execution time and energy consumption of fog nodes in the IoT nodes. As the new model follows a tree structure, each fog node has a small capacity to process data, and the total workload of the fog nodes are distributed. The proposed model TBFC outperforms the linear model by reducing the nodes' energy consumption of and the processing time of nodes.

Using containers as a resource unit in fog computing is better than using virtual machines (VMs) because VMs do not suit the requirements of QoS in fog computing. In [21] the authors proposed a new architecture called a multi-cloud to multifg-fog and implemented two service models that aim to enhance the resource unit in fog computing by applying containers and minimising the service delay. Regarding the two service models, the authors presented a task-scheduling algorithm to balance the energy and schedule requests in real-time. The simulation outcomes show that the proposed architecture and the scheduling algorithm can increase the network lifetime of WSNs by balancing energy, minimising delay and enhancing fog node efficiency.

Ma K et al. [22] proposed a new model called IoT-FCM (a multi-layer IoT-based fog computing) to allocate resources between the fog layer, the terminal layer and a multi-sink version of the least interference beaconing protocol (LIBP) using a genetic algorithm. The proposed model aims to minimise the energy in the terminal layer and improve the fault-tolerance. Comparing the popular max–min and fog-oriented max–min, the outcomes of this study proved that the IoT-FCM shows better results in decreasing fog's distance and the terminal nodes by about 38% and minimising the consumed energy by an average of 150 KWh.

Ghanavati S et al. [23] implemented a new task-scheduling algorithm aiming to decrease both the processing time and the energy consumption for the fog-computing environment to enhance the performance. The proposed method comprises two algorithms: applying the ant mating optimization (AMO) algorithm and optimized distribution to obtain the aforementioned goals. The experimental results of the proposed algorithms showed better results than the bee life algorithm, traditional particle swarm optimisation and genetic algorithm regarding processing time and power consumption. Figure 4 shows a comparison between the aforementioned algorithms regarding the power consumption of the fog nodes.

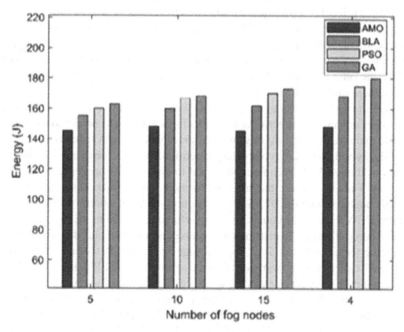

Fig. 4. A comparison between algorithms

Scheduling resources in an environment such as the IoT could be considered one of the NP-Hard problems. In [24] the authors proposed a classification method called fog-based Bayesian classification scheduling (FBCS) to minimise the energy in the IoT environment. The Bayesian classification could be applied in the fog environment to schedule task requirements such as the processing ones. The predicted requirements will be run on virtual machines after the process of classification. Due to the advantages that IfogSim has in terms of the very random and dynamic environment, the authors applied it to the proposed method. In comparison with other methods, the proposed method shows better results in terms of power consumption and executing task cost in the cloud.

One of the hardest things that IIoT service providers face is the availability of energy resources for fog computing services. The most vital factor that might add value to energy consumption in fog systems and enhance the performance for fog services is task scheduling. In [25] the authors proposed an energy-aware metaheuristic algorithm based on harris hawks optimization algorithm and local search strategy (HHOLS) to schedule the tasks in the fog services aiming to enhance the QoS that the users in IIoT applications receive. The proposed algorithm was compared with other algorithms, and the comparison results proved that the proposed algorithm can give better results regarding parameters makespan, energy consumption and cost.

Reddy D et al. [26] proposed a feedback based optimized fuzzy scheduling app-roach (FOFSA) to schedule tasks in fog computing in the IoT environment to reduce processing time and power consumption and enhance the makespan aiming to improve the performance in the IoT applications. The scheduling criteria for the proposed system based on three priorities: Low, Medium and High to offload the tasks to the Cloud. Mat-lab and IfogSim were used to test and run the proposed method. Comparing the osmosis load balancing algorithm (OLB), adaptive task allocation technique (ATAT), dynamic duty scheduling algorithm (DDSA) and optimized fuzzy bee based scheduling algorithm (OFBSA), the proposed method shows better outcomes than the others in terms of the three aforementioned parameters.

Hosseinioun P et al. [27] proposed a new method to save power in distributed systems such as IoT by enhancing the performance in the fog services. The proposed method consists of two main steps. First, ordering tasks without breaking any construction is achieved using of the hybrid IWO-CA evolutionary algorithm. Second, the dynamic voltage and frequency scaling (DVFS) technique was used to estimate the appropriate voltage for the services. The outcomes of the proposed methods show remakeable changes in saving power compared with the DVFS-enabled energy-efficient workflow task scheduling algorithm (DEWTS) and the enhanced energy-efficient scheduling (EES) algorithm.

The resource allocation in distributed systems gets more complex due to the diversity of computing servers, such as cloud, fog and edge layers. In [28] the authors proposed a new approach called energy-aware fog resource optimization (EFRO) model to adapt the QoS requirements in fog services for the IoT devices by minimising energy consumption and executing time. The basic principle of the proposed design is to select the appropriate computing service for the tasks based on the workload, whereas the heavy workload will be processed in the cloud and the middle and light workloads will be processed in the fog and edge layers respectively. The proposed method outperforms the two existing MESF and RR methods regarding energy efficiency by 54.83 and 71.28, respectively.

In addition to the advantages that the fog computing services have added to improve the communication network for IoT nodes, nonorthogonal multiple access (NOMA) has emerged as a promising solution to enhance the spectrum efficiency. Fog computing and NOMA can collaborate to improve the performance of the IIoT by minimising delays and power consumption. In [29] the authors proposed an online learning fashion to offload the tasks in the IIoT via NOMA to multiple nearby fog nodes. The authors proposed an iterative algorithm to schedule the tasks and allocate the subcarrier in each time episode.

RAHBARI D et al. [30] proposed a scheduling algorithm called greedy knapsack-based scheduling (GKS) to allocate recourses accurately in the fog network. The GKS algorithm behavior is based on priorities and profits: the profits in this situation are based on the bandwidth and CPU utilization. IFogsim was used as a simulation tool to apply the theory, and the results show that the proposed algorithm is better than the first-come-first-served (FCFS) in terms of sensor lifetime and energy consumption. Efficient mapping for services among cloud and fog resources can play a vital role in enhancing energy consumption and response time in the environment of cloud and fog computing.

Hassan H et al. [31] proposed a new policy called MinRe for service placement problem (SPP) in the environment of cloud and fog computing. The new policy classifies services into two main categories critical and normal services. MinRes proposed to reduce the response time in the critical services, and MinEng proposed to minimise the power consumption in the fog environment. The simulation results show that the new policy enhanced the energy consumption, deadline of services and average response time by up to 18%, 14% and 10%, respectively.

4   Energy Efficiency in the Smart Grid in IoT Concept

In this section we review recent studies in the literature about how the effective use of smart meters and E Bills can contribute to enhancing the work process in the smart grid. Figure 5 shows how these three areas are linked.

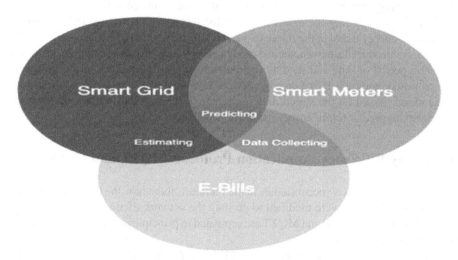

Fig. 5. Intersection of research

Smart grid (SG) has added a value to the traditional grid (TG) and can play a vital role in improving power management for distributes. SG distinguishes from the TG in many aspects. In TG, there is no direct communication between distributors and consumers; however, in SG, consumers can track and monitor electric usage in their buildings easily via smartphone apps. SG can contribute to reducing the number of operations and cost management for distributors. The main objective of the smart grid is to gather the collected data from the SG and filter these data to extract the necessary information by utilising advanced communication technologies aiming to enhance the grid performance. The most important data in the SG are the energy usage of consumers that can be collected by smart meters [32].

Electricity demand has notified a significant increase due to the massive increase in population and urbanisation. Energy monitoring systems can play an important role in saving energy and tracking the usage of electric power. IoT systems can assist developers and researchers in obtaining their objectives in reducing power consumption in buildings and industries. In [33] the authors proposed a low-cost energy monitoring system that aims to save energy by addressing the devices that consume a massive amount of power and defining the devices that can be switched off by using the MIT Platform-based App. The consumed power was calculated using Wi-Fi-enabled ESP8266, which can also identify each device in the system by IP addressing. The proposed method calculates only the energy consumption of the loads.

The cognitive IoT (CIoT) can be described as the ability of a system to make decisions based on historical data and to learn to predict upcoming events in the future. In [34] the authors proposed a smart monitoring system to monitor home appliances via the Internet. The proposed method obtains its objectives depending on three phases. A Raspberry Pi is used to read and calculate the consumed power energy for each home appliance. Google Colab is used to store the training data in order to build the TensorFlow-based Long Short-term Memory (LSTM) model. A neural network model is used to identify any abnormal energy consumption from users based on the collected data.

Effective energy management can assist distributors in predicting and estimating consumers' energy usage in the future to provide full supply for their consumers. In [35] the authors introduced a new method to predict energy usage for consumers in the future in a short period of time and send these predictions to distributors for further analysis. The proposed method is based on edge devices to collect data and then send these data to the cloud. Based on the stored data in the cloud, the authors used a deep learning framework to predict future energy usage for distributors.

5   Energy Efficiency, Application Protocols MQTT and CoAP

In this section we review recent studies in the literature about how the CoAP and MQTT applications protocols were modified to prolong the network lifetime in IoT networks. Figure 6 shows how CoAP and MQTT are separated in principle and how they are linked to the applications protocols.

The process of finding resources for CoAP applications to get frequent updates from nodes about the current reading is split into two main mechanisms: distributed and centralised resources discovery. In the former, the devices send direct queries to find a resource. In the latter, the devices process all queries through one common resource. In the centralised resources discovery, nodes require several updates about the server's

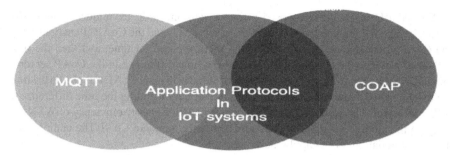

Fig. 6. Intersection of research

status, and theses updates consume power. In [36] the authors modified the standard time for nodes to update the server about the current reading, which is 10 s. The proposed method aims to prolong the network lifetime by minimising the time for nodes to update the CoAP server. Therefore, the battery level of a node is divided into four levels: High (update every 10 s), Medium (update every 20 s), Low (update every 40 s) and critical (update every 80 s). As a result, the proposed approach succeeds in prolonging the network lifetime by about 10%.

Mardini W et al. [37] modified the standard CoAP mechanism to update the CoAP server about the current reading in the centralised resource. In the standard CoAP, the nodes update the CoAP server every 10 s. However, in the proposed approach, the IoT devices send data to the server only when there is a change in the reading environment from the previous one. The simulation results showed that the proposed method enhanced the network lifetime compared to the standard CoAP protocol and the dynamic tuning approach by 33% in the former and by 8% in the latter.

Jin W et al. [38] proposed a sleep scheduling method to control the status of sleep-awake on CoAP, aiming to improve the IoT systems' energy efficiency. Moreover, the work has a slight modification in the IoT middleware layer to obtain the objective in the CoAP, using resource directory (RD) and message queue (MQ) broker to update the IoT nodes synchronicity about the sleep status. RD discovers information for the registered IoT nodes in the CoAP server. MQ acts as a chain to link the IoT nodes to the web client application using the publish-subscribe method. CoAP node can send data to the MQ and switch it to sleep mode. Then, the CoAP client can request the received data from the CoAP node to the MQ to get the data before changing the status to sleep mode. The authors have not applied any experiment in the proposed method to compare their proposed method with existing protocols.

Lai W et al. [39] proposed a method for CoAP proxies called group-based message management (GMM) to enhance the performance of sending notification from IoT devices to client devices. The proposed mechanism is based on three modules. Module1: Clustering the client devices into groups based on their demands, and each. Module2: Adjusting the range of the cache memory such that a proxy can use notifications to respond to requests. Module3: All notifications that a client device requires from different IoT nodes are combined. The simulation result showed that, by reducing the number of notifications; the proposed module improves devices' energy efficiency.

Vishakha D et al. [40] proposed a time synchronisation technique in the CoAP protocol to avoid delays between the CoAP server (node) and the CoAP client (gateway). The CoAP client updates the CoAP server about the current time, and then the time difference between the current time and then the time difference in the CoAP server is counted as a time delay. In order of avoiding the time delay, the CoAP server fills the time gap to be updated synchronously with the CoAP client by adding the time difference to the CoAP server. The authors succeeded in improving the energy efficiency of WSNs by applying the modified coap protocol compared to the standard CoAP.The authors used NS2 as a simulation tool to apply their theory.

A. Ludovici et al. [41] proposed a new approach to enhance the average delay performance, energy consumption, and delivery ratio in the CoAP application protocol. The authors applied their approach in a real wireless sensor network in an e-health app. The main point of the proposed approach is to use the priority effectively in the CoAP application protocol. There are four levels of priority and two types of notifications Critical and Non-Critical. Each level of priority requires a specific type of notification or both types. This approach succeeded in reducing server notifications to the observer, as not all levels require all types of notifications, which leads to achieving their objectives.

Randhawa R et al. [42] proposed a security protocol called Object Security of CoAP (OSCoAP) to address the issues of proxies in the IoT devices while using CoAP. Proxies are used to make the communication between clients and servers in the CoAP protocol more flexible and scalable; they work as a chain to link clients to servers for better performance. OSCoAP protects these proxies to make transmission between clients and servers more secure by encrypting and decrypting messages while exchanging data. The implementation results show that the proposed approach makes the memory more efficient, enhances the battery life by up to 30%, and makes it up to 10 times energy efficient.

Selvi M et al. [43] proposed a new protocol called EES-MQTT (Energy Efficient and Secured MQTT) to the network's quality from a security perspective. The base function of the proposed protocol is to enhance the authentication process during transmission by removing the malicious nodes. By using the MQTT.fx simulation tool and the Eclipse Paho, the experimental results showed that the energy efficiency in EES-MQTT slightly improved compared with the standard protocol MQTT. Therefore, making the IoT system more secure might be a key to save power.

Gupta S et al. [44] proposed a new schema to prolong the network lifetime in IoT systems by addressing the issue of offloading. Offloading the tasks from the gateway nodes to the cloud centre might lead to consuming more, and the proposed scheme succeeded in solving this issue compared to the existing protocols. The scheme used Message Queue Telemetry Transport (MQTT) protocol, and in this protocol, it will be able to decide to offload based on the topic classifying, which could be considered as early offloading. There are two main classifications for tasks at the topic level in MQTT. Tasks that require quick response with low computing will be offloaded to the fog nodes. Tasks that require storage and heavier computing will be offloaded to the cloud.

The number of bytes that are transmitted between IoT devices and fog nodes directly affects the energy performance in the IoT networks. Therefore, in [45] the authors proposed a data predictor in the gateway nodes built over the MQTT protocol, aiming to forecast future data to estimate the amount of required data for different IoT applications. ML algorithms are used to achieve the aforementioned goals. Theses algorithms are processed on the fog nodes when the computing level is low and, on the Cloud, when the level of computing is high, based on the IoT applications. The simulation results showed that the accuracy degree contributed to decreasing the power consumption in the IoT networks, as the data coming from the IoT is minimised accordantly in comparison with the traditional MQTT.

Schutz B et al. [46] proposed a new approach to address the gap of the packet loss in the WSNs by integrating seed-based Random Linear Network Coding with MQTT for Sensor Networks (MQTT-SN). Radio update time in the WSNs could be counted as a costly way in transmitting data, so devices try to reduce the number of radio updates to save power. This approach uses an optimization method called seed-based intrasession Network Coding to forward error correction and prolong the network lifetime by reducing radio updates. The proposed approach applied in a real agricultural scenario, and the result showed that the radio updates could be reduced up to 38.24%.

Packet loss (PL) could be counted as one of the issues that have to be addressed to enhance the performance in the IoT environment while exchanging messages in application protocols such as MQTT and CoAP.PL increases the system's workload in general and consumes more power due to data retransmission and replicating the same message until reaching the destination. PL occurs for many reasons, such as security attacks and timeout. There is a direct link between PL and energy consumption; if the PL increases, the power consumption will increase accordingly, and the opposite is true. Therefore, reducing PL in application protocols in IoT networks is a targeted point to satisfy the QoS requirements and save power [47].

Selvi M et al. [43] proposed a new protocol called EES-MQTT (Energy Efficient and Secured MQTT) to address security issues. The new approach provides better authentication servers, and it can identify intruders and remove malicious nodes. In addition to making the system more secure, the proposed method succeeds in enhancing the other three parameters, namely, Node Energy Consumption, Node Lifetime and Packet delivery ratio, compared with the standard MQTT. The secret behind this, EES-MQTT aims to reduce the number of malicious nodes to minimise their impact, resulting in better packet delivery and less dropped packets.

Researchers have verified that using security systems in the IoT environment requires additional power and increases the whole system's workload even if these systems are lightweight. Researchers aim to protect IoT devices from external attacks without consuming more power. It is vital when working on modifying security systems to minimise the power consumption to be aware that these modifications do not impact the security level. In [48] the authors the Elliptic Curve Cryptography (ECC) in the secured MQTT protocol in fog network to prolong the network lifetime by reducing the encryption energy consumption. The authors also reduce the replicated packets in the replay attacks by using the wake-up pattern to save power [48]. Based on this study and previous studies, we could say that there is a link between security levels and energy in the environment of IoT devices.

6 Conclusion and Future Work

Improving the energy efficiency of IoT devices through working directly on Watt, Joule and hardware modifications is not the only way. Additionally, it can be obtained by working deeply on various competing angels. However, to achieve more accurate results and find more gaps to address, it is vital to target one area to work on and review it deeply to avoid distractions with other areas. In this paper, we carried out a comprehensive survey on previous studies related to enhancing the energy performance of IoT systems from the four most critical angles: fog computing, clustering, and routing in WSNs, Smart grid and MQTT and CoAP application protocols. There is no doubt that there are more than these four areas. However, we limited the number of research areas to assist developers in selecting the research area that they are more interested in when aiming to promote the energy performance of IoT systems. Future studies will propose solutions for the energy inefficiency of IoT networks. Implementation tools such as Cooja and Nodejs will be used to validate the proposed solutions.

References

1. Sen, S., Koo, J., Bagchi, S.: Trifecta: security, energy efficiency, and communication capacity comparison for wireless IoT devices. IEEE Internet Comput. **22**, 74–81 (2018)
2. Perković, T., Damjanović, S., Šolić, P., Patrono, L., Rodrigues, J.: Meeting challenges in IoT: sensing, energy efficiency, and the implementation. In: Yang, X.-S., Sherratt, S., Dey, N., Joshi, A. (eds.) Fourth International Congress on Information and Communication Technology. AISC, vol. 1041, pp. 419–430. Springer, Singapore (2020). https://doi.org/10.1007/978-981-15-0637-6_36Q!R
3. Abdul-Qawy, A.S.H., Almurisi, N.M.S., Tadisetty, S.: Classification of energy saving techniques for IoT-based heterogeneous wireless nodes. Procedia Comput. Sci. **171**, 2590–2599 (2020)
4. Xiong, Z., Wang, H., Zhang, L., Fan, T., Shen, J.: A ring-based routing scheme for distributed energy resources management in IIoT. IEEE Access **8**, 167490–167503 (2020)
5. Zhang, X., Li, J., Qiu, R., Mean, T.-S., Jin, F.: Optimized routing model of sensor nodes in internet of things network. Sens. Mater. **32**, 2801–2811 (2020)
6. Pereira, H., Moritz, G.L., Souza, R.D., Munaretto, A., Fonseca, M.: Increased network lifetime and load balancing based on network interface average power metric for RPL. IEEE Access **8**, 48686–48696 (2020)
7. Khan, F.A., Ahmad, A., Imran, M.: Energy optimization of PR-LEACH routing scheme using distance awareness in internet of things networks. Int. J. Parallel Prog. **48**, 244–263 (2020)
8. Abdullah, S., Asghar, M.N., Ashraf, M., Abbas, N.: An energy-efficient message scheduling algorithm with joint routing mechanism at network layer in Internet of things environment. Wireless Pers. Commun. **111**, 1821–1835 (2020)
9. Iqbal, S., Qureshi, K.N., Kanwal, N., Jeon, G.: Collaborative energy efficient zone-based routing protocol for multihop Internet of Things. Trans. Emerging Telecommun. Technol. **33**, e3885 (2020)
10. Safara, F., Souri, A., Baker, T., Al Ridhawi, I., Aloqaily, M.: PriNergy: a priority-based energy-efficient routing method for IoT systems. J. Supercomput. **76**, 1–18 (2020)
11. Shen, J., Wang, A., Wang, C., Hung, P.C., Lai, C.-F.: An efficient centroid-based routing protocol for energy management in WSN-assisted IoT. IEEE Access **5**, 18469–18479 (2017)

12. Xu, Y., Yue, Z., Lv, L.: Clustering routing algorithm and simulation of internet of things perception layer based on energy balance. IEEE Access **7**, 145667–145676 (2019)
13. Ouhab, A., Abreu, T., Slimani, H., Mellouk, A.: Energy-efficient clustering and routing algorithm for large-scale SDN-based IoT monitoring. In: ICC 2020–2020 IEEE International Conference on Communications (ICC), pp. 1–6. IEEE (2020)
14. Tang, L., Lu, Z.: DS evidence theory-based energy balanced routing algorithm for network lifetime enhancement in WSN-assisted IOT. Algorithms **13**, 152 (2020)
15. Iwendi, C., Maddikunta, P.K.R., Gadekallu, T.R., Lakshmanna, K., Bashir, A.K., Piran, M.J.: A metaheuristic optimization approach for energy efficiency in the IoT networks. Softw. Pract. Experience **51**, 2558–2571 (2021)
16. Sarma, S.K.: Energy aware Cluster based routing for Wireless Sensor Network in IoT: impact of bio-inspired Algorithm. In: 2020 Third International Conference on Smart Systems and Inventive Technology (ICSSIT), pp. 198–206. IEEE (2020)
17. Reddy, M.P.K., Babu, M.R.: Energy efficient cluster head selection for internet of things. New Rev. Inf. Network. **22**, 54–70 (2017)
18. Chelloug, S.A., El-Zawawy, M.A.: Middleware for internet of things: survey and challenges. Intell. Autom. Soft Comput., 1–9 (2017)
19. La, Q.D., Ngo, M.V., Dinh, T.Q., Quek, T.Q., Shin, H.: Enabling intelligence in fog computing to achieve energy and latency reduction. Digit. Commun. Netw. **5**, 3–9 (2019)
20. Oma, R., Nakamura, S., Duolikun, D., Enokido, T., Takizawa, M.: An energy-efficient model for fog computing in the internet of things (IoT). Internet Things **1**, 14–26 (2018)
21. Luo, J., Yin, L., Hu, J., Wang, C., Liu, X., Fan, X., Luo, H.: Container-based fog computing architecture and energy-balancing scheduling algorithm for energy IoT. Future Gener. Comput. Syst. **97**, 50–60 (2019)
22. Ma, K., Bagula, A., Nyirenda, C., Ajayi, O.: An IoT-based fog computing model. Sensors **19**, 2783 (2019)
23. Ghanavati, S., Abawajy, J.H., Izadi, D.: An energy aware task scheduling model using Ant-Mating Optimization in fog computing environment. IEEE Trans. Serv. Comput. (2020)
24. Heydari, G., Rahbari, D., Nickray, M.: Energy saving scheduling in a fog-based IoT application by Bayesian task classification approach. Turkish J. Electr. Eng. Comput. Sci. **27**, 4167–4187 (2019)
25. Abdel-Basset, M., El-shahat, D., Elhoseny, M., Song, H.: Energy-Aware Metaheuristic algorithm for Industrial Internet of Things task scheduling problems in fog computing applications. IEEE Internet Things J. **8**, 12638–12649 (2020)
26. Arunkumar Reddy, D., Venkata Krishna, P.: Feedback-based fuzzy resource management in IoT using fog computing. Evol. Intell. **14**, 669–681 (2021)
27. Hosseinioun, P., Kheirabadi, M., Tabbakh, S.R.K., Ghaemi, R.: A new energy-aware tasks scheduling approach in fog computing using hybrid meta-heuristic algorithm. J. Parall. Distrib. Comput. **143**, 88–96 (2020)
28. Gai, K., Qin, X., Zhu, L.: An energy-aware high performance task allocation strategy in heterogeneous fog computing environments. IEEE Trans. Comput. **70**, 626–639 (2020)
29. Wang, K., Zhou, Y., Liu, Z., Shao, Z., Luo, X., Yang, Y.: Online task scheduling and resource allocation for intelligent NOMA-based industrial internet of things. IEEE J. Sel. Areas Commun. **38**, 803–815 (2020)
30. Rahbari, D., Nickray, M.: Low-latency and energy-efficient scheduling in fog-based IoT applications. Turkish J. Electr. Eng. Comput. Sci. **27**, 1406–1427 (2019)
31. Hassan, H.O., Azizi, S., Shojafar, M.: Priority, network and energy-aware placement of IoT-based application services in fog-cloud environments. IET Commun. **14**, 2117–2129 (2020)
32. Alhasnawi, B.N., Jasim, B.H.: Internet of Things (IoT) for smart grids: a comprehensive review. J. Xi'an Univ. Archit **63**, 1006–7930 (2020)

33. Rao, B.N., Sudheer, R.: Energy monitoring using IOT. In: 2020 International Conference on Inventive Computation Technologies (ICICT), pp. 868–872. IEEE (2020)
34. Rashid, R.A., Chin, L., Sarijari, M.A., Sudirman, R., Ide, T.: Machine learning for smart energy monitoring of home appliances using IoT. In: 2019 Eleventh International Conference on Ubiquitous and Future Networks (ICUFN), pp. 66–71. IEEE (2019)
35. Han, T., Muhammad, K., Hussain, T., Lloret, J., Baik, S.W.: An efficient deep learning framework for intelligent energy management in IoT networks. IEEE Internet Things J. **8**, 3170–3179 (2020)
36. Yassein, M.B., et al.: Challenges and techniques of constrained application protocol (CoAP) for efficient energy consumption. In: 2020 11th International Conference on Information and Communication Systems (ICICS), pp. 373–377. IEEE (2020)
37. Mardini, W., Yassein, M.B., AlRashdan, M., Alsmadi, A., Amer, A.B.: Application-based power saving approach for IoT CoAP protocol. In: Proceedings of the First International Conference on Data Science, E-learning and Information Systems, pp. 1–5 (2018)
38. Jin, W., Kim, D.: A sleep-awake scheme based on CoAP for energy-efficiency in Internet of Things. JOIV Int. J. Inf. Visual. **1**, 110–114 (2017)
39. Lai, W.-K., Wang, Y.-C., Lin, S.-Y.: Efficient scheduling, caching, and merging of notifications to save message costs in IoT networks using CoAP. IEEE Internet Things J. **8**, 1016–1029 (2020)
40. Khatade, V.D., Askhedkar, M.A.: Time synchronization for CoAP using NS2. In: 2019 5th International Conference on Computing, Communication, Control and Automation (ICCUBEA), pp. 1–4. IEEE (2019)
41. Ludovici, A., Garcia, E., Gimeno, X., Augé, A.C.: Adding QoS support for timeliness to the observe extension of CoAP. In: 2012 IEEE 8th International Conference on Wireless and Mobile Computing, Networking and Communications (WiMob), pp. 195–202. IEEE (2012)
42. Randhawa, R.H., Hameed, A., Mian, A.N.: Energy efficient cross-layer approach for object security of CoAP for IoT devices. Ad Hoc Netw. **92**, 101761 (2019)
43. Selvi, M., Gayathri, A., Santhosh, K.S., Kannan, A.: Energy efficient and secured MQTT protocol using IoT. Int. J. Innov. Technol. Exploring Eng. (IJITEE) **9**, 11–14 (2020)
44. Gupta, S., Garg, R., Gupta, N., Alnumay, W.S., Ghosh, U., Sharma, P.K.: Energy-efficient dynamic homomorphic security scheme for fog computing in IoT networks. J. Inf. Secur. Appl. **58**, 102768 (2021)
45. Peralta, G., Iglesias-Urkia, M., Barcelo, M., Gomez, R., Moran, A., Bilbao, J.: Fog computing based efficient IoT scheme for the Industry 4.0. In: 2017 IEEE International Workshop of Electronics, Control, Measurement, Signals and Their Application to Mechatronics (ECMSM), pp. 1–6. IEEE (2017)
46. Schütz, B., Bauer, J., Aschenbruck, N.: Improving energy efficiency of MQTT-SN in Lossy environments using seed-based network coding. In: 2017 IEEE 42nd Conference on Local Computer Networks (LCN), pp. 286–293. IEEE (2017)
47. Bideh, P.N., Sönnerup, J., Hell, M.: Energy consumption for securing lightweight IoT protocols. In: Proceedings of the 10th International Conference on the Internet of Things, pp. 1–8 (2020)
48. De Rango, F., Potrino, G., Tropea, M., Fazio, P.: Energy-aware dynamic Internet of Things security system based on elliptic curve cryptography and message queue telemetry transport protocol for mitigating replay attacks. Pervasive Mob. Comput. **61**, 101105 (2020)

Social Internet of Things: Security, Management and Trends

Challenges and Issues of the Internet of Things: Factoring Elements from the Social, Political and Information Systems

Arif Ali[1]([⊠]) and Walayat Hussian[2,3] [iD]

[1] Wellington Institute of Technology, Wellington, New Zealand
Arif.ali@weltec.ac.nz
[2] Victoria University Business School, Victoria University, Melbourne, VIC, Australia
[3] University of Technology Sydney, Sydney, NSW, Australia
Walayat.Hussain@uts.edu.au

Abstract. The concept and applications of the Internet of Things or IoT are well-known to those dealing with the technicalities and complexities of IoT. However, for most users, the understanding seems to be limited to the benefits and usability of the devices. In particular, grasping the privacy, security and other relevant issues, especially social issues, remains out of reach for most users. This paper addresses the problem of privacy, security and other relevant issues from users' perspective and suggests three areas needing greater attention in resolving the issues. First, this paper highlights social issues and emphasizes the role of business leaders in dealing with the issues surrounding IoT devices. This paper argues that the onus and obligation lie with the business leaders as social architects to perform their duty of care in a socially responsible manner. Second, IoT is simply an IS product in which people and their views are one of the key elements for achieving the common goal, in this case, of networking of things and people. Ignoring the role of end-users as a critical part of IoT does not help achieve the common purpose. Lastly, given the transnational nature of the issue, governments worldwide are essential stakeholders and hence need to have a proactive and positive approach in the fight against the use of IoT for cybercrimes.

Keywords: Cybercrime · Information systems · IoT security · IoT privacy · Leadership · User adoption of technology

1 Introduction

The Internet of Things (IoT) plays a vital role in the existing and future generation of information, communication and applications. IoT enables various technological devices to connect with sensors and software and exchange data in an intelligent way over the Internet. The technology has revolutionized the industry 4.0 technologies; therefore, the adoption is steadily increasing every next day. Small and big enterprises benefit from IoT due to its wide range of features, including – connectivity, monitoring real-time data

W. Hussain and M. A. Jan (Eds.): IoTaaS 2021, LNICST 421, pp. 73–83, 2022.
https://doi.org/10.1007/978-3-030-95987-6_5

capturing, active engagement, convenience and integrity. However, along with a wide variety of features, the IoT has limitations as well. The biggest challenge of IoT for any business is the security and privacy of data while transmitting from one device to another (Raza et al. 2021). Other challenges are – technical complexity, connectivity and power dependence.

The perception of IoT varies from person to person. The features, benefits and operations of IoT are well-known for those familiar and dealing with its technicalities and complexities (Gao et al. 2020). Therefore, their perspectives and how they look at IoT devices are from a designer, developer, or innovator's point of view. For businesses selling and distributing IoT, the devices are another line of fast selling, profitable products. However, for users, the understanding of the devices remains limited to the benefits and usability of the devices. The privacy, security and other relevant issues remain unfamiliar and unknown to the users. They simply trust the vendors and manufacturers and use the devices. Therefore, it is essential to highlight the shortcomings of IoT from a non-technical perspective.

This paper looks at the problem of privacy, security and other relevant issues from users' perspective and suggests three areas needing greater attention in resolving the issues. The contribution of this paper is that it highlights the user's perspective and emphasizes the need for a holistic approach. Specifically, considering users as key stakeholders and the business leaders as social architects who can offer different perspectives on the challenges. The study analyzes and highlights that IoT is an IS product where people and their views are key elements for achieving the goal of networking while considering the security and privacy of users.

The paper first simplifies the concept of IoT and how it works for users, mainly for domestic purposes. That is followed by highlighting the complexities and challenges for business users, which further leads to the discussion of social issues related to the use of IoT devices. The paper emphasizes the role of business leaders responsible for developing and manufacturing millions of IoT devices and developers and innovators to look at these devices from an Information Systems (IS) perspective. The paper also discusses what governments can do by highlighting the need for coordination at the global level for the fight against the use of IoT for cybercrimes. Both the groups, the business leaders and government policymakers, are social architects, expected to create a better society and consider people first over anything else.

The rest of the paper is organized as follows. Section 2 discusses related literature and concepts. Section 3 highlights common issues of IoT in different sectors. Section 4 discusses possible solutions, and finally, Sect. 5 concludes the paper with future research directions.

2   Related Literature and Concepts

This section discusses existing literature and related concepts that are used in our study. The section is divided into three subsections, as presented in Fig. 1:

– Simplifying IoT
– Applications and Challenges
– Complexities of IoT for Users

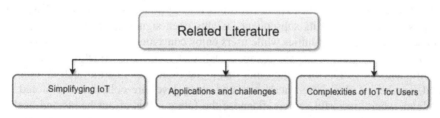

Fig. 1.

The discussion for each subsection is presented as follows:

2.1 Simplifying IoT

Internet of Things, or IoT, is generally defined as devices with network connectivity, collecting user data and sending it over the Internet into the cloud for processing and analyzing and then returning it to the user (Escamilla-Ambrosio et al. 2018; Petrakis et al. 2018). Some examples of the devices could be smartphones, smart fridges, thermostats, baby monitors, smartwatches, other wearables, car Bluetooth, and other similar devices connected with the Internet.

Beyond the physical devices, IoT also includes a person with a heart monitor implant or a farm animal with a chip transponder (Chacko and Hayajneh 2018). The connected devices have their unique identifiers and sensors collecting and transferring data over a network. The devices connect back to a central device such as a smartphone, or a laptop, known as the anchor device, used to control the connected device (Aldahiri et al. 2021).

Across businesses and industries, IoT enables the automation of business processes; it offers analysis and insight based on the data it collects, hence supporting resource monitoring and performance improvement. For example, the aviation industry uses IoT sensors for real-time reporting on the status of an aeroplane engine, i.e. the condition of their equipment. Similarly, city councils use IoT as a part of their smart city projects. For example, city councils use IoT to monitor and gain insights on traffic flow and parking spaces and predict any traffic issues sooner. As a result, the technology helps councils better address bottlenecks, long traffic queues and increase revenue from parking spaces.

2.2 Applications and Challenges

Nowadays, almost every digital product is connected with the Internet as a part of the 'modern technological revolution'. The number of devices is estimated to be around 20 billion (Almadhoun et al. 2018). The devices are transitioning from being an optional luxury feature to being the baseline. That is because we feel technology is beneficial as it saves time, offers convenience and is reliable.

The real application is connecting people to things and things to things in real-time (Coetzee and Eksteen 2011). A typical Internet of Things network can proliferate, resulting in an exponential increase in the variety, velocity, and overall volume of data. The products collect data about the users and store that data in the cloud, where artificial intelligence (AI) enabled analytical programs continuously analyze, make sense out of the data and make conclusions or decisions for the user (Hussai et al. 2021a). For businesses, this data and its subsequent insights open significant value creation and revenue generation opportunities while users enjoy convenience (Showkat et al. 2018).

For example, many users use a smartwatch that collects information about daily activities and every movement and sends that to the cloud. Information such as running speed, number of steps, even heart rate and stress level are collected and stored in the cloud, where powerful servers diagnose the future status of our hearts and health conditions. Another similar example is that the smart fridge with lovely displays offers convenience, allowing users to check the fridge via mobile phone from the office and get items needed for dinner on the way home. In addition, the fridge can help users order groceries 'Just in Time' and notify them about expired products, what users eat, and when. The smart TV is also connected to the Internet and allows users to access videos and contents automatically compiled by the AI from the cloud (Hussain et al. 2020; Hussain et al. 2021b). Similarly, new cars, including their accessories, are already fully connected with the Internet at the time of purchase.

However, there are many challenges for vendors and manufacturers. The real challenge for the Internet of Things environments is how to analyze the large volume of information from all sources and take action in real-time (Davenport et al. 2012; Rathore et al. 2016). The challenge combined with the high expectations created by the Internet, mobile and 24/7 IT environment has made the need for new analytics approaches and technologies more urgent. Achieving desired business objectives requires acting in real-time to take advantage of opportunities and address problems quickly. As identified by Tanford et al. (2012), in the pre-Internet of Things era, an issue in a typical supply chain scenario could be addressed in two to three-day cycles for satisfactory results. However, in the Internet of Things, the time to act is in minutes, seconds or microseconds (Tanford et al. 2012). This explosion of data and the high expectations in the Internet of Things environment means the value of data slips away quickly. Therefore, for businesses, the importance of time to action for Internet of Things applications is crucial. Addressing the critical time to action requirements for businesses and the Internet of Things demands an advanced analytics solution that can unify historical real-time streaming predictive and prescriptive analytics and provide faster analytics and more innovative actions.

2.3 Complexities of IoT for Users

For the business, taking action in real-time based on the IoT-gathered data is crucial. Users at the receiving end of the supply chain have concerns and complexities. Imagine a user arriving home and sitting in front of the fire during winter; the user receives an instant message, an infringement notice from police for driving while intoxicated. While the user is trying to comprehend what is happening, the smartwatch has collected data about the heart rate and translated that into the amount of alcohol in the blood. As the car is connected to the Internet, based on the car and smartwatch data, it was concluded that the user was driving with a certain alcohol level in their blood. While the user has broken the law, the real question is, how did the police know that the user was driving while intoxicated?

As another example, every connected car sends its location to its cloud service provider (Kwak et al. 2015). If somebody manages to hack into the cloud service provider, the hacker can know the location of many cars in a specific country. There is value in this information. First, the hacker can analyze this data and know where the person is living, working, and pinpoint the location of every BMW. Therefore, there is a need for an intelligent prediction system to perform complex predictions. Some recent approaches (Hussain et al. 2021c) introduced a novel ordered weighted aggregation operatore (OWA) in neural network structure to perform complex nonlinear predictions.

These are some examples of what may happen if somebody manages to compromise either the IoT device or the content of information that was delivered from the device to the cloud. As we get many more devices connected with the Internet, the devices can make decisions for users and offer the users services.

Users are aware of the connectivity as it informs their decision to adopt and use. However, they do not necessarily know how the data is exchanged and how the devices can collectively form a digital copy of the user. In fact, IoT devices have been used for cyber-attacks and to act as their proxy without any knowledge of that happening. The recent New Zealand Stock Exchange attack is an example where thousands of devices were used to connect with the Exchange, creating a traffic blockage and resulting in distributed denial of service (DDoS) attacks (New Zealand's Exchange 2020).

That is why it is so essential for innovators and developers to be socially responsible in the development and adoption of information systems devices, including IoT. It is equally important to actively educate the users about the security of their data and devices and possible misuse.

3   Common Issues

Although there is a significant increase in adopting IoT to improve customer service and decision-making efficiency across businesses and industries, all these connected devices have potential technical and non-technical issues. Most importantly, the devices can be hacked and used for committing cybercrimes. In fact, because of the vulnerability of the IoT devices, Meneghello et al. (2019) refers to IoT as the Internet of Threats. The section has divided the common issues into two main sub-sections:

– Security issues
– Privacy issues

3.1   Security

In every device, by default, users are left with no choice but to purchase and integrate the device into their lives. The problem is that the manufacturers expect users to be expert systems administrators. Without any monitoring and standardization and with the race to the top with no boundaries, it is not a matter of if, but when a hacker gains access to one of the IoT devices; often they can access all the user devices and the whole home network gets compromised. First, they access the anchor device and then get everything that is hosted on the anchor device. They can even commit crimes remotely from hacked devices.

From the technical point of view, as the number of connected devices and sharing of information increase, so do issues. Security and privacy remain the top two issues (Atlam and Wills 2020). As described by Atlam and Wills (2020), any bug in a single device can potentially affect an entire IoT system and compromise users' private data. These connected devices produce a considerable amount of data that can be difficult to manage, let alone analyze and gather insights. In addition, competing IoT standards create challenges of getting different devices from different manufacturers to communicate with one another. For example, all standards and frameworks, including IPv6, ZigBee, LiteOS, OneM2M, DDS (data distribution service), and AMQP (advanced messaging queuing protocol), have standardization for IoT devices. While the IoT market is booming exponentially without any limits and users are adopting these devices without any comparison, a lack of standardization and monitoring and control are simply brewing chaos.

3.2 Privacy

We are living in a database society where data about our every move and second is captured. Due to that, there is an increasing likelihood of identity theft. Companies and thieves are making money from every kind of personal information (Labong 2019). For the users, the misuse of their devices and the privacy of their data are significant issues. What most people do not realize is how deeply identity theft can affect their lives. The effect of ID theft on victims is disastrous, taking hundreds of hours to clean up, being emotionally draining and leaving people feeling vulnerable (Weber 2015).

Essentially data is the new oil, and data trafficking is one of the top revenue-generating crimes globally and is just getting worse. Examples of the data breaches such as Equifax, Uber, and alter X are only the tip of the iceberg (Electronic Privacy Information Centre n.d.). The problem is getting worse as there is so much money to be made from identity theft.

Users think that an IoT device like a light bulb, thermostat, or a baby monitor is theirs and that the information is private. However, there are no regulations on almost any consumer device or the data that they collect. Currently, companies do not have to tell users what out of their data collection they are selling, to what third party companies they are sharing information with, and how they are storing the information. Most do not even have to tell users when they or their partner companies have been hacked and that private information is now public. Hence, the bottom line is that users have no clue what information is being sold and who is selling and/or stealing it.

Users assume that the purchaser also owns the information collected by a device. The device software and hardware companies might store our information; however, they have no legal grounds to sell or transfer the information. At the very least, users ought to have the right to opt-out of a company collecting their information and sharing it with others. However, realistically, some companies are spending hundreds of thousands of dollars lobbying their governments to reduce further and relax regulations on data privacy.

The idea of making everyday objects smart is fascinating, however, but the issue is that the information is not stored locally on the user's device and is on the web to communicate with the cloud. Smart devices, such as autonomous lawnmowers, and smart heaters automatically adjusting the room temperature before a user arrives home, are making life easier. However, the devices also let companies analyze the user data mainly for the benefit of their business. The collection and transmission are mainly invisible to ordinary users. The worst case is that companies can remotely control smart devices. These are the most significant concerns with this new technology. Currently, the biggest challenges in the Internet of Things space are security and privacy. Imagine someone with access to a stove could cause it to overheat and maybe even start a home fire, or someone with control over a power plant could cut the power to an entire city. The possibilities seem endless, and the risks involved are not to be taken lightly.

While enjoying the digital assistance and convenience, users should think twice about how much smart technology they want for their homes and family. Users are expected to be expert network administrators and employ expert level measures to ensure their identities remain uniquely theirs. Whoever uses smart technology at home should know what they are dealing with. Smart technology requires smart handling and basically becoming a System Administrator, cataloguing the devices, installing security patches, checking for software updates, changing passwords, and perhaps even setting up protocols to ensure there were no hacking attempts.

4   Possible Solutions

Working on technical solutions is an obvious option; however, the effort is only one part of the solution and requires more comprehensive coverage. Therefore, it becomes short-sighted to only attempt to resolve the issues technically and overlook other possible avenues which can offer solutions. This paper highlights three areas that can complement and offer comprehensive solutions and eventually safe devices to end-users. The areas are related to social and non-technical aspects and are missing from the IoT literature, indicating a gap. The study categorized possible solutions into three sub-sections:

– Leaders as Social Architects
– Treating IoT as an iS Product
– Role of the Government

The discussion of each solution is presented as follows:

4.1 Leaders as Social Architects

Today's human society is being confronted by all sorts of global challenges and issues. Growing digital inequality, the devastation of the natural environment due to e-waste, data privacy breaches and the growing number of cyber security threats are just a few. As mentioned above, with the exponential adoption of IoT devices, security and privacy issues are obviously going to rise. Furthermore, since competition between organizations is increasing and conflicting pressures from stakeholders are mounting, the environmental, social, and ethical impacts of IoT devices will rise. The question is about the role of businesses and business leaders: are they part of the solution or the problem?

The onus and obligation lie with the leaders as the social architects to create a safe environment by performing their duty of care and acting in a socially responsible manner (Muralidharan and Pathak 2018; Siddique and Joseph 2021). The sense of social responsibility is essential and must be considered before any technical adventurism; that is, the crucial requirement and element of human nature before anything else. As described by Nicholson and Kurucz (2019), what makes a person a great leader is their sense of responsibility for people and everything they do. Without such a characteristic, the person is just managing continuous operations and stability of the business with no eyes on the future.

Business leaders shape our future. Twenty years ago, who knew about the social media, social connectivity, and the social dilemma we are living in today? For all those years, the platforms have manipulated our social instincts. The whole younger human generation is being controlled at large and reshaped by social media. Unfortunately, knowingly or unknowingly, social media giants and leaders busy developing the '*social*' networking technology somehow have ignored the '*social*' element. They have started accepting how their social networking platforms have been involved in unethical business activities and have ignored the consequences of social damage. As a result, our society has become more asymmetric.

Therefore, this paper suggests that the business leaders in the IoT industry have the power to design a future without repeating those mistakes of social networking giants. Otherwise, another global issue due to IoT devices is awaiting.

The question is what business leaders in the IoT industry can do to avoid the issue. Besides their business continuity, the leaders can reconceptualize a sustainable growth opportunity for their business. In other words, they can develop a strategy to transition to responsible business practices with sustainability at the forefront of innovation – people first. Admittedly, the road is challenging; however, in the long run, sustainable practice guarantees profits and develops a strong business portfolio that is fit for the future with a positive impact on society.

4.2 Treating IoT as an IS Product

Another avenue and way forward to resolving the issues is to deal with IoT as a product of information systems (IS) instead of a tool. Information Systems is a set of integrated elements that work together towards achieving a common purpose (Papavasiliou 2020). Within the collection of integrated elements, users are a key part of the system (Tambunan et al. 2020).

Moreover, from a systems thinking point of view, systems thinking involves looking at the interconnections between parts of a whole rather than concentrating just on the parts. As described by Wright and Meadows (2008), a system is not just any collection of things, rather an interconnected set of elements that is coherently organized in a way that achieves something – a purpose. Therefore, users or people and their viewpoints are an equal part of a system that enables it to resolve complex situations. Therefore, considering the relationship between people and things is as meaningful and necessary as the structure of the equipment and the particular situation.

Based on that line of thinking, this paper suggests that urgent collective action is needed to tackle cybercrime and the misuse of IoT devices. For that collective action, the users must play a key part in the whole process, from production to the use of the devices. The collective action can be in the form of better information and communication with the users about the vulnerability of the devices. Another possible strategy can be more education on the safe use of the devices. Such kinds of collective action can help minimize, if not eliminate, the unlawful uses of IoT as a service for cybercrime. Most importantly, that is needed because the users need to know about the possible hacking and misuse of their devices if not used securely.

4.3   Role of the Government

Given the transnational nature of misuse of IoT devices for cybercrime and the extent of the damage the criminals can cause, governments around the world are one of the obvious stakeholders. They have significant influence over regulations and policies. However, they seem to be slow in taking a greater level of interest. One can speculate that on the one hand, the nature of Information and Communication Technologies (ICT) is fast-moving; on the other hand, the movement of the machinery of government is slow. The only commonality between both is the complex nature of both – the ICT and machinery of government.

In terms of international conventions, the Budapest Convention adopted by the European Union increased cooperation and sharing of information and knowledge for tackling the challenge of cybercrime. More recently, in December 2019, the United Nations General Assembly adopted a resolution to establish a committee for working towards a comprehensive convention for countering the use of ICT for cybercrimes. The negotiations are starting in January 2022 and are scheduled to conclude in 2024.

While users need such conventions and international agreements, the issue is that the governments are more interested in the areas of national security instead of user protections. There is also a concern that the treaties allow violation of human rights and greater surveillance of people. That is evident due to the fact that some countries are reluctant to take action against cybercrimes within their borders but are showing more interest in international treaties (Brown 2021). As noted in Brown (2021), "cybercrime is dangerous, but a new UN treaty could be worse for rights".

Therefore, it is vital that governments worldwide take vigorous steps to reduce the possibility of the misuse of the devices while preserving the rights of people. First, since governments have the mandate, more close coordination and transnational cooperation between governments are needed for effective and practical steps to minimize the illegal use of IoT devices. However, the pace of formulating and reviewing treaties and conventions has to, at least, match the pace of changes in ICT. In addition, that must not be used for violations of people's rights. Second, they can prioritize the issue and allocate more resources to relevant government agencies fighting against crime. Treaties and conventions will have less impact if the implementing agencies on the ground lack resources. Last but not least, governments and their commerce commissions can develop better checks on the production of secure devices and sharing of information with the users. They also need to prioritize social concerns over trade for tackling the misuse of IoT devices and ICT in general.

5 Conclusion

The objective of all stakeholders in the IoT industry should be to support and uphold broader human values and ethics for cyberspace, a space that functions based on rules, promotes rights of freedom and privacy, and where the users feel secure. For that, it is necessary to not only produce devices that are modern and offer convenience but also proactively seek avenues for discouraging unlawful and misuse of those devices.

In addition to technical solutions, business leaders need to take responsibility for ethical business practices and prioritize people over profit. Similarly, IoT devices need to be treated as a product of information systems in which humans are a key part of the system. Keeping that in mind and working with the users can help in taking collective actions against the misuse of IoT devices. Lastly, governments as crucial stakeholders and influencers can undoubtedly do more.

With all three suggestions, this paper considers that misuse of IoT devices by cyber-criminals and eventual financial, social and emotional impact can be reduced, if not eliminated, entirely. In particular, governments and business leaders have the power to do so.

References

Aldahiri, A., Alrashed, B., Hussain, W.: Trends in using IoT with machine learning in health prediction system. Forecasting **3**(1), 181–206 (2021)

Almadhoun, R., Kadadha, M., Alhemeiri, M., Alshehhi, M., Salah, K.: A user authentication scheme of IoT devices using blockchain-enabled fog nodes. In: 2018 IEEE/ACS 15th international conference on computer systems and applications (AICCSA), pp. 1–8. IEEE, October 2018

Atlam, H., Wills, G.: IoT security, privacy, safety and ethics. In: Farsi, M., Daneshkhah, A., Hosseinian-Far, A., Jahankhani, H. (eds.) Digital Twin Technologies and Smart Cities. IT, pp. 123–149. Springer, Cham (2020). https://doi.org/10.1007/978-3-030-18732-3_8

Brown, D.: Cybercrime is Dangerous, But a New UN Treaty Could Be Worse for Rights (2021). https://www.hrw.org/news/2021/08/13/cybercrime-dangerous-new-un-treaty-could-be-worse-rights

Chacko, A., Hayajneh, T.: Security and privacy issues with IoT in healthcare. EAI Endorsed Trans. Pervasive Health Technol. **4**(14) (2018)

Coetzee, L., Eksteen, J.: The Internet of Things - promise for the future? An introduction. In: 2011 IST-Africa Conference Proceedings, pp. 1–9. IEEE, May 2011

Davenport, T.H., Barth, P., Bean, R.: How big data is different (2012)

Electronic Privacy Information Centre (n.d.). Equifax Data Breach https://epic.org/privacy/data-breach/equifax/

Escamilla-Ambrosio, P.J., Rodríguez-Mota, A., Aguirre-Anaya, E., Acosta-Bermejo, R., Salinas-Rosales, M.: Distributing computing in the internet of things: cloud, fog and edge computing overview. In: Maldonado, Y., Trujillo, L., Schütze, O., Riccardi, A., Vasile, M. (eds.) NEO 2016. SCI, vol. 731, pp. 87–115. Springer, Cham (2018). https://doi.org/10.1007/978-3-319-64063-1_4

Gao, H., Qin, X., Barroso, R.J.D., Hussain, W., Xu, Y., Yin, Y.: Collaborative learning-based industrial IoT API recommendation for software-defined devices: the implicit knowledge discovery perspective. IEEE Trans. Emerging Top. Comput. Intell. **6**, 667–6 (2020)

Hussain, W., Merigo, J.M., Gao, H., Alkalbani, A.M., Rabhi, F.A.: Integrated AHP-IOWA, POWA framework for ideal cloud provider selection and optimum resource management. IEEE Trans. Serv. Comput. (2021a)

Hussain, W., Merigó, J.M., Raza, M.R.: Predictive intelligence using ANFIS-induced OWAWA for complex stock market prediction. Int. J. Intell. Syst. (2021b)

Hussain, W., Merigó, J.M., Raza, M.R., Gao, H.: A new QoS prediction model using hybrid IOWA-ANFIS with fuzzy c-means, subtractive clustering and grid partitioning. Inf. Sci. **584**, 280–300 (2021c)

Hussain, W., Sohaib, O., Naderpour, M., Gao, H.: Cloud marginal resource allocation: a decision support model. Mob. Networks Appl. **25**(4), 1418–1433 (2020)

Kwak, B.I., Han, M.R., Kang, A.R., Kim, H.K.: A study on detection methodology of threat on cars from the viewpoint of IoT. J. Korea Inst. Inf. Secur. Cryptol. **25**(2), 411–421 (2015)

Labong, R.C.: Identity theft protection strategies: a literature review. J. Acad. Res. **4**(2), 1–12 (2019)

Meneghello, F., Calore, M., Zucchetto, D., Polese, M., Zanella, A.: IoT: internet of threats? A survey of practical security vulnerabilities in real IoT devices. IEEE Internet Things J. **6**(5), 8182–8201 (2019)

Muralidharan, E., Pathak, S.: Sustainability, transformational leadership, and social entrepreneurship. Sustainability **10**(2), 567 (2018)

New Zealand's Exchange: Independent reports on NZX IT and cybersecurity completed (2020). https://www.nzx.com/announcements/364459

Nicholson, J., Kurucz, E.: Relational leadership for sustainability: building an ethical framework from the moral theory of 'ethics of care.' J. Bus. Ethics **156**(1), 25–43 (2019)

Papavasiliou, S.J.: A digital transformation governance framework for eGovernment: a systemic approach. Doctoral dissertation (2020)

Petrakis, E.G., Sotiriadis, S., Soultanopoulos, T., Renta, P.T., Buyya, R., Bessis, N.: Internet of things as a service (ITAAS): challenges and solutions for management of sensor data on the cloud and the fog. Internet Things **3**, 156–174 (2018)

Rathore, M.M., Ahmad, A., Paul, A., Rho, S.: Urban planning and building smart cities based on the Internet of things using big data analytics. Comput. Netw. **101**, 63–80 (2016)

Raza, M.R., Varol, A., Hussain, W.: Blockchain-based IoT: an overview. Paper presented at the 2021 9th International Symposium on Digital Forensics and Security (ISDFS) (2021)

Showkat, D., Som, S., Khatri, S.K., Ahluwalia, A.S.: Security implications in IoT using authentication and access control. In: 2018 7th International Conference on Reliability, Infocom Technologies and Optimization (Trends and Future Directions) (ICRITO), pp. 689–694. IEEE, August 2018

Siddique, J., Joseph, P.: The social architect: a new framework for effective activism and social leadership. Cadmus **4**(4) (2021)

Tambunan, S.B., Lores, L., Muda, I.: Factors influencing the establishment of ISO 17799 standards. In: Proceedings of the International Conference of Science, Technology, Engineering, Environmental and Ramification Researches (ICOSTEERR 2018)-Research in Industry 4.0, pp. 1290–1295 (2020)

Tanford, S., Baloglu, S., Erdem, M.: Travel packaging on the internet: the impact of pricing information and perceived value on consumer choice. J. Travel Res. **51**(1), 68–80 (2012)

Weber, R.H.: Internet of things: privacy issues revisited. Comput. Law Secur. Rev. **31**(5), 618–627 (2015)

Wright, D., Meadows, D.H.: Thinking in systems. Earthscan (2008)

Security Requirements in IoT Environments

Ftayem Binglaw[1], Murat Koyuncu[2](✉) ⓘ, and Tolga Pusatlı[3] ⓘ

[1] Graduate School of Natural and Applied Science, Atilim University, Ankara, Turkey
[2] Atilim University, Ankara, Turkey
mkoyuncu@atilim.edu.tr
[3] Cankaya University, Ankara, Turkey

Abstract. The Internet of Things (IoT) is a relatively new concept as it connects things (or objects) that do not have high computational power. The IoT helps these things see, listen, and take action by interoperating with minimal human intervention to make people's lives easier. However, these systems are vulnerable to attacks and security threats that could potentially undermine consumer confidence in them. For this reason, it is critical to understand the characteristics of IoT security and their requirements before starting to discuss how to protect them. In this scope, the present work reviews the importance of security in IoT applications, factors that restrict the use of traditional security methods to protect IoTs, and the basic requirements necessary to judge them as secure environments.

Keywords: Internet of Things · IoT · Security · Security requirements

1 Introduction

IoT security can be defined as all the strategies and technologies that aim to protect any information collected, exchanged, or stored in any IoT system from threats and malicious attacks [1]. This information may face many risks and threats such as theft, tampering, and destruction. Also, the security of IoT components such as sensors, devices, applications, and networks should be considered in the scope of IoT security.

Security considerations are not new in the information technology (IT) context; rather, they are critical components of any technology's success, development and adoption. Security has always been an issue since computers started communicating with each other. However, the scope of coverage of such security has so far been limited, e.g. money and intellectual property, to name two [2, 3]. The advent of the IoT with its complex environment has added a whole new dimension to this problem and, as a result, has faced new and unique security challenges. This complexity is due to various factors such as large number of heterogeneous connected devices, huge data generated and exchanged by these devices, and differences in the communication infrastructure. In addition, IoT devices are made by different manufacturers, use different security policies and communication stacks, and are based on various standards [4]. This has led to the failure in implementing a robust security system for devices, especially since most

© ICST Institute for Computer Sciences, Social Informatics and Telecommunications Engineering 2022
Published by Springer Nature Switzerland AG 2022. All Rights Reserved
W. Hussain and M. A. Jan (Eds.): IoTaaS 2021, LNICST 421, pp. 84–96, 2022.
https://doi.org/10.1007/978-3-030-95987-6_6

of them are not equipped with an effective security mechanism and are not primarily designed to deal with security problems [5].

The IoT is the integration and collaboration of several technologies such as WSN, RFID, cloud computing, Internet, etc. Naturally, it suffers from all the vulnerabilities of these technologies [6]. In addition, as mentioned above, the IoT has its own characteristics which aggravate the security requirements considerably. This leads to an indispensable need to review security requirements specifically from an IoT perspective.

Against this backdrop, the goal of this paper is to answer the following questions:

- Why is it so important to secure the IoT?
- What are the challenges when using the already available technologies to secure and protect information to this end?
- What are the basic security requirements that must be met in IoT to render it secure?

2 Importance of IoT Security

Attacks on IoT devices can sometimes be easy to implement, especially when they target devices with limited resources that represent the majority, such as smart TVs and baby monitors. Resource limitations represent weaknesses and flaws that hackers can use to attack the IoT system as a whole, thereby compromising its overall safety and productivity [5, 7, 8]. In addition, IoT devices may be left to operate in harsh, irregular and even hostile environments without supervision, making them more vulnerable to various security breaches [9]. The common attack strategy on IoT devices is to hack one device that has vulnerabilities, and to take fraudulent actions against other connected devices by impersonating the true identity of the hacked device [5]. As a result, it can be said that the interconnected nature of the IoT means that every insecure device connected to it has the potential to affect the security of the IoT system as a whole [10]. For example, attackers could compromise a home alarm system by intercepting the radio frequency signal used to lock and unlock home windows.

It is common for IoT devices to be targeted by attackers. F-Secure published a report titled "Attack Landscape H1 2019: IoT, SMB Traffic", recording a 300% increase in the number of cyber-attacks on IoT devices in 2019. The attacks usually target IoT devices that are found in homes and workplaces such as medical devices, smart TVs, and smart printers, all of which are considered weak and unsafe against these attacks. More troubling is the fact that attackers find it easy to hack devices as access points to more critical and sensitive networks and systems.

The importance of security in the IoT becomes even clearer with real-life incidents, giving us a better idea about the extent of the impact of IoT security problems on consumers' lives. Here are a few examples:

BMW's ConnectedDrive Vulnerability: In January 2015, a security flaw appeared in the BMW ConnectedDrive System, one that allows drivers whose cars have been accidentally locked to request a remote unlock of their vehicle from the BMW helpline [11]. This flaw allowed the attacker to impersonate the BMW's servers and send instructions to unlock the locked vehicle remotely using a mobile phone network even without any request from the owner.

Hacked IoT Devices: On October 21, 2016, several websites including Twitter, Netflix, Spotify, Airbnb and The New York Times were reported to be inaccessible due to a Distributed Denial of Service (DDoS) attack [12]. To launch this attack, the attacker(s) hacked a number of IoT devices with limited resources and used them to send numerous fake requests to these sites. This overflow burdened the Web sites, rendering them unable to deal with their customers' requests and leading to their temporary shut-down.

Denial of Basic Services: According to Simo Ronella, CEO of Valtia, the company responsible for managing the overall operations and maintenance of damaged properties, in 2016, two buildings in southeast Finland were attacked [13]. This attack deprived residents of heating, which is an essential service in a cold country like Finland, as it temporarily disrupted the computer systems that controlled the central heating and hot water distribution to both buildings using a DDoS attack. According to local reports, this cyber-attack lasted about a week.

Hacked Baby Monitor: According to NBC News, in 2018, a Texas couple experienced a cyber-attack targeting the cameras they used to monitor their four-month-old baby [14]. They heard voices and insults coming from the child's room. Then they heard the voice of a man in their room telling them that their child had been kidnapped. However, when they got to their child's room, they found him alone and asleep.

Exploiting Connected Fax Machines: In 2018, Yaniv Palmas and Eyal Atkin, two security researchers from Check Point, discovered that popular HP Officejet Pro All-in-One fax printers had security flaws [15]. These flaws could allow hackers to steal data across the company's network using a phone line and fax number. They said that attackers could fax files loaded with malware that were specifically created to target networks. Fax vulnerabilities enable this malware to decrypt files and upload them to its memory, which could compromise sensitive information or cause disruption across connected networks.

Hacking Smart Bulbs: The security experts from the University of Texas stated that hackers can make use of Internet-connected light bulbs as a covert channel to exploit the user's private data [16]. Researchers used the LIFX and Phillips Hue smart light systems as a study for this purpose, stating that hackers could launch an attack by manipulating the infrared light upon creating a communication channel between the smart lights and a device that senses infrared light. Then, by installing a malicious agent on the phone, they could encode private data and transfer them through the infrared covert channel.

These are just several examples of what attacks targeting the IoT can do. The consequences of the attacks may be more dangerous when they target applications that directly affect human life, such as e-health applications or smart transportation applications, which may cause accidents that threaten people's lives. IoT devices do not only collect and manage critical personal information such as users' names and telephone numbers, medical records and prescriptions, but also monitor user activities (e.g., when users are at home) [17, 18]. Therefore, users should ensure that IoT devices and the services they provide are free from vulnerabilities and defects threatening user's security, especially as this technology is becoming more and more common in daily life [10, 19, 20]. For this reason, ensuring security in IoT products should be a major stakeholder priority and a goal to be achieved. Otherwise, without IoT security and privacy guarantees, related solutions are unlikely to be widely adopted by stakeholders despite their benefits [21].

3 Factors that Restrict the Use of Traditional Security Methods to Protect IoT

It is well known that protecting the information stored and exchanged among devices and within a network is not a new problem as there have always been concerns for cyber-attacks targeting information. However, security has remained as a hot topic since ready-made solutions are not always satisfactory. The IoT security requires the development and creation of new solutions designed to suit the nature of this technology or, at best, solutions modified from old ones. This is because the common Internet-connected devices differ from IoT devices in terms of functionality and device resources such as memory, power source, and data processing capability. For example, a laptop differs from a baby monitor and a smartphone differs from a smart door lock. This difference makes it difficult to use traditional security, that was originally designed to protect these systems, to protect the IoT; security in this respect has to be stronger because IoT devices are connected to the physical world and, at the same time, they are not designed to withstand the new threats that this world faces on a daily basis. This section visits some of the important features that distinguish the IoT from well-known information systems as reported in [5, 10, 22–25].

3.1 Mobility

Most IoT devices are portable and often connect to the Internet via a wide range of service providers. As most of these devices are mobile, this ability can cause disconnection from a specific network, release its IP address, connect to another network, and get a new IP address. Therefore, a stable network connection cannot always be expected in such an environment. This factor makes it difficult and complicated to verify the identity of every device trying to connect to the network. In addition, what resources such a device can access, and what risks it may bring to the network are other issues to be considered.

3.2 Heterogeneity

The IoT is a heterogeneous and complex system that combines many products from different manufacturers; hence, the different technologies. These products differ from each other in terms of resources (software and hardware), security policies, and functionality. Therefore, interaction and interoperability become difficult due to the lack of a common platform. This gives rise to the problem of creating a common standard for IoT security architecture accepted by all vendors and manufacturers. Creating this architecture would enhance the interoperability of the security functions of all components of the IoT system. Obviously, the success of this will depend on collaboration among companies to create a global standard that significantly facilitates IoT network security.

3.3 Scalability

Scalability is related to the ability of the system, with all the software and hardware it contains, to meet the large increase in the number of devices and the vast amount of information circulating in addition to the increasing demand for services.

The things connected to the IoT are increasing daily and their number is expected to reach about 14.7 billion devices by 2023 [26]. This significant increase in the number of devices is matched with an increase in the number of users and an increase in the services they demand. In addition, the amount of information that users share will increase by a major amount. Such dual increase in both information and devices will lead to other problems, including providing unique addresses for devices, where the information is stored, and how to control and monitor it. On the other hand, a lot of these devices will be deployed in areas where it may be impossible or impractical to provide physical security, making it easier for intruders to physically compromise the devices on the network. In short, limited scalability makes it difficult to monitor, identify, and protect IoT devices.

3.4 The Possibility of Being Tampered

Current security solutions focus primarily on protection from remote attackers, and are based on the fact that these individuals cannot physically access the devices. This is mostly true for desktop computers and servers that are usually kept in closed buildings, or mobile devices that rarely leave their owners' pockets. However, this is not the case for IoT devices that may be located in many remote areas left unattended. In most cases, attackers can gain easy physical access to them to extract secrets, modify programs, or add malicious data.

3.5 Limited Resources

The implementation of a robust security mechanism in an IoT system depends on the availability of strong security in each IoT device. It is well known that the availability of robust security methods in any device depends to a large extent on having sufficient resources to support it, such as having adequate power supply, memory space, and processing capability.

The IoT devices are not initially built for being secure; nor are they always designed to be smart and to exchange information with other devices. As discussed previously, traditional methods may not always work; for instance, those used to secure computers cannot be used to secure IoT devices such as coffee machines, refrigerators, door locks, etc. One of the reasons is that these devices contain a limited amount of resources, unlike computers. Most IoT devices are simple, resource-constrained things that often perform one function, such as turning lights on/off or measuring the oxygen level in the blood. Such lack of resources inhibits the implementation of complex security solutions. On the other hand, since traditional security solutions are designed to run on computers, smartphones, and other devices with larger resources, they are not suitable for IoT devices with limited resources.

The devices in the IoT have many limitations and restrictions that control the level of security they can provide. This may be due to the manufacturers' strategy to produce inexpensive and lightweight smart devices. The resource limitations on IoT devices include hardware restrictions such as computing power, energy supply and memory size; and software restrictions such as O/S security updates, and network limitations due to a variety of the communication protocols and media.

4 Security Requirements for the IoT

In the short term, the IoT is expected to enter various areas of our daily life such as our cities, homes, hospitals and schools. However, this prevalence heavily depends on an important factor, which is the degree of security that the IoT provides to consumers [27]. If IoT service providers want this technology to spread widely, they should think of security requirements when manufacturing or deploying IoT technology. In this way, IoT user can be sure that his sensitive and private information is essentially protected from any kind of abuse. Also, the services and applications provided by the IoT must be available whenever the user needs them.

Table 1. Example IoT threats and possible attack consequences.

Threat	Target	Possible consequences
Eavesdropping	Confidentiality	Disclosure of sensitive data
Eavesdropping	Privacy	Disclosure of private data
Impersonation	Authentication, Authorization	Unauthorized access to data or devices
Tampering	Availability	Physical damage
False data injection	Integrity	May cause false reports and wrong decisions

In order to ensure security in the IoT and to create readily available IoT devices and services, a set of security requirements have to be taken into consideration. Failure to do so could mean failure to provide security and privacy, resulting in serious problems and dire consequences. The minimum main security requirements to be met in any IoT system can be listed as providing confidentiality, integrity, availability, authentication, authorization, and privacy [4, 7, 24, 28–30]. These requirements are extracted considering the most popular potential threats to these systems and their targets as given in Table 1. Note that the table does not include all threats, but only examples; also that, even though these requirements may not be new as regards computer security, they still need to be considered when it comes to IoTs.

4.1 Confidentiality

Confidentiality refers to granting only authorized users the right to access certain information, ensuring the security of that information, and protecting it from disclosure.

Even if this information is stolen, the presence of such a security measure prevents the perpetrators from understanding the stolen data and exploiting it.

IoT devices may deal with sensitive information important to individuals, institutions and governments, including medical records, banking transactions and military secrets. Therefore, the protection of this information is important and is closely related to the user's degree of confidence in the IoT technology and their willingness to use it and benefit from its services. For example, eavesdropping or tampering with information exchanged by health devices may lead to the disclosure of personal health information or even lead to life-threatening situations for individuals. As another example, the data related to the composition of any product that guarantees its quality and distinguishes it from other products should be confidential because its spread can harm the company's reputation and competitive advantage [8].

To achieve confidentiality, protect information and gain user confidence, specific technologies need to be developed, such as encrypting data before it is transmitted, and creating mechanisms for securely distributing cryptographic keys [24, 31, 32]. Most of the techniques used previously to provide confidentiality in the network are considered heavy on the IoT system and, for this reason, cannot be implemented for this purpose. For example, some asymmetric encryption methods, which encode data through a complex calculation that require adequate power and high computational capacity, will not be suitable for use in IoT devices with limited resources. One of the well-known encryption methods is the symmetric key encryption method. In this method, the sender and receiver use the same secret key to encrypt and decrypt the data [33]. However, before defining these technologies, one should take into account the heterogeneous nature of the IoT and the limited resources of most of its devices. In the literature, there are studies to develop symmetric key-based lightweight encryption algorithms aiming to produce solutions to this specific requirement.

4.2 Integrity

This requirement is necessary to give users confidence in the accuracy and completeness of the information provided by the IoT. As mentioned before, the IoT is often based on the exchange of private, sensitive and valuable information among many different devices that greatly affect consumers. For this reason, it is important to ensure that accurate, original, legal, unaltered, timely and complete information reaches consumers [22]. Incorrect information may appear as a result of changing or tampering with the original information, and this change may be intentional or unintentional. In an intentional alteration, a malicious attacker picks up the information before it reaches its target, changes it, and then sends it back to its destination. Thus, the recipient receives information other than what was sent to them from the authorized sender. As a result, the attacker can modify, alter, or completely destroy the data, endangering the integrity of the IoT system, which entails great risks. As for the unintended change, it could sometimes result from a transmission error or unintended noise, or as a result of weather factors [5, 34].

This security requirement is important to the IoT and, if not available, there may be serious consequences. For example, tampering with medical information and readings produced by medical devices, such as an insulin pump or pacemaker, may lead to life-threatening consequences [18]. Apart from this, if the data is not reliable, then it cannot be used for the purposes for which it was designed; hence, any service that relies on this data could be compromised. An even more dangerous incident is using this data without knowing that it has been tampered with, sometimes resulting in wrong decisions, e.g. giving the wrong medication to a patient. Therefore, there is a need to come up with and use technologies whose mission is to verify the integrity of the data provided by the IoT. One simple technique to do so is the Cyclic Redundancy Check (CRC), which ensures data integrity by adding a fixed-length value to detect network errors in the IoT. A request to resend the correct data goes to the sender if this technology observes the arrival of incorrect data [9, 24, 32].

4.3 Availability

The requirement of IoT availability is necessary to provide a fully functional Internet-connected environment. This ensures that services are available to consumers whenever they need them and without interruption [18]. In other words, availability ensures that authorized users can access all related devices, services and data provided by the IoT whenever they need it and without any delay. Availability is essential even in the event of attacks and crashes; it also guarantees the ability to provide minimum services in the event of a power outage and blackout [5, 22]. In IoT, most services are requested in real time, meaning that if the request is not answered in time due to unavailability of the service, this request cannot be rescheduled at any other time [35]. For example, if the information about an intruder in a house is sent to the police station the next day, that information loses its value. Likewise, if the blood glucose meter registers disturbing readings, which are then received late by the doctor, this can result in significant harm to the patient, even death. Therefore, certain techniques should be devised and applied to ensure uninterrupted availability in IoT. Additionally, an IoT system needs to provide backup of vital information to prevent data loss and ensure data availability. Firewalls and IDSs can be installed on a network to prevent attacks and provide availability of IoT devices [32].

4.4 Authentication

Authentication is a major requirement of the IoT because it provides confidence in the devices participating in the IoT network and is critical for improving network performance. This security requirement is for everything intended to connect to an IoT system. Typically, the authentication and identity management work together to manage and secure access to information and resources, and to connect to the network. Identity management identifies objects individually, while authentication enables the IoT objects to confirm the identity of the peer they are communicating with. In other words, authentication enables the recipient to verify whether she or he has actually received the data from the sender who claims who they are. This means ensuring the legitimacy of the data presented in the networks, as well as the legitimacy of the objects sending and requesting that data. In brief, to provide security, no IoT entity should have the ability to directly access available resources unless its identity is authenticated first [5, 7, 32, 34].

The process of authenticating and verifying the identity of an object is a prerequisite for allowing access to resources and requests for any data or service in the IoT. This process ensures that no attacker can enter the network using a false ID and password, and send out false messages. This further demonstrates the importance of having a mechanism that enables the recipient to ensure that the message received comes from a reliable source and, at the same time, enables the senders to ensure that the requester of information is reliable.

The nature of scalability in the IoT is a major concern when authentication is taken into account. Identifying a large number of devices and authenticating each object directly in real time can be a daunting task due to the vast number of objects connected to the IoT [36]. Because of all this, it is necessary to propose a mechanism that effectively deals with the scalability of devices in the IoT environment while enabling entities to confirm each other's identity in every interaction in it. To work around this issue, different schemes and algorithms and pre-shared keys are proposed that are lightweight and do not adversely affect battery life within devices and their performance. For example, symmetric key encryption depends on both parties having the same encryption key to confirm their identity [37, 38]. Also, one of the methods used for authentication is what is known as the 'direct authentication method' for humans and machines. The user can open the office door using biometric identification (such as a fingerprint) or an object within a personal network, such as an ID card or smartphone. The combination of authentication methods can prevent any overall system security loss.

4.5 Authorization

There is sometimes confusion between authentication and authorization requirements although these requirements differ completely in meaning. Authentication means confirmation of identity, while authorization means allowing access to the system. In simple terms, authentication is the process of self-verification, while authorization is the process of checking what the self has access to. Authorization enables determining if the person or object, after authenticating their identity, is permitted to, for example, access, use, or read the resource. These privileges or permissions are determined by the device or by the identity of the users. As such, given proper identity, anyone can access an IoT system while without permission, no one can access any resources in it [5, 39]. Therefore, it can be said that the authorization policy determines which specific resources can be accessed by which entity or user.

Authorization is typically implemented through the use of access control. Access control is important in establishing a secure connection among a number of devices and resources. After determining whether an object has the right to access a specific resource, the access control mechanism either allows or denies it to access the related resource. One important issue that should be addressed in access control is to make it easier to create and modify its rules, and to make these rules easy to understand and follow [7, 40].

4.6 Privacy Requirement

Privacy is the ability to protect data from eavesdropping and to control how it is shared and distributed. It is also concerned with concealing the identity of the owner and the recipient of the information, which is an important aspect especially in the case of personal and sensitive information [28].

Since many people, devices and services communicate and share everything online, such as photos, videos, health records, etc., it has become important to consider privacy as an important security requirement [32]. In an open environment like the IoT, a lot of personal information about individuals can be collected without their knowledge if there are no security measures to prevent this. In an IoT environment, individuals will be able to take advantage of a large number of services that require personal information related to, for example, a consumer. These services may require photos, emails, phone numbers, bank account information, and many more. Moreover, the environment itself may be able to obtain this information automatically as a result of the interconnection among its services and devices. For example, some smart TV companies collect information about their customers in order to assess viewing behavior, usually without the knowledge or desire of customers. In this case, privacy should provide protection to individuals by giving them full control over their personal data. They should know who is responsible for collecting their data and where it is stored, and they should also be notified before such data is shared through the system [4, 39].

The privacy requirement should ensure that consumers' information and identities are in safe hands and completely protected from disclosure or leakage. The inability to access personal data except by the authorized person means that no other authenticated customer who has nothing to do with this information or any other individual can access it [4]. For example, hospital administration personnel need access to patient data for administrative purposes (registration, billing, etc.), but they are not allowed to know anything about the patient's history and health status. In this case, privacy concerns granting employees the right to access information related to their work only without disclosing sensitive medical information not related to their work [20].

IoT has become integral in various applications, namely remote patient monitoring, energy consumption control, traffic control, and smart parking. In all of these applications, users need the protection of personal information related to their movements, habits, and interactions with other people. Therefore, there is an urgent need to propose protocols and administrative frameworks for dealing with privacy, determining who stores them where, and who manages and provides access to information in IoT. For example, individuals' personal information should be destroyed when it is no longer needed. As another solution, all communication between IoT nodes can be encrypted using proper encryption algorithms. This solution ensures that the connection is not open to intruders trying to eavesdrop and, at the same time, guarantees privacy. Access control mechanisms are also among the steps that help protect individuals' privacy. This mechanism controls who has the right to access the data and what action can be taken on it.

5 Conclusions

This paper provides answers related to three key questions listed in the Introduction concerning IoT security. First, the importance of IoT security is explained by providing real-life examples. Then, the reasons that make it difficult to use the available security methods and techniques to protect the IoT are discussed. Finally, the basic security

requirements that should be met in the IoT are elaborated. Since these security requirements are primarily targeted by cyber-attacks, they need special attention to secure any
IoT system.

The findings of this study are as follows: 1) IoT systems are targets of cyber-attacks,
such as eavesdropping, compromising the confidentiality of data exchanged among IoT
nodes. 2) IoT devices are very sensitive to intentional or unintentional data changes.
3) There are different types of attacks which can affect the availability of IoT devices
and service. 4) Authentication and authorization of users and devices become complex
in such a heterogeneous environment. 5) Large amounts of personal information about
individuals can be collected without their knowledge. Considering all these findings,
confidentiality, integrity, availability, authentication, authorization and privacy are taken
as the basic security requirements for an IoT environment.

If enough security measures are in place to protect an IoT system, then the system
can be considered secure. For this reason, it is very important to know such security
requirements in full before starting to implement related actions. With the increasing
use and popularity of IoT devices worldwide, it is only natural and inevitable to guarantee
secure applications before any dire consequences come about as a result of compromised
systems being in use.

References

1. Kouicem, D.E., Bouabdallah, A., Lakhlef, H.: Internet of things security: a top-down survey.
   Comput. Netw. **141**, 199–221 (2018)
2. Cvitić, I., Vujić, M., Husnjak, S.: Classification of security risks in the IoT environment. In: Proceedings of the 26th International DAAAM Symposium, pp. 731–740, DAAAM
   International, Vienna (2016)
3. Patel, K.K., Patel, S.M.: Internet of things-IOT: definition, characteristics, architecture,
   enabling technologies, application & future challenges. Int. J. Eng. Sci. Comput. **6**(5),
   6122–6131 (2016)
4. Razzaq, M.A., Gill, S.H., Qureshi, M.A., Ullah, S.: Security issues in the Internet of Things
   (IoT): a comprehensive study. Int. J. Adv. Comput. Sci. Appl. **8**(6), 383 (2017)
5. Hossain, M.M., Fotouhi, M., Hasan, R.: Towards an analysis of security issues, challenges,
   and open problems in the internet of things. In: IEEE World Congress on Services, pp. 21–28.
   IEEE (2015)
6. Andrea, I., Chrysostomou, C., Hadjichristofi, G.: Internet of Things: security vulnerabilities
   and challenges. In: IEEE Symposium on Computers and Communication (ISCC), pp. 180–
   187. IEEE (2015)
7. Abomhara, M., Køien, G.M.: Security and privacy in the Internet of Things: current status
   and open issues. In: International Conference on Privacy and Security in Mobile Systems
   (PRISMS), pp. 1–8. IEEE (2014)
8. Jha, A., Sunil, M.C.: Security considerations for Internet of Things. L&T Technol. Serv.
   (2014)
9. Krishna, B.S., Gnanasekaran, T.: A systematic study of security issues in Internet-of-Things
   (IoT). In: International Conference on I-SMAC (IoT in Social, Mobile, Analytics and Cloud)
   (I-SMAC), pp. 107–111. IEEE (2017)
10. Iqbal, M.A., Olaleye, O.G., Bayoumi, M.A.: A review on internet of things (IoT): security
    and privacy requirements and the solution approaches. Glob. J. Comput. Sci. Technol. **16**(7)
    (2017)

11. PCWorld: BMW cars found vulnerable in Connected Drive hack. https://www.pcworld.com/article/431610/bmw-cars-found-vulnerable-in-connected-drive-hack.html. Accessed 22 Nov 2021

12. The New York Times: Hackers used new weapons to disrupt major websites across U.S. https://www.nytimes.com/2016/10/22/business/internet-problems-attack.html. Accessed 22 Nov 2021

13. The Hacker News: DDoS attack takes down central heating system amidst winter in Finland. https://thehackernews.com/2016/11/heating-system-hacked.html. Accessed 22 Nov 2021

14. NBC News: Nest camera hacker threatens to kidnap baby, spooks parents. https://www.nbcnews.com/news/us-news/nest-camera-hacker-threatens-kidnap-baby-spooks-parents-n949251. Accessed 22 Nov 2021

15. The Hacker News: Hackers can compromise your network just by sending a Fax. https://thehackernews.com/2018/08/hack-printer-fax-machine.html. Accessed 22 Nov 2021

16. SciTechDaily: Warning: smart light bulbs could open up your personal information to hackers. https://scitechdaily.com/warning-smart-light-bulbs-could-open-up-your-personal-information-to-hackers/. Accessed 22 Nov 2021

17. Yang, Y., Wu, L., Yin, G., Li, L., Zhao, H.: A survey on security and privacy issues in Internet-of-Things. IEEE Internet Things J. **4**(5), 1250–1258 (2017)

18. Mosenia, A., Jha, N.K.: A comprehensive study of security of internet-of-things. IEEE Trans. Emerg. Top. Comput. **5**(4), 586–602 (2016)

19. ENISA: Baseline security recommendations for IoT in the context of Critical Information Infrastructures. https://www.enisa.europa.eu/publications/baseline-security-recommendations-for-iot. Accessed 15 Sept 2021

20. Sfar, A.R., Natalizio, E., Challal, Y., Chtourou, Z.: A roadmap for security challenges in the Internet of Things. Digit. Commun. Networks **4**(2), 118–137 (2018)

21. Miorandi, D., Sicari, S., De Pellegrini, F., Chlamtac, I.: Internet of things: vision, applications and research challenges. Ad Hoc Netw. **10**(7), 1497–1516 (2012)

22. Mahmoud, R., Yousuf, T., Aloul, F., Zualkernan, I.: Internet of things (IoT) security: current status, challenges and prospective measures. In: 10th International Conference for Internet Technology and Secured Transactions (ICITST), pp. 336–341. IEEE, London (2015)

23. Haroon, A., Shah, M.A., Asim, Y., Naeem, W., Kamran, M., Javaid, Q.: Constraints in the IoT: the world in 2020 and beyond. Constraints **7**(11), 252–271 (2016)

24. Al-Sharekh, S.I., Al-Shqeerat, K.H.A.: Security challenges and limitations in IoT environments. Int. J. Comput. Sci. Netw. Secur. **19**(2), 193–199 (2019)

25. Elrawy, M.F., Awad, A.I., Hamed, H.F.A.: Intrusion detection systems for IoT-based smart environments: a survey. J. Cloud Comput. **7**(1), 1–20 (2018). https://doi.org/10.1186/s13677-018-0123-6

26. Cisco, Cisco Annual Internet Report (2018–2023), White paper. https://www.cisco.com/c/en/us/solutions/collateral/executive-perspectives/annual-internet-report/white-paper-c11-741490.pdf. Accessed 15 Sept 2021

27. Shamsi, K., Mazhar, A.: IoT implementation using secure communication protocols. Int. J. Comput. Eng. Res. (IJCER) **7**(12), 2250–3005 (2017)

28. Ngu, A.H., Gutierrez, M., Metsis, V., Nepal, S., Sheng, Q.Z.: IoT middleware: a survey on issues and enabling technologies. IEEE Internet Things J. **4**(1), 1–20 (2016)

29. Vasilomanolakis, E., Daubert, J., Luthra, M., Gazis, V., Wiesmaier, A., Kikiras, P.: On the security and privacy of Internet of Things architectures and systems. In: International Workshop on Secure Internet of Things (SIoT), pp. 49–57. IEEE, Vienna (2015)

30. Batalla, J.M., Vasilakos, A., Gajewski, M.: Secure smart homes: opportunities and challenges. ACM Comput. Surv. (CSUR) **50**(5), 1–32 (2017)

31. Chinanu, U.E., Oche, O.E., Okah-Edemoh, J.O.: Architectural layers of internet of things: analysis of security threats and their countermeasures. Sci. Rev. **4**(10), 80–89 (2018)

32. Lin, J., Yu, W., Zhang, N., Yang, X., Zhang, H., Zhao, W.: A survey on internet of things: architecture, enabling technologies, security and privacy, and applications. IEEE Internet Things J. **4**(5), 1125–1142 (2017)
33. Ashraf, Q.M., Habaebi, M.H.: Autonomic schemes for threat mitigation in Internet of Things. J. Netw. Comput. Appl. **49**, 112–127 (2015)
34. Laeeq, K., Shamsi, J.A.: A study of security issues, vulnerabilities and challenges in internet of things. In: Securing Cyber-Physical Systems, 1st edn. CRC Press (2015)
35. Kozlov, D., Veijalainen, J., Ali, Y.: Security and privacy threats in IoT architectures. In: Workshop on Security Tools and Techniques for Internet of Things (SeTTIT). ACM, Oslo (2012)
36. Khattak, H.A., Shah, M.A., Khan, S., Ali, I., Imran, M.: Perception layer security in Internet of Things. Futur. Gener. Comput. Syst. **100**, 144–164 (2019)
37. Rehman, S.U., Khan, I.U., Moiz, M., Hasan, S.: Security and privacy issues in IoT. Int. J. Commun. Networks Inf. Secur. **8**(3), 147 (2016)
38. Zhao, K., Ge, L.: A survey on the internet of things security. In: Ninth International Conference on Computational Intelligence and Security, pp. 663–667. IEEE, Emeishan (2013)
39. Joshitta, R.S.M., Arockiam, L.: Security in IoT environment: a survey. Int. J. Inf. Technol. Mech. Eng. **2**(7), 1–8 (2016)
40. Roman, R., Najera, P., Lopez, J.: Securing the internet of things. Computer **44**(9), 51–58 (2011)

Reinforcement Learning Based Intelligent Management of Smart Community Grids

Muhammad Khalid[1]([⊠]), Mir Bilal Khan[2], Liaquat Ali[3], and Faheem Ahmed[4]

[1] Jacobs University Bremen, Campus Ring 1, 28759 Bremen, Germany
Khalid.csd.uob@gmail.com
[2] University of Hertfordshire, Collage Lane, Hatfield AL10 9AB, UK
[3] Department of Computer Science and IT, University of Balochistan, Quetta 87300, Pakistan
[4] Department of Computer Science - UBIT, University of Karachi, Sindh, Pakistan

Abstract. The fundamental goal and commitment of this article is the exploitation of our perception-based intelligent management method. An examination with 39 elective methodologies was performed, exhibiting the upsides of our methodology as far as interpret able and precise fuzzy principle-based DSGC strength forecast then revealing the chain of importance of DSGC-framework's characteristic criticalness. Shrewd networks are strong, self-recuperating systems that authorized bidirectional circulation of vitality and data inside the utility framework. Therefore, prosumer supervision involves growing attentiveness between scholars in current years. At that point, this evaluation process of nearby market interest is tackled by deep reinforcement learning and deep Qlearning techniques with experience replay system. This idea discovers the safety of upcoming energy frameworks touching near to coordinating extra parts of sustainable power source elements. Particularly, we can manage cold-start clients with less social connections. Later on, we will distinguish further data from informal community to viably tackle client cold-start issues. Moreover, we will investigate the effect of complex data on client utilization conduct to assemble a stable recommender system. The subsequent part presents logical examinations of Internet of Things (IoT)applications in the power business. For the logical examination relevant investigation, brilliant local area meter information-driven and autonomous models are made to figure the likely kilowatt (kW) limit decline from DR. At long last, I bring up open inquiries to empower further exploration.

Keywords: Big data · Wind power · SGD · SVM

1 Introduction

The following and preceding task of the research of which this report is a section centers around dispersal of big-data and data-mining applications in the electric utility industry and commitment of the power business at workshops, conferences, research development and innovation roadmap 2017–2026, webcasts, and so on. Industry gatherings furnish partners with a chance to audit in big-data, new programming advances, and uses of

W. Hussain and M. A. Jan (Eds.): IoTaaS 2021, LNICST 421, pp. 97–109, 2022.
https://doi.org/10.1007/978-3-030-95987-6_7

cutting-edge investigation. The discoveries from this examination impress the estimation of big-data and investigation for the "European Network of Transmission System Operations for Electricity". electric industry and recognize applications for prescriptive analysis that utilization AI and Machin Learning (Hussain et al. 2015). Certification of greatest performs in big-data. Reinforcement Learning is class of machine learning methods that has emerged only recently. This involves the exploration of intelligent schemes by attempting to achieve objectives and improving gradually improving its performance toward accomplishing human level or even surpassing humans (Mu et al. 2019b). Deep reinforcement learning has rapid changed field of intelligent systems with numerous accomplishments by the utilization of artificial neural networks algorithms in reinforcement learning (Raza et al. 2021a; Raza et al. 2021b). It enables machine learning to tackle issues that were previously too computationally intensive (Boyd and Crawford 2011). The deep reinforcement learning techniques further improve the conventional reinforcement learning which is asked on Markov decision processes. The relationship between deep reinforcement learning and traditional reinforcement learning is presented. Deep reinforcement learning (DRL) being a blend of deep learning and reinforcement learning, utilizes the concept of DL model training in AI applications. Along these lines, DL, RL, and DRL present an opportunity towards the future improvement of smart grids. In the first place, intermittent nature of wind and solar energy bring numerous difficulties for electric power distribution. Deep reinforcement learning can be an answer for overseeing fluctuating sources, load forecasting, planning, management of energy and so forth. To guarantee secure and stable functionalist of huge power systems under complex and uncertain situations is perhaps the greatest challenge that power engineers need to address today.

Environmental change is forcing the energy producers, governments, businesses, and utility providers to utilize sustainable power sources and improve energy efficiency (Bhattarai et al. 2019; Billinton and Wangdee 2006). To meet the requirement for green energy regulations and to comply with new monetary and ecological constraints, the power infrastructure is slowly changing from the conventional centralized model to increasingly decentralized and innovative smart grids. This concept of smart decentralized power generation and distribution infrastructure is called smart community grid where energy customers may assume the role of prosumers, who produce and sell or offer surplus energy (Landberg 1999; Dabrowski and Fern 2009). The effectiveness of smart grid energy sharing depends upon meaningful prosumers' contribution to the community grid (Ericsson 2010). Energy sharing in community smart grids involves coordination and reliable connections between partners, which inclued prosumers, energy producers, energy market administrator and so on (Manzoor et al. 2017). All these partners must have accessibility to data for monitoring the community grid's energy market citeespe2018prosumer. Thus, to enable the prosumers and other partners in acquiring reliable data is a key aspect of intelligent decision-making by the partners (Espe et al. 2018). Henceforth, the test is to help presumes and partners in acquiring suitable data to be progressively creative, profitable, and have the option to settle on choices which sway their social, natural and financial state (Lu and Hong 2019). In today's conventional retail power distribution infrastructure, customers generally have exceptionally constrained "energy choices" to pick from various kinds of energy providers. Even though the establishment of Distributed Energy Resources (DERs) has gained popularity, in current power sector's, clients or prosumers can only decide to exchange their surplus energy or request to fill deficits from utility providers (Bhattarai et al. 2019). With buying vitality since before retailing vitality extra rear toward the services straightforwardly, the customers or prosumers need to endure some value hole. the way to giving more energy exchanging opportunity and open advancement the retail electricity market is to create client driven plans of action and conceivably a restricted energy exchanging stage. Following this faith in the ebb and flow look into network, the cutting-edge retail power advertise framework will in the end become a level playing field, where all clients have an equivalent chance to effectively participate legitimately (Lu et al. 2019). In order to manage the energy effectiveness issue, the demand-side management (DSM) framework (Mnih et al. 2015) provides the solution by load-moving through planned energy usage that flattens the fluctuating energy demand and also decreases the absolute energy consumption of every client in addition to focusing on dynamic pricing strategy. Moreover, the DSM framework can (Zhao et al. 2016) acquire greater adaptability when performing energy scheduling (Ericsson 2010). Addition of household energy-storing structure (ESS) to photovoltaic (PV) energy generation. Centralised QoE and QoS CQoES framework using a hybrid AHP-IOWA, POWA, UCF and KNN methods (Hussain and Merigó 2022). The proposed method handles nonlinear relationships among selection criteria and intelligently weight customized criteria based on complex attitudinal characteristics of the decision-maker (Hussain et al. 2021a). At present, several mechanisms dealing with DSM issues exist in the literature. However, most of these mechanisms cannot employ Big Data. With the improved computation power, the AI approach, for example, reinforcement learning, can give an extraordinary capacity of learning the control arrangement under various circumstances inside a smart home. Along these lines, the proposed work aims to manage the DSM issue dependent on the home zone and domestic performances using a Deep Q Network (DQN) mediator (Mu et al. 2019b; Mu et al. 2019a) coupled with the human decision maker.

2 Background

2.1 Markov Chain Process

The conduct of a significance community grid system can be displayed as far as the processing jobs executing in the framework whenever. Each undertaking advances through an actual existence cycle in which it is first presented by a client, specialist organizations are found to run the errand, an SLA is haggled with chose provider(s), and the errand is either executed to finishing or fizzles to finish. The condition of the community grid system can be depicted by the conditions of the considerable number of errands that are in the framework at some specific time. This area initially portrays the state change model for an individual undertaking and afterwards shows how the total of numerous assignments states are spoken to in a Markov chain model. This possibly huge model can be compacted, or lumped, into an increasingly succinct portrayal where the elements of the community grid system can be concentrated in a significant manner (Dabrowski and Fern 2009).

2.2 Markov Reward Process

A Markov Reward Process is a Markov procedure through esteem decision, saying what way considerable recompense gathered from side to side approximately specific arrangement that we inspected. An MRP is a tuple. (S, P, R, γ) where S is a limited state space, P is the state transition probability function, R is a reward function where, it says how much instant reward we hope to get from state S at right now. Here is the notion of the return Gt, which is the absolute limited rewards from time step (Shi et al. 2008).

2.3 Markov Decision Process

A MDP is a Markov Reward Process with decisions, it's a situation where in all states are Markov. This is the thing that we need to illuminate (Shi et al. 2008). A MDP is a tuple (S, A, P, R, γ) where S is our state space, A will be a limited arrangement of activities, P is the state transition probability function, R is the reward function where, in (Shi et al. 2008) All the more as of late, reinforcement learning (RL), otherwise called the prototype free mechanism method, has gotten consideration whilst a likely Machin Learning approach on behalf of power-driven vitality management. A spearheading effort in RL-based vitality managing stays Google DeepMind, which existed created utilizing the Reinforcement Learning strategy then consumes survived established toward reduce the power beak through conserving the server farm via around 40percent. Deep Reinforcement Learning (DRL) (that survives, the combination of RL and ANN) pragmatic to the switch of HVAC trendy a structure to diminish the vitality price though keeping up an agreeable customer level as far as the indoor temperature (Shi et al. 2008), just by way of equally the roofed warmth then midair superiority (Shi et al. 2008). A few identifications consume provided details regarding household vitality supervision through DERs utilizing Q-learning, happening which the ESS occurred coordinated near accomplish vitality reserves hip a solitary (Shi et al. 2008) household plus a communal alongside numerous structures (Shi et al. 2008).

3 Methods

This part represents an overview of the deep q-learning algorithm, reinforcement learning and data source and the classes and qualities of data on the smart community grid with an emphasis on large-scale of investigation for DR programs and the job of data normalization in that specific situation and disused the Markov Chain Monte Carlo Simulations. So, we have a numerical model with which system precariousness can be expected. The need for a tool to predict solution unpredictability would have been met, and the double characterization ("stable" versus "unsteady") issue would be unraveled. But the execution of this model depends on noteworthy improvements. A differential condition-based model can be controlled in a few different ways. One customary methodology comprises in running recreations with a mix of fixed qualities for one subset of factors and fixed worth circulations for the rest of the subset. As carefully delineated in Dorin Moldovan (2020).

3.1 Deep Q-Learning Algorithm

In (Hussain 2021), multi-agent RL remained introduced to deal with the household energy utilization. Every mediator compared toward different household apparatuses sorts through nonchargeable, Changeable, plus manageable electric loads, the energy utilization of every machine is improved by the Q-learning method, alongside the current forecasted value of energy by utilizing the ANN. As of late, a novel Q-learning strategy utilizing activity subordinate double heuristic programming was used to resolve the unlimited-time area straight equal-sided follower exclusive of needful data of the technique substances in (Mu et al. 2019b). Cutting-edge (Mu et al. 2019a) Q-learning-based self-organized system existed wherever entirely mediators speak by one another then harmonize alongside pioneer mediator, thusly accomplishing the ideal accord answer aimed at each mediator continuously.

3.2 Shortest Path Using Q-Learning Algorithm

Graphs are numerical structures used to display pairwise relations between objects. A graph is comprised of vertices that are associated with edges. In an undirected graph, I will locate the briefest way between two vertices. Q-learning is a without model reinforcement learning algorithm. The impartial of Q-learning remains toward achievement expertise by a method, whichever indications towards a mediator whatever move near type underneath whatever conditions. The situation does not need a consummate of the background, then its container treaty through questions by stochastic advances plus rewards, exclusive of needful modifications. Q-learning procedure includes a mediator, a usual of positions then a customary of movements for every formal. It utilizes Q-values

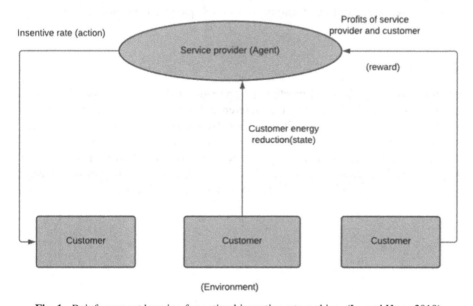

Fig. 1. Reinforcement learning for optimal incentive rate making. (Lu and Hong 2019)

what is more chance at approximately amount toward decide that deed to yield. The reward and conceivable potential rewards of an activity taken (Fig. 1).

4   Result

In the prospect computerized culture, the power source consistency and power value are firmly needed. The power production is experiencing thoughtful modifications. The smart grid as arises the condition necessitate. The outdated power grid is progressively incorporated with the data communication system, supervising and regulator system (Gelazanskas and Gamage 2014; Gorzałczany et al. 2020). Monte Carlo simulation is frequently expended in the dependability assessment of the power system at current. Though, on account of the limitations of large computing resources and gradual conjunction rapidity, it is challenging to use the simulation method in the operational situation (Hussain et al. 2018; Hussain and Sohaib 2019). In reflection of the wide-ranging of the power system and the huge number of mechanisms, the Monte Carlo technique used on the Markov chain was presented into the analysis of power system process consistency assessment in the works (Gungor et al. 2011; François-Lavet et al. 2016). Nevertheless, the Gibbs lesser required for simulation to create the Markov chain can't essentially reward for the limitations of the simulation method.

4.1   Imported Required Libraries

Alongside conventional libraries imported for tensor control, numerical activities and designs improvement, three scikit-learn modules (StandardAero as a scaler, confusion matrix as the model execution metric of decision and KFold as the cross-validation engine) and two Keras profound learning objects (Sequential and Dense) are utilized in this activity.

4.2   Data Set

The dataset picked for this AI practice has an engineered nature and contains results from recreations of grid stability for a reference 4-hub star arrange, as portrayed in (Moldovan 2020; Kenyon et al. 2020). The first dataset contains 10,000 perceptions. As the reference framework is symmetric, the dataset can be expanded in 3! (3 factorial) times, or multiple times, speaking to a change of the three purchasers involving three shopper hubs. The expanded variant has then 60,000 perceptions. It likewise contains 14 essential prescient highlights and two ward factors (Figs. 2 and 3).

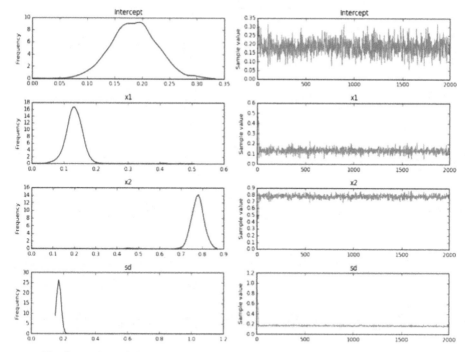

Fig. 2. Markov Chain Monte Carlo to get the improvement over straight averaging

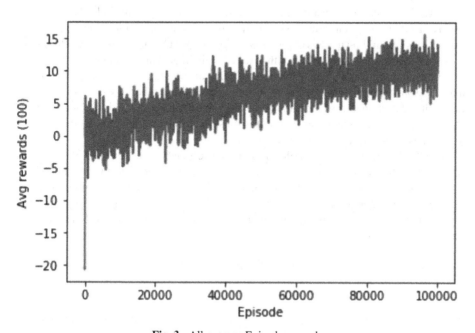

Fig. 3. All average Episode rewards

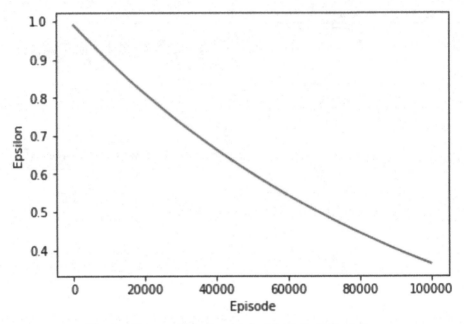

Fig. 4. All average Episode rewards - Monte Carlo simulation

4.3 Monte Carlo Simulation

Monte Carlo simulation is an automatic scientific method that permits individuals to represent a hazard in quantitative analysis and dynamic. Monte Carlo simulations implement risk analysis by building models of potential outcomes by subbing a scope of qualities—a likelihood dispersion—for any factor that has an inalienable vulnerability. It at that point figures results, again and again, each time utilizing an alternate arrangement of random qualities from the probability functions. Contingent on the number of vulnerabilities and the reaches determined for them, a Monte Carlo simulation could include thousands or a huge number of recalculations before it is finished. Monte Carlo simulation produces circulations of conceivable result esteems.

In Actor-Critic, rather than holding up until the finish of the episode as we do in Monte Carlo Reinforce, we make an update at each progression. Since we do an update at each time step, we can't utilize the complete reward R(t). Rather, we must prepare a Critic model that approximates the worth capacity. This worth capacity replaces the reward function in strategy inclination that figures the rewards just toward the finish of the episode (Figs. 4, 5 and Tables 1 and 2).

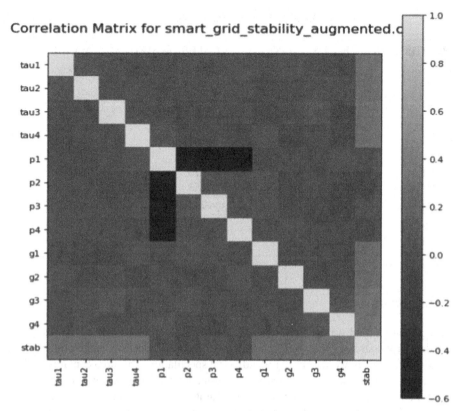

Fig. 5. Distribution graphs (histogram/bar graph) of sampled columns

Table 1. Original dataset (10,000 observation)

ARCHITECTURE	FOLDS	EPOCHS	CONFUSION MATRIX	ACCURACY
24-12-1	10	10	596-28 40-336	93.20%
24-12-1	10	20	605-19 31-345	95.00%
24-12-1	10	50	603-21 35-341	94.40
24-12-1	10	10	604-20 30-346	95.00%
24-12-1	10	20	604-20 31-345	94.90%
24-12-1	10	50	602-22 20-356	95.80%

Table 2. Augment dataset (60,000)

ARCHITECTURE	FOLDS	EPOCHS	CONFUSION MATRIX	ACCURACY
24-12-1	10	10	3795-56 168-1981	96.28%
24-12-1	10	20	3680-73 78-2071	98.00%
24-12-1	10	50	3787-64 67-2058	98.20%
24-12-1	10	10	3864-76 97-2053	97.10%
24-12-1	10	20	3765-83 59-2091	96.95%
24-12-1	10	50	3798-56 68-2083	97.95%

5 Discussion

Although the method we used to study the results of simulations already works quite even though the strategy we used to anticipate the consequences of simulations as of now works very well, we see space for additional speculation. This area contains angles this examination has not tended to which we esteem promising exploration headings. In of our analyses, exactness (the portion of accurately arranged plan focuses) has been around 70%. To get an overall view on the framework, this isn't significant, and our outcomes stay substantial. Be that as it may, when one uses simulations to discover unadulterated stability locales, this might be unacceptable. Considering cost delicate classifiers, which put more accentuation on stable structure focuses, is one potential bearing of exploration. Next, we have utilized the information on framework balance to get the highlights from the underlying information by processing sums. In any case, questions, for example, regardless of whether our structures are ideal in approximately logical, can handle complex nonlinear problems (Hussain et al. 2021a; Hussain et al. 2022), or whether such features can be" naturally stay open. Also, the expansion of investigation for enormous networks, containing more than 10 members, isn't clear.

6 Conclusions

In this study, we address the issue of straightforward and exact expectation of smart framework control stability utilizing our insight-based data mining approach executed as the fuzzy rule-based classifier. Smart Grid Control (DSGC), the subject of this object, has been promoted as an approach to acknowledge demand response. We have gathered the suspicions behind it deliberately, some of which are prohibitive. To wipe out certain suppositions, while simultaneously focusing at straightforward and astute models, we have proposed the accompanying: Reproduce the framework for differing sets of infor-mation values. A reproduction result has been an induction on whether the framework is steady for the data prizes. Make structures from unique contributions, to diminish the number of degrees of opportunity. Request a decision tree algorithm to the information coming about because all things considered. This methodology uncovers new bits of knowledge concerning DSGC, not known from past investigations. For instance, we have discovered that the framework can be steady regardless of whether a few members adjust their vitality utilization with a high deferral, or quick variation is best for dependability under specific conditions. Normalized information strategies can empower proficient, practical utilization of expository data to help coordinated grid exercises, for example, power unwavering quality, grid arranging and tasks, DSM projects, and DR execution evaluation. Big-data analytics could utilize to target clients that have the most DR.with regards to each DR program. Beginning phase prescriptive examination and progressed prescient investigation strategies are accessible to decide the estimation of DR to both the grid and the client.

Moreover, the fundamental suspicions of the DSGC frameworks, for instance, the fixed info issue, correspondence issue, physical model suppositions, and so forth., can be investigated further for improved area expertise that will prompt an improved Machine Learning Classification Model.

References

Bhattarai, B.P., et al.: Big data analytics in smart grids: state-of-the-art, challenges, opportunities, and future directions. IET Smart Grid **2**, 141–154 (2019). https://doi.org/10.1049/iet-stg.2018.0261

Billinton, R., Wangdee, W.: Predicting bulk electricity system reliability performance indices using sequential monte carlo simulation. IEEE Trans. Power Deliv. **21**, 909–917 (2006). https://doi.org/10.1109/TPWRD.2005.861237

Dabrowski, C., Fern, H.: Markov chain analysis for large-scale grid systems. National Institute of Standards and Technology (2009)

Boyd, D., Crawford, K.: Six provocations for big data. In: A Decade in Internet Time: Symposium on the Dynamics of the Internet and Society (2011)

Ericsson, G.N.: Cyber security and power system communication—essential parts of a smart grid infrastructure. IEEE Trans. Power Deliv. **25**, 1501–1507 (2010). https://doi.org/10.1109/TPWRD.2010.2046654

Espe, E., Potdar, V., Chang, E.: Prosumer communities and relationships in smart grids: a literature review, evolution and future directions. Energies **11**, 2528 (2018). https://doi.org/10.3390/en11102528

Gelazanskas, L., Gamage, K.A.A.: Demand side management in smart grid: a review and proposals for future direction. Sustain Cities Soc. **11**, 22–30 (2014). https://doi.org/10.1016/j.scs.2013.11.001

Gorzałczany, M.B., Piekoszewski, J., Rudziński, F.: A modern data-mining approach based on genetically optimized fuzzy systems for interpretable and accurate smart-grid stability prediction. Energies **13**, 2559 (2020). https://doi.org/10.3390/en13102559

Gungor, V.C., et al.: Smart grid technologies: communication technologies and standards. IEEE Trans. Ind. Inform. **7**, 529–539 (2011). https://doi.org/10.1109/TII.2011.2166794

Hussain, W, Merigo, J.M., Gao, H., Alkalbani, A.M., Rabhi, F.A.: Integrated AHP-IOWA, POWA framework for ideal cloud provider selection and optimum resource management. IEEE Trans. Serv. Comput., 1 (2021). https://doi.org/10.1109/TSC.2021.3124885

Hussain, W., Hussain, F.K., Hussain, O.K.: Towards soft computing approaches for formulating viable service level agreements in cloud. Paper presented at the Neural Information Processing (2015)

Hussain, W., Hussain, F.K., Saberi, M., Hussain, O.K., Chang, E.: Comparing time series with machine learning-based prediction approaches for violation management in cloud SLAs. Futur. Gener. Comput. Syst. **89**, 464–477 (2018)

Hussain, W., Merigó, J.M.: Centralised quality of experience and service framework using PROMETHEE-II for cloud provider selection. In: Gao, H., Kim, J.Y., Hussain, W., Iqbal, M., Duan, Y. (eds.) Intelligent Processing Practices and Tools for E-Commerce Data, Information, and Knowledge, pp. 79–94. Springer International Publishing, Cham (2022)

Hussain, W., Merigó, J.M., Raza, M.R.: Predictive intelligence using ANFIS-induced OWAWA for complex stock market prediction. Int. J. Intell. Syst. (2021). https://doi.org/10.1002/int.22732

Hussain, W., Merigó, J.M., Raza, M.R., Gao, H.: A new QoS prediction model using hybrid IOWA-ANFIS with Fuzzy C-means, subtractive clustering and grid partitioning. Inf. Sci. **584**, 280–300 (2022)

Hussain, W., Sohaib, O.: Analysing cloud QoS prediction approaches and its control parameters: considering overall accuracy and freshness of a dataset. IEEE Access **7**, 82649–82671 (2019). https://doi.org/10.1109/ACCESS.2019.2923706

Kenyon, R.W., et al.: Stability and control of power systems with high penetrations of inverter-based resources: an accessible review of current knowledge and open questions. Sol. Energy **210**, 149–168 (2020). https://doi.org/10.1016/j.solener.2020.05.053

Landberg, L.: Short-term prediction of the power production from wind farms. J. Wind Eng. Ind. Aerodyn. **80**, 207–220 (1999). https://doi.org/10.1016/S0167-6105(98)00192-5

Lu, R., Hong, S.H.: Incentive-based demand response for smart grid with reinforcement learning and deep neural network. Appl. Energy **236**, 937–949 (2019). https://doi.org/10.1016/j.apenergy.2018.12.061

Lu, R., Hong, S.H., Yu, M.: Demand response for home energy management using reinforcement learning and artificial neural network. IEEE Trans. Smart Grid **10**, 6629–6639 (2019). https://doi.org/10.1109/TSG.2019.2909266

Manzoor, S., Manzoor, M., Hussain, W.: An analysis of energy-efficient approaches used for virtual machines and data centres. Paper presented at the 2017 IEEE 14th International Conference on e-Business Engineering (ICEBE) (2017)

Mnih, V., et al.: Human-level control through deep reinforcement learning. Nature **518**, 529–533 (2015). https://doi.org/10.1038/nature14236

Moldovan, D.: Horse optimization algorithm: a novel bio-inspired algorithm for solving global optimization problems. In: Silhavy, R. (ed.) Artificial Intelligence and Bioinspired Computational Methods, pp. 195–209. Springer International Publishing, Cham (2020)

Mu, C., Zhao, Q., Gao, Z., Sun, C.: Q-learning solution for optimal consensus control of discrete-time multiagent systems using reinforcement learning. J. Frankl. Inst. **356**, 6946–6967 (2019a). https://doi.org/10.1016/j.jfranklin.2019.06.007

Mu, C., Zhao, Q., Sun, C., Gao, Z.: An ADDHP-based Q-learning algorithm for optimal tracking control of linear discrete-time systems with unknown dynamics. Appl. Soft Comput. **82**, 105593 (2019b). https://doi.org/10.1016/j.asoc.2019.105593

Raza, M.R., Hussain, W., Merigó, J.M.: Cloud sentiment accuracy comparison using RNN, LSTM and GRU. Paper presented at the 2021 Innovations in Intelligent Systems and Applications Conference (ASYU) (2021a)

Raza, M.R., Hussain, W., Merigó, J.M.: Long short-term memory-based sentiment classification of cloud dataset. Paper presented at the 2021 Innovations in Intelligent Systems and Applications Conference (ASYU), Elazig, Turkey (2021b)

François-Lavet, V., Taralla, D., Ernst, D., Fonteneau, R.: Deep reinforcement learning solutions for energy microgrids management (2016)

Shi, W.-H., Shi, W.-H., Shi, W.-H.: Applications of Markov chain Monte Carlo in large-scale system reliability evaluation (2008)

Zhao, Y., Ye, L., Li, Z., Song, X., Lang, Y., Su, J.: A novel bidirectional mechanism based on time series model for wind power forecasting. Appl. Energy **177**, 793–803 (2016). https://doi.org/10.1016/j.apenergy.2016.03.096

Energy Inefficacy in IoT Networks: Causes, Solutions and Enabling Techniques

Ziyad Almudayni[1][(✉)], Ben Soh[2], and Alice Li[2]

[1] Hail University, Hail, Saudi Arabia
20167676@students.latrobe.edu.au
[2] La Trobe University, Melbourne, Australia
{b.soh,a.li}@latrobe.edu.au

Abstract. The Internet of things (IoT) concept can be generally described as the ability of machines to communicate via the Internet to perform tasks. In addition to the communication between devices, humans can remotely control IoT devices via controllers such as smartphones. The main aim of introducing IoT technologies is to make our lives easier and more convenient. Due to the massive increase in both IoT devices and research on enhancing the security and the speed of these devices, there is a strong demand to work in parallel to promote IoT networks' energy efficiency to make IoT systems scalable. This paper outlines the causes of energy inefficiency in IoT systems and proposes some key tools to prolong the network lifetime of these devices.

Keywords: IoT · Routing · Clustering · Offloading · Scheduling

1 Introduction

The Internet of things (IoT) concept can generally be described as the ability of machines to communicate via the Internet to perform tasks. In addition to the communication between devices, humans can remotely control IoT devices via controllers such as smartphones [1]. The main aim of introducing IoT technologies is to make our lives easier and more convenient. In many various fields, the IoT systems can simplify work processes by building automatic systems that can operate without any human interaction, which saves time, money, effort [2]. Due to the massive rise in IoT devices, there is a strong demand to promote IoT networks' energy efficiency. In addition to the number of IoT devices, researchers have developed several complex algorithms to improve other parameters such as security, data rate, and bandwidth, which increase the workload and the consumption of power [3]. From an energy perspective, a study carried out in 2021 by Liu L et al., found that the number of connected IoT devices in use globally will reach 55.7 billion by 2025. Furthermore, these different IoT sensors and devices require various power costs to work normally; for example, a gas sensor requires 500–800 mW for operating normally [4]. From an economic perspective, several studies have shown the importance of IoT in the market and how this technology can lead to successful investments. A recent study predicted that the total investment in IoT technology would increase from USD 130.33 billion in 2015 to USD 883.55 billion in 2022 [5]. Thus, engineering IoT systems to consume less power and cost will encourage providers and consumers to participate in the IoT markets and result in more in successful investments in the IoT markets. From an environmental perspective, all energy sources have a negative impact on our air, water and land [6]. Thus, it is vital to be aware of the power emissions that IoT devices produce and to decrease their impacts as much as possible by reducing the power consumption of IoT systems while ensuring they continue to reaching their objectives, we will mitigate the impacts on the environment. From an industrial perspective, minimising the power consumption of IoT devices will encourage industries to integrate the IoT systems into their environment and to rely more on this technology. From a governmental perspective, introducing IoT systems with this advantage (low power requirements) will encourage organisations such as the Ministry of Health, the Ministry of Transportation to avail from this technology to simplify their work process.

2   The Causes and Solutions for Energy Inefficiency in the IoT Systems

Many technical issues in the IoT systems make the IoT devices consume more power in the IoT networks. Therefore, it is vital that researchers work more deeply on these technical issues to find and address gaps to reduce the amount of power consumed by IoT systems. In this section, thirteen common technical as shown in Fig. 1 for energy inefficiency with initial solutions will be discussed in detail.

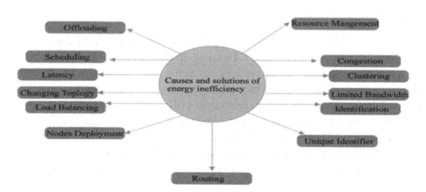

Fig. 1. Causes of energy inefficiency

2.1   Offloading

Offloading in general terms refers to moving things from one state to a different state. Offloading in IoT systems occurs when the tasks move from one fog node to another fog node or from a fog node to the cloud server. Efficient tasks offloading can be considered as one of the main keys to enhancing the QoS and improving parameters such as energy efficiency, delay, data rate and more. From an energy perspective, inefficient offloading of the IoT tasks leads to an increase in processing time, resulting in a greater consumption of power. This might also lead to an increase in the load on fog nodes while other nodes remain empty if the tasks are not distributed equally. Therefore, it is necessary to take the offloading into account to reduce the power used by IoT devices [7]. Researchers have been working to develop the offloading strategies to achieve the best decision-making about whether the tasks are processed on the fog or the cloud; this decision could be counted as the key to improve the offloading [8].

2.2 Scheduling

Tasks in IoT systems can be allocated based on various scheduling criteria to handle the resources and functions in a specific amount of time. Constraints and objectives are the two main features that have to be fulfilled to solve must of the scheduling problems. The scheduling mechanism is another keys to improving the QoS in IoT systems [9]. Due to the nature of heterogeneity and the number of IoT tasks and functions, efficient tasks scheduling makes IoT systems more organized and less heterogeneous, which leads to a decrease in the processing time, and as the processing time decreases the power consumption of the IoT systems will decrease accordingly. Inefficient tasks scheduling makes work in IoT systems more complicated and less efficient as well as consuming more power and processing time. Researchers need to be aware of this point to improve the QoS of IoT from an energy perspective as well as to improve other parameters, such as bandwidth and data rate.

2.3 Latency

Latency in general terms is when a system can not complete a process by the submission time. In other words, there is a delay. From an IoT perspective, as IoT applications require real-time processing to deliver services to the end-user, delays might lead to a large impact and affect the system's process negatively, so the response time has to be as short as possible to satisfy the QoS requirements [10]. Latency and power consumption in the IoT systems are related, so when the latency in systems is high, the IoT devices and network nodes will consume more power; the opposite is also true. The reason for this is the delays in the system will cause an increase in the processing time, which leads to more power consumption. As researchers, we must seek minimise the response time for IoT communication as much as possible to save more power for the IoT systems.

2.4 Changing Topology

The wireless network is the fundamental method of communication that most IoT devices use. Due to the dynamic nature of the IoT environment, the wireless network topology updates its structure frequently, and the number of IoT nodes is updated from time to time. These changes affect the efficiency and reliability of data transmission [11]. A change in the network topology might affect the energy's performance in the IoT environment as

IoT devices and network nodes consume more power during these changes. The process of an IoT device joining and leaving a wireless network for the IoT devices consumes energy, researchers have to be aware of this and strive to make the IoT network as steady as possible to minimise the amount of joining and leaving. When there is a change in the IoT network topology, the number of the required network nodes for the IoT devices might change from time to time, for instance, a smart building might require 50 network nodes in winter while the same building might require 70 network nodes in summer. Prediction algorithms could play an important role in solving this problem by estimating the number of the required network nodes in all different scenarios.

2.5 Load Balancing

Load balancing in general terms can be defined as systems' ability to distribute the workload of things, humans, machines and nodes equally. From an IoT perspective, load balancing can be achieved when the workload is distributed equally between routes in the network rooting and between nodes in computing services and between the IoT devices. As the traffic in the IoT networks increases accordingly with the rise in the number of processes in an IoT system, load balancing can play an essential role in minimising traffic in the network by distributing the workload over several IoT nodes and routes [12]. From an energy perspective, efficient load balancing can contribute to estimating the required nodes, routes, and devices. This estimation results in reducing the power consumption of the IoT devices, as there will be no extra nodes, routes and devices. Inefficient load balancing is one of the main reasons for losing power in IoT systems as there might be more active empty nodes where routes are not needed if the IoT system's workload is not balanced effectively. Also, there might be greater loads on nodes and routes, while others have less or zero loads, which leads to greater power consumption. There are two types of load balancing: static load balancing and dynamic load balancing. In the former, the load distribution and balancing are based on data that have been stored before the start of the system. In the latter, the system distributes the load equally during real-time [13].

2.6 Node Deployment

The structure of network nodes is one of the first steps that a designer has to be aware of when establishing a network system. There are three main structures in IoT systems and fog services for the deployment of nodes: cluster, peer to peer, and master–slave [14]. Selecting the appropriate structure for an IoT system enhances the QoS and improves the performance in terms of data rate, bandwidth, security and energy consumption. From an energy perspective, the inefficient selection of a network node structure might affect the energy consumption performance and lead to consuming more power as there might be extra nodes more than needed and some nodes might have extra loads while others empty. To satisfy the QoS requirements and improve the performance of IoT communications, when selecting the structure of deployments designers need to consider certain things such as the amount and type of tasks, the number of IoT devices and sensors and the workloads [15].

2.7 Resource Management

Adequate resource management of IoT devices could be considered one of the key factors to enhance the IoT systems' performance and satisfying the QoS requirements. These resources are managed and powered by tiny operating systems such as TinyOS, FreeRTOS and Contiki. For each IoT device, there are five main components of resources management: process management, memory management, energy management, communication management and file management. For instance, when aiming to reduce power consumption and enhance energy efficiency of an IoT system, we can focus on energy resource management. This can be achieved by improving the network protocols and OS scheduling modes such as the CPU's sleep mode when the queue is empty. Researchers have to be aware of all the different layers of IoT architecture to save more power or any different parameters, and inefficient resource energy management might cause in losing more power and make the network lifetime shorter, so it is vital to be aware of this point [16].

2.8 Congestion Control IoT

IoT networks include various types of networks such as wireless sensors networks, adhoc networks and vehicular ad hoc networks. The complexity of these networks will cause traffic and increase the size of the network, which leads to congestion in the IoT network and delays in communication [17]. Congestion in the IoT network negatively affects the IoT system's performance, thus decreasing the level of QoS in the system. Effective routing protocols could be counted as one of the main keys to avoid congestion in the network by selecting the best and the shortest path and controlling these paths when sending and receiving data [18]. From an energy perspective, congestion in the IoT network node results in the use of more power due to the increase in the processing and transferring of data in the node. It is vital to handle the congestion problem in IoT networks by effectively controlling the routing paths and balancing the network nodes' workload to prolong the network lifetime of IoT networks [19].

2.9 Clustering

Clustering is a key to enhancing the overall performance of the IoT networks. Without clustering, all IoT nodes send data packets to the base station, leading to more power consumption. There are two types of nodes in clustering: cluster heads (CH) and cluster members. CHs work as a centre point to aggregate data from the cluster members (neighboring nodes) to the base station, leading to saving power. Machine learning, fuzzy logic and other approaches can be utilised to select the appropriate CH and the number of nodes in each cluster [20].

2.10 Routing

The route in the network is the path from the source (sender) to the destination (receiver), and routing is the process of following these paths when sending and receiving data packets in the network. As deployment of IoT devices is heterogeneous in nature, finding the shortest path is one of the primary ways to satisfy the QoS requirements in IoT networks. From an energy perspective, the power consumed by a transmission when forwarding data packets from the source to the destination via long paths is higher than the forwarding through shorter paths. Therefore, it is vital to take advantage of using optimizing algorithms such as ant colony optimization algorithm to find the shortest path in order to save power and prolong the network lifetime [21].

2.11 Limited Bandwidth

Minimizing the bandwidth in IoT networks is essential. Limiting the bandwidth in IoT systems can play an essential role in enhancing the QoS of IoT technologies. Power consumption and the speed of real-time processing in IoT networks show significant improvements when the bandwidth is limited. The average range of the bandwidth in most of the IoT networks is about 200 kbit/s [22]. It is vital to minimize the bandwidth of the IoT network without affecting the delivered services for end-users, as all the requested services from end-users have to arrive on time.

2.12 Identification of IoT Devices

All devices and nodes in the IoT environment have to be identified in all layers of IoT. The IoT nodes are distinguished from one to another in terms of many aspects like performance, properties, functions and more. As IoT nodes are dissimilar in their methods, it is important to identify each node in the IoT environment to understand the behavior of the IoT network nodes. Identification in the IoT devices is one of the main challenges in IoT systems due to the high number of IoT devices [23]. Therefore, the process of identification has to be as simple as possible to reduce the work complexity in IoT networks.

2.13 Unique Identifier

IoT has contributed to increasing the number of connected devices via the Internet to reach to billions. Network identifiers (NIs) allow IoT nodes to communicate and transmit data by addressing each node in the network. NIs systems such as IPv4, IPv6, 16-bit and ZigBee are distinguished from each other in the way and size of addressing. IPv4 is widely considered as the most addressing system to define each node in IoT systems. However, this addressing system is not reliable when applied to a large number of IoT devices because it is 32 bits long and has limited addressing the devices, which is about 4.3 billion. IPv6 (128-bit) provides more spaces than IPv4, however, using a long identifier for small IoT networks is wasteful because 128-bits is too large to be utilised to define only 100 IoT nodes. It is vital to have a unique identifier as these distinguishes in addressing and protocols can lead to technical issues in compatibility and interoperability [24].

3   Enabling Technologies

Enabling technologies are the tools that can be used to solve any technical issues. This section focuses on the tools that can be used to solve technical issues in IoT systems and, especially, to improve the energy efficiency of these systems. Six of the most important tools are listed below in more detail; however, it is important to be aware that there are than these six tools (see Fig. 2.).

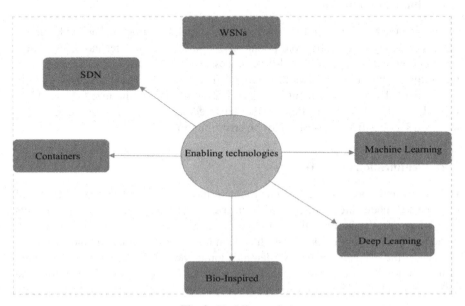

Fig. 2.   Enabling tools

3.1   Software-Defined Networking

SDN is a software tool that is used to manage and control networks virtually. The control plane and the data plane, which work separately, are the main parts of SDN. The control plane manages the network routes, and the data plane is responsible only for forwarding the data. SDN has added value to the network management by reducing the cost and efforts as these managements can be done without any physical interactions [25]. SDN has the potential to simplify network management and programmability and this advantage might add value to the IoT network management and make the system less complex for example by scheduling and the work load of tasks and activities in the IoT networks. SDN can also improve the IoT network's energy efficiency by managing sensor nodes and IoT devices as well as by controlling the duty cycles and sleep-scheduling mechanisms for low rate WPAN [26].

3.2 Containers

Containers can be defined as light virtual operating systems that can be run on various systems such as IoT, fog computing and more. The main objective of establishing containers is to manage each single point in the system, including IoT nodes and fog nodes. The management of resources such as CPUs, power, and memory and more in IoT nodes or fog nodes can be easily done through containers when they are established in the fog or IoT system. In addition to the management of resources, containers can control, monitor, and schedule the tasks. The containers can play an important role in enhancing the performance of IoT or fog system and making the system more scalable to increase the number of devices in the network [27]. There is a potential to improve the energy efficiency of both the fog nodes and the IoT nodes to satisfy the QoS requirements by effectively managing resources such as power, CPUs, I/O and memory through containers.

3.3 Wireless Sensor Networks (WSNs)

A WSN consists of a group of sensor nodes that can process, communicate and store data. The main purpose of sensor nodes is to detect and sense the changes in the surrounding areas in the environments such as temperature, humidity etc., and transfer data between IoT nodes. The end-user is updated frequently about the current state of the environment from the data collected by sensor nodes and can take actions accordingly. Lack of energy resources, lack of memory and a limited physical range are the main things that the WSNs suffer from [28]. It is vital to improve the performance of the WSNs to satisfy the QoS requirements by significantly improving the energy efficiency of networks and other parameters such as security. This can be achieved by working deeply in the network such as improving the clustering and distribution of WSNs, and selecting the shortest path between the nodes to send and receive data.

3.4 Machine Learning

Machine learning analyses historical data to predict future events and make intelligent decisions. In IoT systems, ML and AI can act as the brain of the IoT network to handle and control the system and perform tasks [29]. There are three main categories of machine learning: supervised learning, unsupervised learning, and reinforcement learning: each has its own features that benefit the IoT system and improve the overall performance of the system. The main objective of supervised learning is to classify things such as tasks in the IoT networks or any other system, which can be done by using labeled data. The IoT networks can benefit from supervised learning by classifying the tasks into categories to enhance the performance of scheduling in IoT nodes, fog nodes and resources management. Unsupervised learning obtains to cluster things by using unlabeled data where a machine figures out the output. It can add value to the IoT networks by, for example by clustering in the WSNs to reduce the power consumption and improve the network's performance. Reinforcement learning can be defined as the ability of agents to interact in the environment to take actions; it can be used to design the routing protocols in IoT systems to satisfy the QoS requirements [30].

3.5 Deep Learning

Deep learning (DL) aims to analyse a large volume of data to predict events and perform tasks in a complex environment. Due to its multilayer structure, DL can be considered as advanced type of machine learning. As IoT systems deal with a large value of data, DL can perform better performance than ML, and it can also solve different problems automatically by extracting new features [31]. DL uses artificial neural networks (ANNs) to process and analyse data, which has inputs, hidden layers and outputs. The neural network's hidden layers act as the brain of the network to analyse and process the inputs data to generate the outputs as solutions, tasks, and events. DL can add advantages to most IoT applications; including those in healthcare, agriculture and educations. This DL technology has numerous features, such as image recognition, voice recognition and indoor localization. As IoT systems have limited energy, developers have to be aware that DL techniques demand a large amount of resources such as battery energy, memory and processors [32]. Therefore, the DL algorithms have to be as simple as possible to limit power consumption and take the advantage of finding solutions for energy inefficiency.

3.6 Bio-Inspired Algorithm

Bio-inspired optimization algorithms are a promising tool for solving and developing computing techniques by using biological principles such as genetic bee colony (GBC) algorithm, fish swarm algorithm (FSA). Biology optimization algorithms are capable of solving complex machine learning problems in science and engineering [33]. From a network perspective, these biology algorithms have played a vital role in enhancing and providing solutions for communication protocols between devices. For example, most of the routing and clustering problems in the wireless sensor network have been solved using these algorithms. These bio-inspired optimization algorithms have added values to IoT systems and contributed to enhancing the IoT system's overall performance [34]. Therefore, we as researchers have to take advantage and benefit from these biology algorithms to solve and develop our energy efficiency problems by employing these algorithms.

4 Conclusion and Future Work

Developing any layers from the four architecture layers can enhance the IoT system's energy efficiency and all other parameters. Thus, from a computing perspective, it is vital to know that saving power in IoT systems can be achieved without working directly on watts, voltage and joules. Instead, working on and developing other parameters that are more related to computing and networking, such as latency and capacity, can achieve the aim of saving energy. Also, improving these parameters can be accomplished without working on them directly. The conclusion of this paper is to suggest that researchers who are aiming to improve the IoT systems' power consumption should work more deeply in such areas as scheduling, offloading, node deployment, resource management, routing, and clustering. Future studies will review previous studies related to improving the energy efficiency of IoT networks from different aspects to help researchers target research areas to address gaps.

References

1. Khan, M.A., Salah, K.: IoT security: review, blockchain solutions, and open challenges. Future Gener. Comput. Syst. **82**, 395–411 (2018)
2. Nižetić, S., Šolić, P., González-de, D.L.-D.-I., Patrono, L.: Internet of Things (IoT): opportunities, issues and challenges towards a smart and sustainable future. J. Cleaner Prod. **274**, 122877 (2020)
3. Sen, S., Koo, J., Bagchi, S.: TRIFECTA: security, energy efficiency, and communication capacity comparison for wireless IoT devices. IEEE Internet Comput. **22**, 74–81 (2018)
4. Liu, L., Guo, X., Lee, C.: Promoting smart cities into the 5G era with multi-field Internet of Things (IoT) applications powered with advanced mechanical energy harvesters. Nano Energy, 106304 (2021)
5. Tsai, C.-W.: SEIRA: an effective algorithm for IoT resource allocation problem. Comput. Commun. **119**, 156–166 (2018)
6. Bilgen, S.: Structure and environmental impact of global energy consumption. Renew. Sustain. Energy Rev. **38**, 890–902 (2014)
7. Yousefpour, A., Ishigaki, G., Gour, R., Jue, J.P.: On reducing IoT service delay via fog offloading. IEEE Internet Things J. **5**, 998–1010 (2018)
8. Jiang, J., Li, Z., Tian, Y., Al-Nabhan, N.: A review of techniques and methods for IoT applications in collaborative cloud-fog environment. Secur. Commun. Networks **2020** (2020)
9. Aburukba, R.O., AliKarrar, M., Landolsi, T., El-Fakih, K.: Scheduling Internet of Things requests to minimize latency in hybrid Fog–Cloud computing. Future Gener. Comput. Syst. **111**, 539–551 (2020)
10. Ma, Z., Xiao, M., Xiao, Y., Pang, Z., Poor, H.V., Vucetic, B.: High-reliability and low-latency wireless communication for internet of things: challenges, fundamentals, and enabling technologies. IEEE Internet Things J. **6**, 7946–7970 (2019)
11. Marietta, J., Mohan, B.C.: A review on routing in internet of things. Wireless Pers. Commun. **111**, 209–233 (2020)
12. Tseng, C.H.: Multipath load balancing routing for Internet of things. J. Sens. **2016** (2016)
13. Kaur, M., Aron, R.: A systematic study of load balancing approaches in the fog computing environment. J. Supercomput., 1–46 (2021)
14. Mahmud, R., Kotagiri, R., Buyya, R.: Fog computing: a taxonomy, survey and future directions. In: Di Martino, B., Li, K.-C., Yang, L.T., Esposito, A. (eds.) Internet of everything. IT, pp. 103–130. Springer, Singapore (2018). https://doi.org/10.1007/978-981-10-5861-5_5
15. Zahmatkesh, H., Al-Turjman, F.: Fog computing for sustainable smart cities in the IoT era: caching techniques and enabling technologies-an overview. Sustain. Cities Soc. **59**, 102139 (2020)
16. Musaddiq, A., Zikria, Y.B., Hahm, O., Yu, H., Bashir, A.K., Kim, S.W.: A survey on resource management in IoT operating systems. IEEE Access **6**, 8459–8482 (2018)
17. Bhandari, K.S., Hosen, A., Cho, G.H.: CoAR: congestion-aware routing protocol for low power and lossy networks for IoT applications. Sensors **18**(11), 3838 (2018)
18. Verma, L.P., Kumar, M.: An IoT based congestion control algorithm. Internet Things **9**, 100157 (2020)
19. Bhandari, K.S., Hosen, A., Cho, G.H.: CoAR: congestion-aware routing protocol for low power and lossy networks for IoT applications. Sensors **18**, 3838 (2018)
20. Srivastava, V., Tripathi, S., Singh, K., Son, L.H.: Energy efficient optimized rate based congestion control routing in wireless sensor network. J. Ambient Intell. Humanized Comput. **11**, 1325–1338 (2020)
21. Radhika, S., Rangarajan, P.: On improving the lifespan of wireless sensor networks with fuzzy based clustering and machine learning based data reduction. Appl. Soft Comput. **83**, 105610 (2019)

22. Raj, J.S., Basar, A.: QoS optimization of energy efficient routing in IoT wireless sensor networks. J. ISMAC **1**, 12–23 (2019)
23. Zikria, Y.B., Yu, H., Afzal, M.K., Rehmani, M.H., Hahm, O.: Internet of Things (IoT): operating system, applications and protocols design, and validation techniques. Elsevier (2018)
24. Aswale, P., Shukla, A., Bharati, P., Bharambe, S., Palve, S.: An overview of Internet of Things: architecture, protocols and challenges. In: Satapathy, S.C., Joshi, A. (eds.) Information and Communication Technology for Intelligent Systems. SIST, vol. 106, pp. 299–308. Springer, Singapore (2019). https://doi.org/10.1007/978-981-13-1742-2_29
25. Liu, G., Quan, W., Cheng, N., Zhang, H., Shen, X.: VLI: variable-length identifier for interconnecting heterogeneous IoT networks. IEEE Wireless Commun. Lett. **9**, 1146–1149 (2020)
26. Qafzezi, E., Bylykbashi, K., Ikeda, M., Matsuo, K., Barolli, L.: Coordination and management of cloud, fog and edge resources in SDN-VANETs using fuzzy logic: a comparison study for two fuzzy-based systems. Internet Things **11**, 100169 (2020)
27. Li, Y., et al.: Enhancing the internet of things with knowledge-driven software-defined networking technology: future perspectives. Sensors **20**, 3459 (2020)
28. Aruna, K., Pradeep, G.: Performance and scalability improvement using IoT-based edge computing container technologies. SN Comput. Sci. **1**, 1–7 (2020)
29. Singh, H., Bala, M., Bamber, S.S.: Augmenting network lifetime for heterogenous WSN assisted IoT using mobile agent. Wireless Netw. **26**, 5965–5979 (2020)
30. Younan, M., Houssein, E.H., Elhoseny, M., Ali, A.A.: Challenges and recommended technologies for the industrial internet of things: a comprehensive review. Measurement **151**, 107198 (2020)
31. Khattab, A., Youssry, N.: Machine learning for IoT systems. Internet Things (IoT), 105–127 (2020)
32. Li, H., Ota, K., Dong, M.: Learning IoT in edge: deep learning for the Internet of Things with edge computing. IEEE Network **32**, 96–101 (2018)
33. Mohammadi, M., Al-Fuqaha, A., Sorour, S., Guizani, M.: Deep learning for IoT big data and streaming analytics: a survey. IEEE Commun. Surv. Tutorials **20**, 2923–2960 (2018)
34. Darwish, A.: Bio-inspired computing: algorithms review, deep analysis, and the scope of applications. Future Comput. Inf. J. **3**, 231–246 (2018)
35. Hamidouche, R., Aliouat, Z., Gueroui, A.M., Ari, A.A.A., Louail, L.: Classical and bio-inspired mobility in sensor networks for IoT applications. J. Network Comput. Appl. **121**, 70–88 (2018)

IiCE: A Proposed System Based on IoTaaS to Study Administrative Efficiency in Primary Schools

Hamad Almaghrabi[1(✉)], Alice Li[2], and Ben Soh[1]

[1] Computer Science and Information Technology, LaTrobe University,
Melbourne, VIC, Australia
{h.almaghrabi,B.Soh}@latrobe.edu.au
[2] La Trobe Business School, LaTrobe University, Melbourne, VIC, Australia
A.Li@latrobe.edu.au

Abstract. Although many studies are conducted for ICT systems for educational organisations, there is a lack of understanding of ICT systems' usage for school administration. Infrastructure IT support Communication Experience and Training (IiCE) is a proposed framework based on the ICT that subsumes the IoT intending to improve the primary school administration tasks. This study is conducted on Saudi public primary schools. This study aims to investigate the current state of ICT systems used in primary schools' administration to provide a framework for the ICT systems usage. We carried out an electronic survey and analysed more than 500 responses. We include a detailed analysis reflecting different school members roles, including teachers, school principals, administrative assistants and parents. The findings of this study highlight the limitations in the existing ICT systems for school administration and provide a holistic understanding of influencing factors. Decision-makers for Saudi educational organisations can use the findings with the proposed framework to better understand the current situation of ICT systems and provide better solutions.

Keywords: Information and communication technology · School administration · Primary schools · School management · Education · IoTaaS · IoT · ICT

1 Introduction

Information Communication Technology (ICT) is a broad term that refers to any type of computer and communications hardware and software, which are used to create, store, transmit, interpret, and alter data in various formats [1]. While computers are typically linked with the phrase, it is also applied to a wide range of other media, including mobile devices, TVs, radios, seniors, IoTs and even

W. Hussain and M. A. Jan (Eds.): IoTaaS 2021, LNICST 421, pp. 121–138, 2022.
https://doi.org/10.1007/978-3-030-95987-6_9

prints [2]. The extensive access to computers has increased the accessibility and the usage of information, similarly communicate with others and produce new knowledge and cultural artifacts [2]. The effects of ICT and technology on education, curriculum, classroom and students have been studied in a comprehensive manner in the literature such as [1, 3–6]

Although the use of ICT from the education and learning point of view has been discussed comprehensively by a good number of studies [7–16], there is a dearth in the literature about using ICT for school administration purposes [1, 15–19]. For example, Hoque et al. [1] conducted a study for the use of ICT in school management of Maldivian schools. They considered 26 school teachers and 3 principals in their sample study and targeted high schools in Maldives. The research shows that while certain Maldivian schools have ICT facilities and technology, ICT is not effectively employed in school management for educational purposes, but is used to some level for daily administrative tasks. Despite the benefits and importance of using ICT for school administration, there is no usage framework has been given in this study. It also does not consider all the stakeholders of the ICT systems such as students or administrative assistance. Another study by Hoque et al. [5] to determine the areas of ICT utilisation among Malaysian school teachers and principals. They considered 215 teachers and 45 principals who were studying Masters in Educational Management Program and have an experience of being a teacher. The sample represents the whole Malaysia. However, it assumes that all the teachers and principals are of high level of education. The findings of this research demonstrate the needs for establishing a clear policy for ICT in schools. Another study for ICT in Greek kindergarten schools is conducted by Prokopiadou [6]. Their goal is to assess the level of ICT infrastructure available, as well as the variables that influence ICT application in school management. Their finding highlights the importance of the need to establish an appropriate framework for ICT usage in school administration.

The usage of ICT for administrative purposes in schools and especially in primary schools does not have enough attention yet. Although an ICT usage framework in school management is still not established it is vital to understand the comprehensive situation of current ICT systems. To address this need the main goal of this study is to explore and investigate the current situation of using ICT for school administration. The domain of this work is public Saudi primary schools. The ultimate aim is to find the highest factors that affect the schools' use of ICT for administration purposes. This is important to fill the gap and provide better understanding of the ICT systems in primary schools and thus establish an appropriate framework for ICT usage for school administration purposes. The use of ICT for administrative purposes in schools, especially primary schools, has received insufficient attention in the literature [1, 15–19]. Students typically attend primary school for six years, which is one of the most extended terms of study. In this article, we addressed the most often cited factors that influenced ICT use in schools. These components fall into four categories: infrastructure, information technology (IT) support, communication, and experience and training.

2   Background

In this section we address the most often cited factors that influence ICT use in schools. These components can be categorised into four groups: infrastructure, information technology support, communication, and experience and training.

2.1   Infrastructure

Infrastructure refers to hardware such as computers, scanners, photocopiers, printers, and projectors, as well as critical software that facilitates school management, teaching and learning [6]. The most common factors reported in previous studies to affect the ICT infrastructure in schools are the internet concoction and Security and privacy.

Internet connectivity is crucial for ICT technology because it is used by the great majority of services and organisations; users may suffer when attempting to use ICT systems if the internet connection is repeatedly disrupted. This had been discussed in the literature, and they highlighted the importance of computer and internet connection for the ICT systems [5, 6]. Stable and reliable internet connection should be provided to schools to allow the staff using ICT [1, 11]. Schools in developing countries without reliable internet connections are struggling to use ICT to manage schools' tasks [6, 12]. Moreover, the high cost of internet connection, particularly broadband connectivity, had a negative impact on students, schools staff and families use of ICT systems alike [6, 20–22]. They continued by emphasising that the bulk of internet users reside in major cities, with Internet penetration in villages and rural areas remaining at a bare minimum [6, 21, 22].

Additionally, past studies noted the benefit of having an internet connection that includes good and dependable technical assistance, customer service, and emergency and routine maintenance [6, 20–22]. As motioned in [6, 7, 20–22] it can be devastating for ICT users, especially those in schools, if there is insufficient support for the internet connection, such as technology support, equipped maintenance teams, and effective customer service. Another study arrives at similar conclusions that schools in urban areas maintain a digital advantage compared with schools in rural areas. Indeed, the lack of technological infrastructure such as a stable internet connection with high speed makes it hard for schools and their users to deal with ICT systems [6, 21–23]. Numerous schools in remote locations may have trouble using ICT due to power issues, as electricity is not always accessible throughout the day in these areas. The authors in [6, 24] emphasis that developing a sufficient infrastructure, in this context, refers to acquiring a decent internet connection, which is critical for schools and their users to use ICT systems efficiently.

ICT users' security and privacy must be well maintained during their usage, hence should take enough attention through the design and implementation. Securing ICT systems and ensuring the availability of vital education services would boost user satisfaction on all levels, including students, teachers, principals, and stakeholders, enabling uninterrupted usage of ICT systems

[12,20,22,25,26]. When the ICT systems did not match the users' needs and expectations, they were more exposed to cyber-attacks. For example, the current ICT systems do not help users to do their duty easily; consequently, they will use an out-source software application that is not secure and not authorised by the ministry. As a result of the use of third-party applications, the users' security and privacy are in greater risk [12,20,22,25,26].

In Arab countries, in most cases, there is a very high restrictions on the internet [12,20,22,25,26]. Internet users are highly constrained. In Saudi Arabia, for example, the government has declared that it will seek to protect its citizens from immoral Internet content, as a result, the government spends more in the firewalls and security systems [22]. While there is no dispute about the efficiency of investment in security systems and ICT, this does not guarantee that the ICT users will be completely protected from cyber-attacks [12,14,20,22,25,26]. ICT systems and all the digital technology will remain within the risk circle and the online terrorism such as disrupting communication, compromising security, phishing, stealing the users' information, destroying devices [22,27].

In previous studies [10,24] they mentioned that due to the massive influx of social media into people's everyday lives, it has become a fundamental component in educational organizations and ICT systems. ICT systems are not isolated from the rest of cyber technology; rather, they are an integral component of it and are directly or indirectly affected by other factors in the cyber world [12,24,28]. To illustrate, social media can be utilised in conjunction with ICT in schools for administrative purposes if handled properly [12,24,28]. Almost every school has an account on the social media. In addition, the school members are very likely to have accounts as well on social media. According to [12,24,28,29] there are no clear regulations that regulate the use of social media platforms in the name of a school. Therefore, using social media platforms in schools will not be based on a clear path; instead, that would be more according to individuals' views [12,24,28,29]. In addition, these unmonitored uses could cause a critical breach to the whole system and ICT in particular in terms of security and users' privacy that has been discussed in [30,31]. In previous studies [30,31] they continued to state that, social media applications require access to users' information or to other applications such as files; hence, users' privacy will be jeopardised, and the likelihood of ICT systems being breached dramatically increases. Information in educational organisations are critical as any organisation. With the prevalence of social media in schools and an insufficient understanding of how to use ICT technology to meet users' requirements, the possibility of data and circulars being leaked extremely increases [5,30,31].

Educational organisations use many different ICT systems; thus, they come up with higher risks regarding the security of the system and the users' privacy [12,20,22,25,26]. In addition, there could be more than one storage to store the information that may be due to the systems architecture. Many educational organisations use many different systems for administration purposes; moreover, these systems could be different from one department to another while they are in the same ministry [12,14,20,22,25,26]. The risk of using many different systems and third-party applications is extremely high, whereas using reliable ICT systems that are authorised and maintained by the ministry are safer and more secure [12,14,20,22,25,26]. Hence, schools members should avoid using ICT systems or applications not authorised by the ministry.

2.2 IT Support

IT support is a vital part of the life cycle of the ICT systems but not available all the times. According to [7,16,23,32–34] ICT systems in schools must provide a "friendly environment" which includes providing technical support, encouraging ICT utilisation, and offering required training. It is crucial to maintain all components of ICT, both hardware and software, and ensure that technical support is available when users experience difficulties that have been discussed in [7,16,23,32–34]. Usually, there is no specialised IT support staff to facilitate ICT systems in schools. Instead, that will be assigned to the principal or a school member to play that role in addition to their responsibilities in the school. Schools' principals may be unable to address ICT technical issues due to their workload, a lack of essential expertise, or a fear of being distracted from their duties as school administrators. Moreover, school members might not solve ICT issues repeatedly as that could waste their time or put extra work on their shoulders as this is not their primary role in the school [32,33,35–37].

Some schools in poor and developing countries are lack of finance required for technical support such as countries in South America and Africa. Governments in these countries are not capable to provide IT support to each school, consequently, this can lead to useless ICT systems [6,7,12]. In addition, schools that are located in remote areas may wait for weeks or months to get the support. That is because IT experts are mainly located in the urban area where the education departments usually are located [6,7,12].

School principals are not authorised by the education department to take action that could solve the ICT issues such as communicate with local IT providers. In other words, unauthorised access to the ICT systems could cause major consequences to the school principals as well as to the other administration members. IT support in schools contributes to the sustainability and viability of ICT and improves school administration [7,14,28,38,39].

ICT users lack the opportunity to express their needs and goals when building and designing ICT systems. It is imperative that ICT systems reflect the needs of the users and make their daily responsibilities easier to perform, which will increase their productivity. In other words, the users in schools should have a chance to express and explain their needs during the design and implementation steps since they are the primary users of the ICT systems [17,23,39–42]. Moreover, users in rural schools may not get even a single chance to pass their thinking about the structure or the design of the ICT till the education ministry or the department inform them to start using them in their daily work [13,17,21,41].

2.3   Communication

Lack of proper communication among the education ministry or any organisation will lead to coming up with weak and insufficient ICT systems [5,43–45]. Communication is one of the fundamental steps during building ICT systems because these systems are designed to assist users in carrying and achieving the planned goals. So, if there is no proper communication channel between the users and the systems developers, that will lead to useless systems [5,36,43,45]. For instance, [19] demonstrated that while school principals may possess a high level of knowledge about certain aspects of their schools' ICT systems, they are not sufficiently involved in ICT projects and implementation phases due to a shortage of communication.

At educational organizations, decisions are made by the higher departments, in general, are without communication with lower-level users. Usually, managers make decisions about the design and construction of ICT systems. In addition, they may ask users to use a specific system, and then after a while, they will tell them to stop using it. These ICT systems may have been designed and implemented very well from the technical point of view, resulting in high performance; however, they may not be user-friendly, especially for those without IT experience. For example, in educational organizations, most of the ICT systems users are teachers with a low amount of IT background. Furthermore, if the school members did not engage during the design and the implementation, they could not efficiently utilise the ICT systems [5,6,16,23,26,34,46].

The lack of communication also casts a shadow on parents, and the surrounding community [5,8,38,47]. According to [47], a lack of communication between schools and families results in weak interaction or, in the worst-case scenario, a loss of this interaction. They continued by emphasising that the majority of schools that lack effective connection with students' families struggle to persuade them to adopt new ICT systems as a result of the families being excluded from the planning and design phases [47]. According to a prior study, technology alone does not guarantee improved outcomes, and that moving to ICT systems without positive communication with prospective stakeholders results in inefficient ICT technologies [11]. Negative implications for student accomplishment have also crept in as a result of non-existent or ineffective communication between educational institutions and parents, as declared in [8,10,47].

In the educational process, the main focus is on students. ICT systems can help students and their families. First, ICT systems provide a reliable channel for the school and the families to communicate with respect to their privacy and security. ICT systems also can improve the students' communication skills and their relationship with teachers, the school administration team and other students. Additionally, ICT can help teachers and parents to keep track of the student's progress and provide the necessary support by keeping students more connected to their schools [12,13,46,47]. Many studies show that students who have access to the ICT achieve better results, consequently, ICT systems would positively involved in school administration [12,13,46,47]. Communication using ICT systems can help schools and educational organisations to improve the curriculum to match the students' skills. For example, for students who are shy or have difficulties expressing themselves in front of their classmates in face-to-face communication, ICT could help them overcome that issue and increase their confidence dramatically while they are interacting with the administrations' team, teachers, and their friends in the school [12,13,46,47].

ICT systems helped schools very much during tough times to maintain the accessibility of E-learning to their students. For example, during times of crisis, such as the Coronavirus pandemic, all educational organisations globally suspended traditional face-to-face schooling. The optimum option was to transition to remote learning, and ICT serves as the foundation for remote learning. Schools without powerfully built ICT equipment failed to communicate with their students quickly. Thus, the students learning has been negatively affected [8,12,16,40,43,47–49].

2.4 Experience and Training

Experience and training are essential to use ICT systems in a superior manner. The authors of [8,23,32,34,37] reported that training is a fundamental procedure for the users of ICT systems in school and educational organisations. Previous studies also have emphasised that schools principals were less knowledgeable users of ICT technology [23,34,50]. Using ICT for school administration is based on the school principals and their motivation to be active leadership. However, some of them feel they are overwhelmed by using the ICT systems without enough experience or training [19,34,50].

The previous research [19] shows that ICT users with experience and knowledge are more likely to be motivated about using ICT systems in schools, particularly for administration goals. Training and experience did not get enough attention in programs conducted to prepare school leaders. Additionally, there is no intensive training for the school principals during their work as school leaders besides being ICT leadership [34,37,50]. That is because they do not have time for attending workshops or training courses within their responsibilities as school leaders. Previous studies have shown that ICT training courses, most of the time held in urban areas that are difficult for the rural school principals to attend [6,21,26,26,34,37,50].

Training courses and workshops about using ICT should not be only for school principals but must include other stakeholders, such as parents and teachers. Mandatory use for ICT by the leaders and the school staff without enough training or solid background of dealing with technology could be problematic, as well as if they start to use it as they have to, they will not be confident [19]. That will make using ICT weaker in schools for administration purposes. In [2,5,38] they discussed the shortfall of training. Although schools try their best based on their capabilities to assist the parents and other users to utilise ICT systems, parents and families struggle or face difficulties using them [5,38].

3 Methodology

The fundamental objective of this study is to explore the current situation of the ICT systems in Saudi public primary schools and provide a framework of ICT systems as tools for school administration. To fulfil this goal we conducted this work in an exploratory and descriptive nature. In the following subsections we explain the sampling design, instrument design and data collection.

3.1 Sampling Design and Population

This study's intended audience comprises employees of Saudi Arabia's public primary schools and parents of children enrolled in these schools. Users from inside the educational circle are considered internal users, whereas families are considered external users. 42% of the public primary schools are located in three large regions in Saudi Arabia, and the rest 10 regions share the remaining 58%. These central regions are Riyadh province, Makkah province and Ash-Sharqiya province. The other regions are not as developed as these three large regions. We consider Makkah province schools for this study as a representative sample. Makkah province has a more diverse nature in terms of demographics and geography.

Given the size of the population, we chose to design the study using a random sampling of the entire population. Total population sampling is a purposive sampling that implies investigating the entire population for a specific set of qualities, features, experiences, knowledge, skill, and exposure to an event. Nonetheless, according to [18] there are two instances in which complete population sampling may be appropriate: (1) the population size is small and (2) the population have a common unique characteristic. In our case, users who are using ICT systems in primary schools are unique characteristics.

3.2 Instrument Design

A questionnaire is a self-report instrument that can be used to collect data from a large number of respondents in a cost-effective and timely manner [51]. It can be used to gather both qualitative and quantitative data. We used a quantitative questionnaire with closed-ended questions to achieve precise and accurate responses. Based upon a 5-point Likert-type scale, anchors in the questionnaire ranged from 1 to 5 to indicate the degree of agreement. Moreover, the questionnaire has been given to a panel of 3 experts for validation, and the comments were just a few [52].

The questionnaire aimed to obtain information on different aspects, including available ICT infrastructure, available IT support, available ICT communication channels and training programs available for ICT systems. It also addressed the effect of each mentioned factor. Moreover, it gathers the knowledge and technical skills of ICT systems users in schools.

Table 1. Demographic information of the respondents

	Question	Frequency	Percentage
1	**You are older than 18 years:**		
	Yes	514	95,90%
	No	22	4.10%
2	**Your education level is:**		
	Secondary school degree or lower	75	14.59%
	Diploma degree	40	7.78%
	Bachelor degree	305	59.34%
	Higher degree	94	18.29%
3	**You are working or worked in an education sector:**		
	Yes	236	45.91%
	No	278	54.09%
4	**Your role in the school is:**		
	School principal	38	9.43%
	Teacher	267	66.25%
	Administrative assistance	53	13.15%
	School Deputy Headmaster	16	3.97%
	Other	29	7.20%
5	**You are working in:**		
	Primary schools	138	46%
	Secondary schools	92	32%
	Intermediate schools	59	22%

3.3 Data Collection

The questionnaire link was distributed using social media applications such as WhatsApp, Twitter and Telegram. These are the most widely utilised platforms in Saudi Arabia. More than 1000 respondents responded to the poll in total. The optimal sample size is 400 participants [53]. However, the total number of completed responses is 555.

3.4 Results and Discussion

The study's goal was to analyze the use of ICT in Saudi public primary schools' management and provide a framework for its usage.

4 Demographic Information

Table 1 shows the demographic information of the respondents. Almost all of the respondents are older than 18 years old, with more than 95%. Around 60% of the

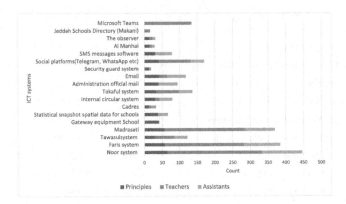

Fig. 1. Common ICT systems used in Saudi public primary schools

respondents hold a bachelor's degree, while 15% of them hold a master's degree, and just 3% have a PhD degree. Lower portion of respondents are with lower educational degrees include primary and intermediate, secondary or diploma degree. In addition, 54% of the participants work in educational organisations, and the rest are parents of children in primary schools. Interestingly, 46% of parents are not working in educational sector.

Among people who work in educational organisations only 46% of the respondents work in primary schools. In terms of their role at schools, 66% are teachers, about 9% work as school principals, 13% are administrative assistance, about 4% are school deputy headmaster, and the other 8% are working in school administration team such as librarian, activity pioneer, and clerk. The high portion of the respondents are teachers while the rest are of different roles in school administration. This low percentage for school administrators is expected because each school is associated only with one principal, and few number of other assistants.

4.1   Current ICT Infrastructure

Numerous ICTs are utilised extensively in educational administration and management, particularly in primary schools. The results show that the most commonly ICT system used in Saudi primary schools is Noor system with about 80.36%, followed by Faris with 69.19%, Madrasati with 66.49%, Tawasul system with about 22% and social media with 31%. Figure 1 presents a summary of the existing ICT systems with their extent of use in terms of each rule in the school.

Noor system is an electronic system to administrate the students' results. It provides reports for the students and some services for teachers such as internal and external transportation. Also, Noor system provides some services for parents, including the registration of students in public schools. Faris system is used to manage the human resources data. Madrasati is a virtual learning system introduced by the Saudi education ministry during the recent Coronavirus

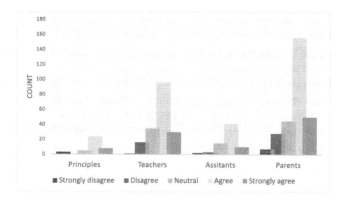

Fig. 2. Security and Privacy levels in current ICT systems for school administration

pandemic. Microsoft Teams is used by the teachers mostly. So, schools principals and other administration members seems to not use it often.

This result shows a high diversity in the available ICT systems, more than 15 systems are currently in use with different extent. This diverse highlight the issues discuses in the background section. It is difficult to maintain consistent with all of these systems. Although there are the official emails there is another ICT system for communication, which is Tawasul. However, users tend to use the social media for communication such as WhatsApp and Twitter more than the email or the official system. This is very important observation to investigate. It highlights the issue of privacy and security concerns with ICT systems. This can also means the current ICT systems with this range failed to match the users' needs, forcing them to find or use alternatives.

In addition, around 70% agreed that their schools use social media to distribute new rules or new administrative circulars. In Saudi context that is not authorised, and it is against the rule of the education ministry. Moreover, that would increase the probability of breaching the users' privacy and threaten the organisations' security. As can be seen, the organisation email is not considered a communication medium in educational organisations. Around 32% of the participants use Twitter as the primary channel to contact the school while about 35% of the participants use WhatsApp. Additionally, more than 46% of the parents agreed, and 11% strongly agreed that social media is the first communication medium. Email is more secure and can help protect the users' privacy much better than unauthorised applications; however, lower portion of participants reported the use of Emails [5, 18, 22, 30, 33].

About 50% of the participants agreed that the internet connection impacts their use of the current ICT systems. 22% of the participants strongly agreed that the internet connection influences their usage of ICT systems [5, 21, 22, 44]. The rate of using ICT systems has been fluctuated in schools due to the infrastructure and the internet connection in particular. Moreover, users with low or lack of internet connection will not be enthusiastic about using ICT systems. In addition, they could consider that as time and effort wasting [5, 21, 22, 44].

The findings of the question related to the privacy and security of current ICT systems reveal a good agreement by all users on sustaining a private and secure services, as illustrated by Fig. 2. However, as there are some people think these services are not very secure that is an indicate of an issue. Another angle that it could be an unaware of the risk of using this kind of systems especially with the proportion of parents where they mainly rely on third-party applications to communicate with schools.

4.2   Effectiveness of Current IT Support

Around 41% of the participants agreed, and 25% strongly agreed that there is enough IT support with current ICT systems. In contrast, 16% disagreed, and 5% strongly disagreed that the current IT support is insufficient or unavailable. Roughly 25% of the participants are neutral about IT support. Limited or lack of IT support could reduce the users' of using ICT systems. Additionally, IT support plays an essential role in maintaining the ICT systems regularly, reducing the IT problems and increasing the ICT systems efficiency [5, 6, 37, 45].

Users could stop using ICT systems if they did not find IT support to help them come up with any challenges they could face. Solving the ICT systems technical issues could impact the staff performance when they spend time and effort to resolve the ICT technical problems. The school members could hesitate to solve these IT issues independently, but they are not authorised and face the consequences [5, 6, 37, 45].

4.3   Communication Using ICT Systems

By Communication we target two perspectives: First, is the communication via ICT systems for the school management, Second, is the communication about ICT systems design and implementation.

For communication using ICT systems most participants, about 70%, are agreed on that the current ICT systems help them to share their knowledge and experiences with others easily and quickly. They also think the systems help them to save time while doing the daily work. Regarding communication with higher departments to express their needs, 54.07% of the users chose that ICT enhances communication speed and makes it more accessible. Just 43% answered that ICT helped them to get feedback from the higher departments faster. Communication plays a very critical role in the organisation. Thus, the participants' responses clearly show that communication with higher departments is not that strong and it is not in the spotlight [14, 18, 36, 41, 47].

In general, more than 70% of the participants, who are working in schools administration, agreed that they are satisfied with using current ICT systems. In contrast, around 10% are not satisfied with the current ICT systems, and just 20% are neutral about using ICT systems in schools for the administration process. ICT systems developers, planners, designers and decision-makers should take into account the users' needs and the usage from different stakeholders. ICT systems will be insufficient when they do not meet the users' expectations; moreover, that could lead to less productivity. In addition, that may lead to resource wasting [11, 16, 19, 26, 45, 47, 54].

4.4 ICT Users' Experience and Training

The finding shows that the weakest point in ICT systems usage for school administration is the required experience and training. Based on the survey results about the previous experience with the current ICT systems, more than 60% of the participants reported they were not experienced with the systems. Additionally, only 33% of the respondents agreed they get enough training of using the ICT system. The majority of the respondents think they are not receiving enough training.

The continuous training on how to use the ICT systems is essential for the practical and efficient utilisation of ICT systems. Providing proper training will increase the efficiency of the staff. Additionally, that will help in reducing waste and save resources [21, 23, 26, 32, 34, 37, 55].

4.5 IiCE Framework

AS we discussed their are four main factors that mainly affect the usage of ICT systems in school administration. Based on the exploration and analysis of the current states of the ICT systems we propose the Infrastructure IT support Communication Experience and Training (IiCE) framework for ICT systems usage in school administration, as shown in Fig. 3.

The main components of the IiCE are: users and factors. The users can be external or internal. External users include parents who have a children who is a student in a primary school. Internal users are mainly school members such as: school principle, teachers, and administrative assistants. The factors can be internal or external. External factors are the factors affecting the ICT systems out of educational organisation domain. The ICT infrastructure is considered to be an external factor. Internal factors are the elements within the educational organisations. These include IT support, communication and experience and training. The ICT systems are supposed to dynamically process the external and internal user requirements and provide proper feedback within the consideration of the external and internal factors. The proposed IiCE framework can help the ICT systems developers, designers, educational organisation members as well as decision makers to understand the ICT systems workflow within the organisation and provide better solutions.

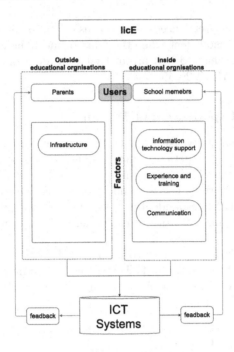

Fig. 3. IiCE suggested framework

5   Conclusion

In this study, we explored the current situation of ICT in Saudi Arabia primary schools. We categorised the factors affecting ICT systems in school managements into four groups. Then we proposed the IiCE framework to better understand the ICT systems in schools in terms of users and factors. The IiCE could help the schools principals to improve the administration process by providing a holistic understanding for the systems flow. Some of the findings are:

- ICT systems can help to provide more attractive and motivate workplace members, regardless of their role.
- There is a huge diverse in the existing ICT systems which is problematic in terms of consistency and privacy.
- The schools' administration process can be more effective if the ICT systems are built and designed in accordance with the aspirations of the users.
- There is a lack of communication between the users of ICT systems and the providers.
- There is a lack of sufficient training for ICT systems which impacts the user satisfaction with the current systems.

For future work we will consider the extension of the proposed IiCE framework to include more details about the policy and regulations to maintain better ICT systems utilisation. Then we will apply the framework on some schools in the domain of the study for richer evaluation. Another future work will also investigate the dominance of social media channels in school communications.

References

1. Hoque, K.E., Samad, R.S.A., Siraj, S., Ziyadh, A.: The role of ICT in school management of Maldives. New Educ. Rev. **27**(1), 270–282 (2012). ISSN 17326729
2. Sincar, M., Hauge, T.E., Norenes, S.O., Blau, I., Shamir-Inbal, T.: Digital competences and long-term ICT integration in school culture: the perspective of elementary school leaders. In: 6th International Computer and Instructional Technologies Symposium, Gaziantep, Turkey, vol. 18, no. (3), pp. 1273–1284 (2015). ISSN 15737608. https://doi.org/10.1007/s10639-015-9456-7. https://doi.org/10.1080/13603124.2014.963689
3. Brannigan, N.: Enhancing leadership capacity in ICTs in education through technology enabled collaboration. Retrieved **5**(2015), 28 (2010)
4. Ghavifekr, S., Afshari, M., Siraj, S., Seger, K.: ICT application for administration and management: a conceptual review. Procedia Soc. Behav. Sci. **103**, 1344–1351 (2013). ISSN 18770428. https://doi.org/10.1016/j.sbspro.2013.10.705
5. Hoque, K.E., Razak, A.Z.A., Zohora, M.F.: ICT utilization among school teachers and principals in Malaysia. Int. J. Acad. Res. Progressive Educ. Dev. **1**(4), 17–34 (2012)
6. Prokopiadou, G.: Using information and communication technologies in school administration: researching Greek Kindergarten Schools. Educ. Manag. Adm. Leadersh. **40**(3), 305–327 (2012). ISSN 17411432. https://doi.org/10.1177/1741143212436953
7. Almalki, G., Williams, N.: A strategy to improve the usage of ICT in The Kingdom of Saudi Arabia Primary School. Int. J. Adv. Comput. Sci. Appl. **3**(10), 42–49 (2012). ISSN 2158107X. https://doi.org/10.14569/ijacsa.2012.031007
8. Blau, I., Presser, O.: E-leadership of school principals: increasing school effectiveness by a school data management system. Br. J. Educ. Technol. **44**(6), 1000–1011 (2013). ISSN 00071013. https://doi.org/10.1111/bjet.12088
9. De Brock, E.O., Box, P.O.: Integrating real practical experience in ICT education. J. Inf. Syst. Educ. **12**(3), 133–140 (2001)
10. Hauge, T.E., Norenes, S.O.: Collaborative leadership development with ICT: experiences from three exemplary schools. Int. J. Leadersh. Educ. **18**(3), 340–364 (2015). ISSN 14645092. https://doi.org/10.1080/13603124.2014.963689
11. Hayes, D.N.A.: ICT and learning: lessons from Australian classrooms. Comput. Educ. (2007). ISDSN 03601315. https://doi.org/10.1016/j.compedu.2005.09.003
12. Kozma, E., Kozma, R.B.: ICT policies and educational transformation. Unesco. Org, 1–24, (2010). http://www.unesco.org/new/fileadmin/MULTIMEDIA/HQ/ED/ICT/pdf/ICTpoliedtran.pdf
13. Light, D.: The role of ICT in enhancing education in developing countries: findings from an evaluation of the Intel® teach essentials course in India, Turkey, and Chile. J. Educ. Int. Dev. **4**(2), 52–66 (2009)
14. Mitomo, H. (ed.): Telecommunications Policies of Japan. AICR, vol. 1. Springer, Singapore (2020). https://doi.org/10.1007/978-981-15-1033-5
15. Passey, D.: ICT and school management: a review of selected literature. Lancaster University: Department of Educational Research (2002). Accessed 16 July 2008

16. Vanderlinde, R., van Braak, J., Tondeur, J.: Using an online tool to support school-based ICT policy planning in primary education. J. Comput. Assist. Learn. **26**(5), 434–447 (2010). ISSN 02664909. https://doi.org/10.1111/j.1365-2729.2010.00358.x

17. Mcleod, S., Richardson, J.W., Hua Chang, I.: The effect of principals' technological leadership on teachers' technological literacy and teaching effectiveness in Taiwanese elementary schools. Educ. Technol. Soc. **15**(2), 328–340 (2012). ISSN 11763647. https://doi.org/10.1177/105268461102100204

18. Seyal, A.H.: A preliminary study of school administrators' use of information and communication technologies: Bruneian perspective. Int. J. Educ. Dev. Using Inf. Commun. Technol. **8**(1), 29–45 (2012). ISSN 1814-0556. http://search.ebscohost.com/login.aspx?direct=true&db=eric&AN=EJ1084147&site=ehost-live

19. Stuart, L.H., Mills, A.M., Remus, U.: School leaders, ICT competence and championing innovations. Comput. Educ. **53**(3), 733–741 (2009). ISSN 03601315. https://doi.org/10.1016/j.compedu.2009.04.013

20. Dutta, S., Coury, M.E.: ICT challenges for the Arab world. The Global Information Technology Report. World Trade, pp. 116–131 (2002)

21. Khalid, M.S., Nyvang, T.: A change agent's facilitation process for overcoming the barriers of ICT adoption for educational administration - the case of a rural-Bangladesh vocational institution. Australas. J. Educ. Technol. **30**(5), 547–561 (2014). ISSN 14495554. https://doi.org/10.14742/ajet.626

22. Sait, S.M., Al-Tawil, K.M., Sanaullah, S., Faheemuddin, M.: Impact of internet usage in Saudi Arabia: a social perspective. Int. J. Inf. Technol. Web Eng. **2**(2), 81–107 (2007). ISSN 15541045. https://doi.org/10.4018/jitwe.2007040104

23. Weng, C.-H., Tang, Y.: The relationship between technology leadership strategies and effectiveness of school administration: an empirical study. Comput. Educ. **76**, 91–107 (2014)

24. Blau, I., Barak, A.: How do personality, synchronous media, and discussion topic affect participation? Educ. Technol. Soc. **15**(2), 12–24 (2012). ISSN 14364522

25. Qureshi, H.Z., Abro, M.Q.M.: Efficient Use of ICT in administration a case from Mehran University of Engineering and Technology, Jamshoro, Pakistan. Int. J. Econ. Commer. Manag. **4**(10), 540–550 (2016). http://ijecm.co.uk/

26. Yu, C., Prince, D.L.: Aspiring school administrators' perceived ability to meet technology standards and technological needs for professional development. J. Res. Technol. Educ. **48**(4), 239–257 (2016)

27. Vanderlinde, R., Dexter, S., Van Braak, J.: School-based ICT policy plans in primary education: elements, typologies and underlying processes. Br. J. Educ. Technol. **43**(3), 505–519 (2012). ISSN 00071013. https://doi.org/10.1111/j.1467-8535.2011.01191.x

28. Mcleod, S., Richardson, J.W.: The dearth of technology leadership coverage. J. School Leadersh. **21**(2), 216–240 (2011). ISSN 1052-6846. https://doi.org/10.1177/105268461102100204

29. Wang, Y.: Social media in schools. J. Cases Educ. Leadersh. **16**(1), 56–64 (2013). ISSN 1555-4589. https://doi.org/10.1177/1555458913478424

30. Dormann, M., Hinz, S., Wittmann, E.: Improving school administration through information technology? How digitalisation changes the bureaucratic features of public school administration. Educ. Manag. Adm. Leadersh. **47**(2), 275–290 (2019). ISSN 17411440. https://doi.org/10.1177/1741143217732793

31. Krutka, D.G., Carpenter, J.P.: Why social media must have a place in schools. Kappa Delta Pi Record **52**(1), 6–10 (2016). ISSN 21631611. https://doi.org/10.1080/00228958.2016.1123048

32. Alturkostany, M., Iinuma, M.: The application of technology in the Saudi national program "Tatweer" to improve public education. In: ACM International Conference Proceeding Series, pp. 177–184 (2018). https://doi.org/10.1145/3178158.3178166
33. Condie, R., Munro, R.K.: The impact of ICT in schools-a landscape review (2007)
34. Shah, M.: Impact of management information systems (MIS) on school administration: what the literature says. Procedia Soc. Behav. Sci. **116**, 2799–2804 (2014). ISSN 18770428. https://doi.org/10.1016/j.sbspro.2014.01.659
35. Anderson, R.E., Dexter, S.: School technology leadership: an empirical investigation of prevalence and effect. Educ. Adm. Q. **41**(1), 49–82 (2005). ISSN 0013161X. https://doi.org/10.1177/0013161X04269517
36. Asiabaka, I.P.: Access and use of information and communication technology (ICT) for administrative purposes by principals of government secondary schools in Nigeria. Res. **2**(1), 43–50 (2010)
37. Esplin, N.L., Stewart, C., Thurston, T.N.: Technology leadership perceptions of Utah elementary school principals. J. Res. Technol. Educ. **50**(4), 305–317 (2018)
38. Blau, I., Shamir-Inbal, T.: Digital competences and long-term ICT integration in school culture: the perspective of elementary school leaders. Educ. Inf. Technol. **22**(3), 769–787 (2016). https://doi.org/10.1007/s10639-015-9456-7
39. Oyaid, A.A.: Education policy in Saudi Arabia and its relation to secondary school teachers' ICT use, perceptions, and views of the future of ICT in education. Open Res. Exeter, 300 (2009). ISSN 1471-2156. http://hdl.handle.net/10036/69537
40. Cvitić, I., Peraković, D., Periša, M., Jurcut, A.D.: Methodology proposal for proactive detection of network anomalies in e-learning system during the covid-19 scenario, 143–151 (2022)
41. Omotayo, F.O., Chigbundu, M.C.: Use of information and communication technologies for administration and management of schools in Nigeria. J. Syst. Inf. Technol. **19**(3–4), 183–201 (2017). ISSN 17588847. https://doi.org/10.1108/JSIT-06-2017-0045
42. Tondeur, J., van Keer, H., van Braak, J., Valcke, M.: ICT integration in the classroom: challenging the potential of a school policy. Comput. Educ. **51**(1), 212–223 (2008). ISSN 03601315. https://doi.org/10.1016/j.compedu.2007.05.003
43. Alyami, R.H.: Educational reform in the Kingdom of Saudi Arabia: Tatweer Schools as a unit of development. Literacy Inf. Comput. Educ. J. **5**(2), 1515–1524 (2014). https://doi.org/10.20533/licej.2040.2589.2014.0202
44. Anderson, R.E., Dexter, S.L.: School Technology Leadership: Incidence and Impact. Escholarship Org (2000). http://www.crito.uci.edu/tlc/html/findings.html
45. Young, C., McNamara, G., Brown, M., O'Hara, J.: Adopting and adapting: school leaders in the age of data-informed decision making. Educ. Assess. Eval. Accountability **30**(2), 133–158 (2018). ISSN 18748600. https://doi.org/10.1007/s11092-018-9278-4
46. Stevenson, K.R.: Educational trends shaping school planning, design, construction, funding and operation. National Clearinghouse for Educational Facilities (2010)
47. Hohlfeld, T.N., Ritzhaupt, A.D., Barron, A.E.: Connecting schools, community, and family with ICT: four-year trends related to school level and SES of public schools in Florida. Comput. Educ. **55**(1), 391–405 (2010). ISSN 03601315. https://doi.org/10.1016/j.compedu.2010.02.004

48. Albion, P.R., Tondeur, J., Forkosh-Baruch, A., Peeraer, J.: Teachers' professional development for ICT integration: towards a reciprocal relationship between research and practice. Educ. Inf. Technol. **20**(4), 655–673 (2015). ISSN 15737608. https://doi.org/10.1007/s10639-015-9401-9

49. Gülbahar, Y.: Technology planning: a roadmap to successful technology integration in schools. Comput. Educ. **49**(4), 943–956 (2007). ISSN 03601315. https://doi.org/10.1016/j.compedu.2005.12.002

50. Alenezi, A.: Technology leadership in Saudi schools. Educ. Inf. Technol. **22**(3), 1121–1132 (2016). https://doi.org/10.1007/s10639-016-9477-x

51. Brown, J.D., et al.: Using Surveys in Language Programs. Cambridge University Press, Cambridge (2001)

52. Papanastasiou, E.C., Angeli, C.: Evaluating the use of ICT in education: psychometric properties of the survey of factors affecting teachers teaching with technology (SFA-T 3). Educ. Technol. Soc. **11**(1), 69–86 (2008). ISSN 14364522

53. Whitehead, A.L., Julious, S.A., Cooper, C.L., Campbell, M.J.: Estimating the sample size for a pilot randomised trial to minimise the overall trial sample size for the external pilot and main trial for a continuous outcome variable. Stat. Methods Med. Res. **25**(3), 1057–1073 (2016). ISSN 14770334. https://doi.org/10.1177/0962280215588241

54. Higgins, J.: ICT in school administration and management. In: The ICT Teacher's Handbook, pp. 141–154 (2013)

55. Buabeng-Andoh, C.: Factors influencing teachers' adoption and integration of information and communication technology into teaching: a review of the literature. Int. J. Educ. Dev. Using Inf. Commun. Technol. **8**(1), 136–155 (2012). ISSN 1814-0556

Heterogeneous Institutional Shareholding, Internal Control and Corporate Social Responsibility: Evidence from Chinese Listed Companies

Xin Zhang[1,2](✉)

[1] Lyceum of the Philippines University,, Muralla Street, Intramuros, Manila, Philippines
zhang2567yk@163.com
[2] Zhengzhou Shengda University, Zhengzhou, Henan, China

Abstract. The study analyzes the impact of heterogeneous institutional share-holding on corporate social responsibility (CSR) performance and corporate internal control (IC), and explores the mediating effect of internal control between heterogeneous institutional shareholding and CSR performance. The results show that Pressure-resistant institutional shareholding significantly improves CSR fulfillment degree and the effectiveness of internal control, while Pressure-sensitive institutional shareholding has no significant promoting effect on CSR fulfillment and IC effectiveness. Effective IC has a significant mediating effect between Pressure-sensitive institutional shareholding and CSR fulfillment. Finally, it is suggested that the structure of institutional investors should be optimized, and the shareholding ratio of Securities investment funds, qualified foreign institutional investors (QFII) and Social security funds should be enhanced to improve CSR performance and IC effectiveness. And the mediating effect of IC between institutional ownership and CSR fulfillment should be promoted, to strengthen the consciousness of enterprises to take the initiative to enhance CSR performance.

Keywords: Institutional ownership · Heterogeneity · Internal control · Mediation effect · CSR

1 Introduction

As China's economic development has entered a new era, enterprises need to fulfill their social responsibilities to achieve stable employment, improved people's livelihood, cultural prosperity and a sound ecological environment. According to the stakeholder theory, CSR activities mean taking the responsibilities for share-holders, suppliers, employees, customers, the government, communities and the environment. Enterprises have gradually increased the awareness of product safety and ecological protection. And CSR fulfillment is a measure to meet challenges and minimize risks, as well as a core resource to achieve differentiation strategy [1–4].

© ICST Institute for Computer Sciences, Social Informatics and Telecommunications Engineering 2022
Published by Springer Nature Switzerland AG 2022. All Rights Reserved
W. Hussain and M. A. Jan (Eds.): IoTaaS 2021, LNICST 421, pp. 139–158, 2022.
https://doi.org/10.1007/978-3-030-95987-6_10

Corporate IC and institutional shareholding are two major systems in China's capital market [5]. As an institutional arrangement, effective IC ensures the operation compliance, asset safety and reliable financial information, improves the operation efficiency and effect, and promotes the realization of development strategy. In China, institutional investors have become an important force in the capital market. Institution-al investors have formed a diversified development pattern. In the "Report on Governance Development of Listed Companies in China", China Securities Regulatory Commission [6] pointed out that institutional investors mainly include Securities investment funds, Social security funds, QFII, Securities dealers and Insurance companies, etc.

With reference to the research of Brickley et al., Chen et al., Puspa et al. and Liang, this study classifies Securities investment funds, Social security funds and QFII as Pressure-resistant institutional investors, which have no commercial relationship with the invested companies and have stronger independence by and large [7–10]. And Insurance companies, Securities brokers, financial companies and Non-financial listed companies are classified as Pressure-sensitive institutional investors, which have commercial relations with the invested companies. On this basis, this study analyzes the relations among heterogeneous institutional ownership, IC and CSR, and explores the joint mechanism of internal and external governance on CSR performance. From the perspective of IC effectiveness, this study empirically tests the mediating effect of IC between heterogeneous institutional ownership and CSR performance, to further improve the relevant institutional norms and explore effective pathways to improve CSR performance.

2   Literature Review, Theoretical Basis, and Research Hypothesis

2.1   Heterogeneous Institutional Shareholding and CSR Performance

As the invested enterprises' major shareholders, institutional investors often have professional investment teams and more capital reserves. However, there is no consensus on institutional investors' role in the capital market. One view is that the short-term profit-seeking behavior of institutions reduces the governance level of investee enterprises. Institutional investors do not fully participate in corporate governance actively, and there are some negative shareholders who "vote with feet" [11]. Institutional investors play an active role as the "crash accelerator" rather than "market stabilizer" [12]. The alternative view is that institutional investors supervise the management and major shareholders, and actively participate in corporate governance by submitting proposals or negotiating with the management [13]. Institutional investors have advantages in information collection and analysis, and can identify opportunistic behaviors of the management, which is conducive to improving corporate financial performance [14, 15]. Compared with the regular announcements issued by enterprises and irregular research reports issued by intermediary agencies, institutional investors play a governance role by obtaining the latest operational information and monitoring the production and operation of enterprises [16, 17].

If institutional investors are considered as a whole, the heterogeneity of institutional types will be covered up [18]. Different types of institutional investors have different behavior characteristics and investment strategies. The rational differentiation of heterogeneous institutional investors is a means to study the effect of institutional governance

[19]. Pressure-resistant institutions actively promote enterprises to fulfill their social responsibilities, while pressure-sensitive institutions often fail to articulate independent opinions on CSR issues [20]. Due to the specific source of funds and strict regulatory control, Pressure-resistant institutions do not have business connection with the invested companies other than investment, and pay more attention to obtaining authentic and reliable information disclosure, to supervise the actual CSR implementation. On the contrary, Pressure-sensitive institutions often have business relationships with the invested companies. Usually, they are unwilling to give up the benefits brought by the business relationships, and take a neutral attitude towards CSR issues, or support the attitude of management and controlling share-holders, then lack the motivation to promote CSR performance. Based on the above analyses, the following research hypothesis is proposed.

Hypothesis 1. Pressure-resistant institutional ownership can significantly enhance CSR performance, while Pressure-sensitive institutional ownership has no significant promoting effect on CSR performance.

2.2 Heterogeneous Institutional Shareholding and IC Effectiveness

Institutional investors perform the supervision duties by holding listed enterprises' shares [21, 22]. Institutional investors participate in corporate governance by submitting proposals based on their strong abilities of information screening and interpretation. Institutional shareholding reduces the propensity of enterprises to violate regulations and increases the possibility of being inspected [23]. According to the efficient supervision hypothesis, institutional investors, as an important external governance force, exert their governance effect by "voting with hands". Through investigation activities deeply, institutional investors can learn the internal environment, risk assessment, business activities, information and communication, internal supervision and other information, then combine their own advantages in information processing, and integrate the information from other sources, to form an objective evaluation on IC actual operation [24].

Because of different investment objectives, investment concepts and styles, heterogeneous institutions will have different investment styles and governance effects. Heterogeneous institutional investors have different preferences for IC effectiveness [25]. IC is an important part of corporate governance, and IC defects cause internal governance failure. Pressure-resistant institutions focus on the long-term development of enterprises, and are motivated to help enterprises improve corporate governance. However, Pressure-sensitive institutional shareholding has a short-term tendency, and cannot play its role in corporate governance. Only when institutions hold shares stably, can they transform from passive holding to active investment, and actively participate in corporate governance to supervise the behaviors of the management [26], to promote IC effectiveness and enhance the ability to deal with operational risks. Therefore, compared with Pressure-sensitive institutions, the higher the shareholding ratio of Pressure-resistant institutions, the greater the positive impact on IC, which will help to strengthen external supervision and improve IC effectiveness. Based on the above analyses, the following research hypothesis is proposed.

Hypothesis 2. Pressure-resistant institutional shareholding can significantly enhance IC effectiveness, while Pressure-sensitive institutional shareholding has no significant promoting effect on IC effectiveness.

2.3 Heterogeneous Institutional Shareholding, IC Effectiveness and CSR Performance

Pressure-sensitive institutions have commercial relations with investee companies other than investment, and may participate in corporate governance negatively, in order to maintain such relations. Pressure-resistant institutions are relatively independent investors who supervise the "insiders" and the management, to promote more standardized and effective operation, and then improve IC effectiveness. As an endogenous supervision mechanism, effective IC links enterprises and the market, and alleviates the information asymmetry between enterprises and external investors [27, 28]. Effective IC enhances the quality and efficiency of information communication, forms a good division of responsibilities, and improves the quality of internal governance [29, 30].

Effective IC has a promoting effect on enterprises to effectively fulfill social responsibilities, which can alleviate the conflicts between enterprises and stakeholders, protect stakeholders' rights and interests, and promote enterprises to maintain a stable development [31]. Enterprises' favorable development changes the zero-sum game under the "competitive economy" into the position-sum competition under the "collaborative economy", alleviates the contradiction between stakeholders' scattered needs and corporate overall interests, and maximizes the return on capital input from stakeholders. Effective IC is helpful to reduce stakeholders' risk expectation. As a result, the level of protection for stakeholders is enhanced, and CSR performance tends to improve. Meanwhile, considering Hypothesis 2 above, this study forms a mediating path between heterogeneous institutional ownership and CSR performance, that is, effective IC presents a significant mediating effect between Pressure-resistant institutional ownership and CSR performance. Based on the above analyses, the following research hypothesis is proposed.

Hypothesis 3. Effective IC has a significant mediating effect in the process of Pressure-resistant institutions promoting CSR performance, but this effect is not reflected between Pressure-sensitive institutional owner-ship and CSR performance.

3   Data Sources and Variable Definition and Model Setting

3.1   Data Sources

The listed companies publicly traded in Shanghai and Shenzhen stock markets from 2011 to 2018 are se-lected as the sample. Where, the data of IC effectiveness are from DIB IC and risk management data-base, other data from CSMAR China Stock Market research database, Wind Information terminal. The data are eliminated according to the following standards: Finance and insurance; ST, *ST class. Finally, 4856 groups of annual-individual data Are obtained as the effective observations. The continuous variables are Wionsorize treated with bidirectional 1% quantiles, to avoid the adverse effects of abnormal observations.

3.2 Definition of Variables

Explained Variable. The real social responsibility of an enterprise to its stakeholders is reflected in the cash actually paid to the stakeholders under the given income conditions [32]. Therefore, with reference to the research of Li et al., the ratio of cash paid by an enterprise for shareholders, creditors, employees, customers, consumers, suppliers, communities and other stakeholders to the average total number of shares in the current period is taken as the specific value of CSR performance (CSRP) [33]. The specific calculation meth-od is shown in Eq. (1).

$$CSR\,performance(CSRP) = (Cash\,paid\,for\,dividends\,or\,profits\, +\, Cash\,expenses\,for$$
$$business\, +\, Cash\,paid\,for\,interests\, +\, Cash\,payments\,to\,and\,for\,employees\, +\, Cash\,used$$
$$to\,pay\,for\,goods\,or\,services\, +\, Cash\,for\,tax\,payment)/Average\,total\,shares\,at\,the$$
$$beginning\,and\,end\,of\,the\,period$$

$$(1)$$

Explanatory Variable. The shareholding ratio of Pressure-resistant institutions (Resist) and that of Pressure-sensitive institutions (Sensitive) are measured respectively by taking the percentage of their shareholding quantity in the company's circulating A-shares. Resist and Sensitive disclosed in the semi-annual and annual reports are aver-aged, respectively, to evaluate the annual shareholding status of institutions, and smooth the adverse impact of the difference in the length of institutional shareholding on the conclusions as much as possible.

Mediating Variable. This study adopts DIB IC index of listed companies to measure IC effectiveness. The higher the index, the more effective IC.

Control Variable. With reference to the research of Puspa et al. [9] and Li et al. [33], Asset-liability ratio, Total asset turnover, Sales growth rate, Comprehensive leverage, Ownership concentration, the proportion of independent directors, Audit opinion, Enterprise size, Executive compensation, Property attribute are taken as the control variables. Also, the annual effect and industry effect are controlled in the regression. Table 1 shows the variable name and description.

3.3 Model Setting

With reference to the research of Puspa et al. and Li et al., the following Models 1, 2 and 3 are con-structed to test Hypotheses 1, 2 and 3 respectively [9, 33]. To alleviate the endogenous problem caused by reverse causality, the control variables - LEV, TAT, GROWTH, DTL, AUDIT, and LnSALARY are taken as the first-order lags in regression. In Model 2, to maintain the dimensional consistency between the explained variable and explanatory variables, the value of IC is the standardized value of DIB IC index divided by 100, by referring to the research of Chen et al. (2018) [34].

Mode 1.

Table 1. Variable name and description.

Nature	Symbol	Name	Computing method
Explained variable	CSRP	CSR performance	As shown in Eq. (1)
Explanatory variable	Resist	Pressure-resistant institutional shareholding ratio	Total number of shares held by Pressure-resistant institutions/A-shares in circulation, expressed in percentage
	Sensitive	Pressure-sensitive institutional shareholding ratio	Total number of shares held by Pressure–sensitive institutions/A-shares in circulation, expressed in percentage
Mediating variable	IC	IC effectiveness	DIB · IC index
Control variable	LEV	Asset-liability ratio	Total liabilities/total assets
	TAT	Total asset turnover	Operating income/average total assets; Average total assets equal to the average of total assets at the beginning and end of the period
	GROWTH	Sales growth rate	(Current sales revenue - previous sales revenue)/previous sales revenue
	DTL	Comprehensive leverage	Financial leverage × operating leverage
	ShrZ	Ownership concentration	The shareholding ratio of the largest shareholder to that of the second largest shareholder
	IN_DIRECTOR	The proportion of independent directors	The proportion of independent directors in the board of directors
	AUDIT	Audit opinion	Dummy variable set according to the audit opinion type. The value for the standard unqualified opinion is 1; otherwise 0
	LnASSET	Enterprise scale	The natural logarithm of total assets at the beginning of the year
	LnSALARY	Executive compensation	The natural logarithm of the total annual salaries of directors, supervisors, and executives

(*continued*)

Table 1. (*continued*)

Nature	Symbol	Name	Computing method
	STATE	Property attribute	Dummy variable, the value for state-owned enterprises is 1; otherwise, 0
	YEAR	Year	Annual effect
	IND	Industry	industry effect. In accordance with the "Guidance on Industry Classification of Listed Companies (revised in 2012)", industry dummy variables are set up according to categories
	ε		Random perturbation term

$$CSRP_{i,t} = \alpha 0 + \alpha 1\, Resist_{i,t}(Sensitive_{i,t}) + \alpha 2 LEV_{i,t-1} + \alpha 3 TAT_{i,t-1} + \alpha 4$$
$$GROWTH_{i,t-1} + \alpha 5\, DTL_{i,t-1} + \alpha 6\, ShrZ_{i,t} + \alpha 7 IN_{DIRECTOR_i} + \alpha 8\, AUDIT_{i,t-1} +$$
$$\alpha 9 LnASSET_{i,t} + \alpha 10 LnSALARY_{i,t-1} + \alpha 11 STATE_{i,t} + \alpha 12 \sum_t YEAR + \alpha 13 \quad (2)$$
$$\sum_t IND + \varepsilon_{i,t}$$

Mode 2.

$$IC_{i,t} = \beta 0 + \beta 1\, Resist_{i,t}(Sensitive_{i,t}) +$$
$$\beta 2 LEV_{i,t-1} + \beta 3 TAT_{i,t-1} + \beta 4\, GROWTH_{i,t-1} + \beta 5 DTL_{i,t-1} + \beta 6 ShrZ_{i,t} +$$
$$\beta 7 IN_{DIRECTOR_i,t} + \beta 8\, AUDIT_{i,t-1} + \beta 9 LnASSET_{i,t} + \beta 10 LnSALARY_{i,t-1} +$$
$$\beta 11 STATE_{i,t} + \beta 12 \sum_t YEAR + \beta 13 \sum_t IND + \varepsilon_{i,t}$$

$$(3)$$

Mode 3.

$$CSRP_{i,t} = \delta 0 + \delta 1\, Resist_{i,t}(Sensitive_{i,t}) + \delta 2\, IC_{i,t} + \delta 3 LEV_{i,t-1} + \delta 4 TAT_{i,t-1} +$$
$$\delta 5\, GROWTH_{i,t-1} + \delta 6 DTL_{i,t-1} + \delta 7\, ShrZ_{i,t} + \delta 8\, IN_{DIRECTOR_i} + \delta 9\, AUDIT_{i,t-1} +$$
$$\delta 10 LnASSET_{i,t} + \delta 11 LnSALARY_{i,t-1} + \delta 12 STATE_{i,t} + 13 \sum_t YEAR + \delta 14 \quad (4)$$
$$\sum_t IND + \varepsilon_{i,t}$$

Also, Models 1, 2 and 3 are adopted to test the possible mediating effect of IC between institutional ownership and CSR performance. The coefficient $\alpha 1$ in Model 1 is the total effect of Resist (Sensitive) on CSRP. In Model 2, the coefficient $\beta 1$ is the effect of Resist

(Sensitive) on the mediating variable – IC. In Model 3, the coefficient δ2 is the effect of IC on CSRP after Resist (Sensitive) is taken into account; and the coefficient δ1 is the direct effect of Resist (Sensitive) on CSRP after IC is controlled. With reference to the research of Wen and Ye, the mediating effect of IC between heterogeneous institutional shareholding and CSR performance can be described by the schematic diagram shown in Fig. 1 [35].

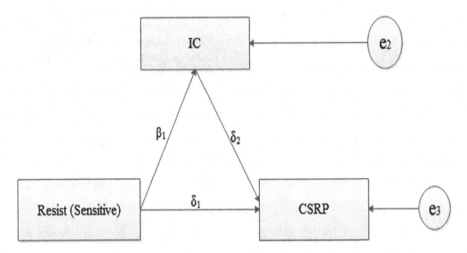

Fig. 1. Schematic diagram of mediating effect.

4 Descriptive Statistics and Correlation

4.1 Descriptive Statistics

Table 2 reports the descriptive statistical results. For the explained variables, in models 1 and 3, the mean (standard deviation) of CSRP is 8.211 (10.834), the maximum (minimum) is 73.688 (0.588), showing that CSR performance is uneven and there is a big gap among different enterprises. In model 2, the mean of IC is 6.781, implying that the sample enterprises' IC is generally at a medium effective level. And maximum (minimum) of IC is 8.866 (3.430), the IC effectiveness varies greatly among sample enterprises, and the some enterprises' IC effectiveness needs to be further improved.

For the explanatory variables, the mean (maximum) of Resist is 7.40% (51.34%); and the mean (maximum) of Sensitive is 2.44% (91.80%). In general, the average shareholding ratio of Pressure-resistant institutions is higher than that of Pressure-sensitive institutions, however, the maximum of Pressure-sensitive institutional shareholding ratio is higher than that of Pressure-resistant institutions. Institutional investors are more and more involved in corporate governance, but due to the different nature of various institutions, they cannot be regarded as a homogenous whole. Different institutions have different investment preferences and patterns, which have different impacts on invested enterprises. Meanwhile, the control variables are sufficiently different. In general, the sample is well differentiated, providing a beneficial basis for subsequent regression.

Table 2. Descriptive statistics.

Variable	Mean	Median	Maximum	Minimum	Deviation	Observations
CSRP	8.211	4.702	73.688	0.588	10.834	4856
IC	6.781	6.851	8.866	3.430	0.729	4856
Resist	7.396	3.967	51.339	0.000	9.029	4856
Sensitive	2.440	0.512	91.797	0.000	7.117	4856
LEV	41.542	40.951	86.081	4.666	18.808	4856
TAT	0.746	0.638	2.866	0.079	0.469	4856
GROWTH	15.323	11.810	152.917	−47.780	24.875	4856
DTL	1.986	1.476	11.703	0.819	1.624	4856
ShrZ	10.694	4.517	96.065	1.020	16.159	4856
IN_DIRECTOR	0.368	0.333	0.800	0.231	0.054	4856
AUDIT	0.995	1.000	1.000	0.000	0.069	4856
LnASSET	22.461	22.275	26.024	19.867	1.190	4856
LnSALARY	5.227	5.229	6.981	3.450	0.682	4856
STATE	0.463	0.000	1.000	0.000	0.499	4856

4.2 Correlation

Table 3 reports the correlations between the variables. In model 1 and 3, the correlation between Resist and CSRP is positive and significant (0.098, $p < 0.01$), and that between Sensitive and CSRP is not significant (0.007, $p > 0.10$). Compared with Pressure-sensitive institutions, Pressure-resistant institutional ownership is more likely to significantly improve CSR performance. In model 2, the correlation between Resist and IC is positive and significant (0.200, $p < 0.01$); and that between Sensitive and IC is positive and significant (0.031, $p < 0.05$). Compared with Pressure-sensitive institutions, Pressure-resistant institutional ownership is more likely to strengthen external supervision to enhance IC effectiveness. In model 3, the correlation be-tween IC and CSRP is positive and significant (0.235, $p < 0.01$). Effective IC is conducive to build an institu-tional environment to improve CSR performance.

For the control variables, in models 1 and 3, LEV (0.428), TAT (0.674), ShrZ (0.042), LnASSET (0.366), LnSALARY (0.254) and STATE (0.218) are positively and significantly ($p < 0.01$) correlated with CSRP. And GROWTH, IN_DIRECTOR are positively and significantly correlated with CSRP (0.034, $p < 0.05$; 0.024, $p < 0.10$). In model 2, LEV (0.080), TAT (0.219), GROWTH (0.159), DTL (-0.172), IN_DIRECTOR (0.053), AUDIT (0.134), LnASSET (0.218), LnSALARY (0.117) and STATE (0.087) are significantly ($p < 0.01$) correlated with IC. And ShrZ is positively and significantly correlated with IC (0.035, $p < 0.05$). These correlations indicate that the selection of control variables is very necessary, which ensure the rationality of models 1, 2 and 3 constructed above.

Table 3. Descriptive statistics.

Variable	CSRP	IC	Resist	Sensitive	LEV	TAT	GROWTH	DTL	ShrZ	IN_DIRECTOR	AUDIT	LnASSET	LnSALRY	STATE
CSRP	1.000													
IC	0.235***	1.000												
Resist	0.098***	0.200***	1.000											
Sensitive	0.007	0.031**	−0.016	1.000										
LEV	0.428***	0.080***	−0.115***	−0.007	1.000									
TAT	0.674***	0.219***	0.090***	−0.043***	0.258***	1.000								
GROWTH	0.034**	0.159***	0.241***	−0.038***	−0.008	0.095***	1.000							
DTL	−0.019	−0.172***	−0.218***	−0.043***	0.316***	−0.068***	−0.149***	1.000						
ShrZ	0.042***	0.035**	−0.164***	0.049***	0.129***	0.041***	−0.093***	0.059***	1.000					
IN_DIRECTOR	0.024*	0.053***	0.032*	−0.025*	0.051***	−0.005	0.015	0.043***	0.014	1.000				
AUDIT	0.020	0.134***	0.005	0.017	−0.016	0.048***	0.012	−0.050***	0.016	−0.015	1.000			
LnASSET	0.366***	0.218***	−0.028*	0.036**	0.524***	0.082***	−0.026*	0.106***	0.047***	0.097***	−0.003	1.000		
LnSALARY	0.254***	0.117***	0.139***	0.022	0.138***	0.1820***	0.0278**	−0.140***	−0.095***	0.058***	0.025*	0.474***	1.000	
STATE	0.218***	0.087***	−0.131***	0.079***	0.265***	0.105***	−0.142***	0.064***	0.233***	0.003	0.040***	0.282***	0.064***	1.000

*** Significant at 1%; ** Significant at 5%; * Significant at 10%.

Also, it is shown that the maximum of the correlations is 0.524. This maximum exists between LEV and LnASSET, which is less than the threshold of 0.800. This shows that there is no serious multicollinearity in models 1, 2 and 3, which provide a reliable guarantee for subsequent regression.

5 Model Regression Analysis

5.1 Analyses of Model 1's Regression Results

As shown in Table 4, in columns 2 and 3, the coefficient on Resist is positive and significant (0.045, p < 0.01), indicating that Pressure-resistant institutional shareholding significantly improves CSR performance. Pressure-resistant institutions have no potential commercial relationship with the invested enterprises, and can effectively reduce the agency costs by using their own professional knowledge and governance capabilities. Pressure-resistant institutions have the motivation and ability to guide enterprises to actively carry out CSR activities, and safeguard the legitimate rights and interests of stakeholders. However, the coefficient on Sensitive is not significant statistically (0.023, p > 0.10), implying that Pressure-sensitive institutional shareholding has not yet improved CSR perf0ormance. Pressure-sensitive institutions are unwilling to give up the interests generated by the business relationship with the invested enterprises, so they inevitably adopt a neutral attitude towards CSR issues, or succumb to the attitude of the management and control-ling shareholders, and then lack the motivation to continuously promote CSR activities. Hypothesis 1 above is verified.

For the control variables, in columns 2 and 3, the coefficients on L.LEV are positive and significant (0.046, p < 0.01; 0.048, p < 0.01), showing that creditor governance plays a positive role in promoting enterprises to fulfill social responsibilities. And those on L.TAT are positive and significant (5.683, p < 0.01; 5.674, p < 0.01). In columns 3, the coefficient on L.GROWTH is positive and significant (0.007, p < 0.05). The good asset turnover and sales growth trend are the favorable factors to strengthen CSR performance. While realizing their own development, enterprises should give full attention to strengthening CSR performance, which is conducive to better enhancing enterprise value [36]. In columns 2 and 3, the coefficients on are positive and significant (1.339, p < 0.01; 1.070, p < 0.05). The larger the scale of enterprises are, the more diversified and complex their product varieties and geographical distribution will be. Therefore, they will face more supervision from stakeholders such as the government, media and social organizations. Furthermore, large-scale enterprises usually pay more attention to CSR performance while pursuing entrepreneur profits. Besides, the coefficient on L.DTL is negative and significant (−0.091, p < 0.05; −0.099, p < 0.05), suggesting that the excessive operational risk has an adverse effect on the sustainable operation, which may have a negative effect on CSR performance. And those on STATE is negative and significant −0.905, p < 0.05; −0.895, p < 0.05). The possible reason for this situation is that the excessive separation of residual claims and control rights makes the strategic decision-making team of state-owned enterprises lack the corresponding incentive mechanism of property rights [37]. As a result, the management decisions and behaviors may have a short-term tendency, weakening the enthusiasm to improve CSR performance. The coefficients on other control variables are not statistically significant.

Table 4. Regression results for models 1, 2 and 3.

Variable	Model 1		Model 2		Model 3	
	Coef. (S.E.)	Coef. (S.E.)	Coef. (S.E.)	Coef. (S.E.)	Coef. (S.E.)	Coef. (S.E.)
Intercept	−29.556** (12.280)	−23.006* (12.200)	9.430*** (1.367)	10.966*** (1.411)	−34.251*** (12.718)	−28.948** (12.739)
Resist	0.045*** (0.013)		0.011*** (0.002)		0.040*** (0.013)	
Sensitive		0.023 (0.052)		−0.008 (0.006)		0.028 (0.051)
IC					0.498*** (0.133)	0.542*** (0.130)
L.LEV	0.046*** (0.012)	0.048*** (0.012)	−0.0002 (0.157)	0.043 (0.158)	0.046*** (0.012)	0.048*** (0.012)
L.TAT	5.683*** (0.860)	5.674*** (0.868)	0.050 (0.091)	0.048 (0.092)	5.658*** (0.861)	5.648*** (0.868)
L.GROWTH	0.005 (0.003)	0.007** (0.003)	0.002*** (0.001)	0.003*** (0.001)	0.004 (0.003)	0.005* (0.003)
L.DTL	−0.091** (0.041)	−0.099** (0.041)	−0.002 (0.009)	−0.004 (0.009)	−0.091*** (0.040)	−0.097** (0.041)
ShrZ	0.005 (0.012)	0.003 (0.012)	−0.001 (0.001)	−0.002 (0.001)	0.006 (0.012)	0.004 (0.012)
IN_DIRECTOR	3.038 (2.342)	3.087 (2.349)	−0.637 (0.462)	−0.641 (0.461)	3.355 (2.367)	3.435 (2.375)
L.AUDIT	−0.443 (0.676)	−0.412 (0.668)	0.359 (0.279)	0.366 (0.281)	−0.621 (0.693)	−0.611 (0.689)
LnASSET	1.339*** (0.485)	1.070** (0.479)	−0.077 (0.058)	−0.139** (0.060)	1.378*** (0.486)	1.146** (0.484)
L.LnSALARY	−0.135 (0.298)	−0.117 (0.304)	−0.001 (0.045)	0.006 (0.045)	−0.134 (0.297)	−0.120 (0.302)
STATE	−0.905** (0.389)	−0.895** (0.378)	0.095 (0.143)	0.081 (0.141)	−0.952** (0.378)	−0.939** (0.373)
YEAR/IND	YES	YES	YES	YES	YES	YES
Observation data	4249	4249	4249	4249	4249	4249
Within_R^2	0.157	0.151	0.126	0.116	0.165	0.161
F_Statistics	25.91***	24.78***	20.01***	18.25***	26.43***	25.61***

*** Significant at 1%; ** Significant at 5%; * Significant at 10%

Robust standard errors in brackets are clustered at corporate level.

5.2 Analyses of Model 2's Regression Results

In columns 4 and 5, the coefficient on Resist is positive and significant $(0.011, p < 0.01)$, indicating that Pressure-resistant institutional shareholding can restrain IC defects, and improve IC effectiveness. Pres-sure-resistant institutions are important participants in corporate governance, and play an active supervisory role on the management, which is conducive to improving corporate internal governance and reduc-ing operation risk. However, the coefficient on Sensitive is not significant statistically $(-0.008, p > 0.10)$. There is a commercial interest relationship between Pressure-sensitive institutions and invested enterprises other than investment, which makes them lack the motivation to continuously promote IC effectiveness. Hypothesis 2 above is verified.

For the control variables, in columns 4 and 5, the coefficients on L.GROWTH are positive and significant $(0.002, p < 0.01; 0.003, p < 0.01)$. When the development trend of enterprises is good, they have a higher level of governance, which strengthens IC construction process. Besides, in column 5, the coefficient on LnASSET is negative and significant $(-0.139, p < 0.05)$. In general, the control chain of large-scale enterprises is longer, which is easy to cause serious insider control, and thus adversely affect IC effective-ness. The coefficients on other control variables are not statistically significant.

5.3 Analyses of Model 3's Regression Results

In columns 6 and 7, the coefficient on Resist is positive and significant $(0.040, p < 0.01)$; that on Sensitive is not significant statistically $(-0.028, p > 0.10)$. Compared with Pressure-sensitive institutions, Pressure-resistant institutions urge senior executives to attach importance to the long-term development, and enhance CSR fulfillment through the strategic decision-making. And the coefficients on IC are positive and significant $(0.498, p < 0.01; 0.542, p < 0.01)$, showing that effective IC is an important means to safeguard the legitimate rights and interests of stakeholders. Therefore, effective IC has a significant mediating effect between institutional shareholding and CSR performance, which is only reflected between Pressure-resistant institutional shareholding and CSR fulfillment, but not for Pressure-sensitive institutional share-holding. Hypothesis 3 is verified. Compared with Pressure-sensitive institutions, Pressure-resistant institutions urge enterprises to build an effective IC system, to actively pay attention to the expecta-tions and demands of different stakeholders in addition to economic interests, and then fully improve CSR performance. With reference to Wen and Ye, the non-parametric per-centile Bootstrap (1000) meth-od for deviation correction is adopted [35]. Furthermore, the confidence interval of $\beta1 \times \delta2$ in 95% confidence is estimated to be $[0.007, 0.016]$. Where, $\beta1 \times \delta2$ is the product of the effects of Resist on IC and IC on CSRP. Also, the effect magnitude of the mediating effect is about 12.17% (i.e. $\beta1 \times \delta2/\alpha1 = 0.011 \times 0.498/0.045$).

For the control variables, the coefficient on L.LEV, L.TAT, L.GROWTH, L.DTL, LnASSET and STATE are statistically significant, and the conclusions on are consistent with those from model 1.

6   Robustness Test

6.1   Analysis Based on Propensity Score Matching (PSM) Sample

This study set dummy variables - DResist and DSensitive as the explained variables of logistic regression. When Pressure-resistant (Pressure-sensitive) institutional shareholding ratio is greater than the correspond-ing industry - annual median, DResist (DSensitive) is 1; otherwise, DResist (DSensitive) is 0. Meanwhile, LEV, TAT, GROWTH, DTL, ShrZ, IN_DIRECTOR, AUDIT, LnASSET, LnSALARY, STATE, industry and annual dummy variables are selected as covariates to screen out the treatment group and control group. Different from the matching of a single index, PSM condenses multiple features into a "tendency score" value", and promotes the overall matching of multiple features, to obtain the same or similar paired sam-ple in the main feature variables, to reduce the adverse impact of other possible interference factors on the conclusions. Based on Models 4 and 5, the propensity scores are calculated. Then, 2098 and 2095 pairs of paired observations are obtained for DResist and DSensitive, according to the nearest neighbor matching principle of one-to-one correspondence. On this basis, the regressions on Models 1, 2 and 3 are conducted again according to PSM sample. Table 5 reports the regression results.

Table 5. Table captions should be placed above the tables

Variable	Model 1		Model 2		Model 3	
	Coef. (S.E.)	Coef. (S.E.)	Coef. (S.E.)	Coef. (S.E.)	Coef. (S.E.)	Coef. (S.E.)
Intercept	−29.865**	26.511**	9.556***	11.285***	36.637***	33.000**
	(12.370)	(12.670)	(1.389)	(1.481)	(12.887)	(13.138)
Resist	0.046***		0.011***		0.038***	
	(0.013)		(0.002)		(0.013)	
Sensitive		0.023		−0.008		0.028
		(0.052)		(0.006)		(0.051)
IC					0.515***	0.582***
					(0.138)	(0.135)
YEAR/IND	YES	YES	YES	YES	YES	YES
Observation data	4164	4141	4164	4141	4137	4151
Within_R2	0.152	0.148	0.129	0.119	0.163	0.159
F_Statistics	24.36***	23.50***	20.18***	18.14***	25.23***	24.68***

*** Significant at 1%; ** Significant at 5%; * Significant at 10%

Mode 4

$$DResisti, t = \gamma 0 + \gamma 1\, LEVi, t - 1 + \gamma 2\, TATi, t - 1 + \gamma 3\, GROWTHi, t - 1 + \gamma 4\, DTLi, t - 1 + \gamma 5\, ShrZi, t +$$
$$\gamma 6\, IN_{DIRECTORi}, t + \gamma 7\, AUDITi, t - 1 + \gamma 8\, LnASSETi, t + \gamma 9LnSALARYi, t - 1 + \gamma 10\, STATEi, t +$$

$$\sum_{\gamma 11} YEAR \sum_{\gamma 12} \sum_{t} IND + \varepsilon i, t$$

$$(5)$$

Mode 5.

$$DSensitivei, t = \lambda.0 + \lambda 1\, LEVi, t - 1 + \lambda 2\, TATi, t - 1 + \lambda.3\, GROWTHi, t - 1 + \lambda 4\, DTLi, t - 1 + \lambda 5\, ShrZi, t$$
$$+\lambda 6IN_{DIRECTORi}, t + \lambda 7\, AUDITi, t - 1 + \lambda 8\, LnASSETi, t + \lambda\, SLnSALARYi, t - 1 + \lambda 10\, STATEi, t$$

$$\sum_{t} YEAR \sum_{t} \sum_{t\lambda 12} IND + \varepsilon i, t$$

$$(6)$$

In Models 1, 2 and 3, the coefficients on Resist are positive and significant (0.046, $p < 0.01$; 0.011, $p < 0.01$; 0.038, $p < 0.01$); those on Sensitive are not statistically significant (0.023, $p > 0.10$; -0.008, $p > 0.10$; 0.028, $p > 0.10$). Pressure-resistant institutional ownership can significantly improve CSR performance and IC effectiveness, while Pressure-sensitive institutional ownership has no significant promoting effect on CSR performance and IC effectiveness. Hypotheses 1 and 2 are verified again. In Model 3, the coefficients on IC are positive and significant (0.515, $p < 0.01$; 0.582, $p < 0.01$). Effective IC supervises the management to improve CSR performance. Based on these results, this study believes that effective IC has a significant mediating effect between Pressure-resistant institutional ownership and CSR performance. The size of the mediating effect is about 12.31% ($\beta 1 \times \delta 2/\alpha 1 = 0.011 \times 0.515/0.046$). However, this mediating effect is not reflected for Pressure-sensitive institutional ownership. Hypothesis 3 is verified again.

Robust standard errors in brackets are clustered at corporate level.

6.2 Tests Based on Heckman Two-Stage Regression

Institutional investors can choose to increase or decrease the shares of listed enterprises according to CSR performance. In order to weaken the adverse effects of such "self-selection", with reference to Dhaliwal et al. and Dai, Heckman's two-stage regression is adopted for re-analysis [38, 39].

In the first stage, the Probit regression models (Models 6 and 7) are constructed, and the inverse Mills ratio (IMR) is estimated. In Models 6 and 7, DResist and DSensitive have the same meanings as in Sect. 6.1. As the institutional shareholding ratio in the previous period obviously affects that in the current period, but may have a weak impact on CSR activities in the current period, the first-order lags of Resist and Sensitive are introduced respectively in Models 6 and 7. Meanwhile, with reference to Hu and Yang and Li et al., "Whether CSI 300 share" (HS) is added as an instrumental variable for institutional shareholding ratio [40, 41]. The CSI 300 index provides authoritative investment guidance for investors to track and select portfolios. The stocks selected for the CSI 300 index tend to have higher levels of ownership by institutional investors. On this basis, the exclusion restriction of the Heckman model can be met. In the second stage, the IMRs estimated in the first stage are added into the original models to test the impact of institutional ownership on CSR performance. Table 6 reports the test results of the Heckman two-stage regression.

Table 6. Model 1–Model 3 Heckman two-stage model verification results.

Variable	Model 1		Model 2		Model 3	
	Coef. (S.E.)	Coef. (S.E.)	Coef. (S.E.)	Coef. (S.E.)	Coef. (S.E.)	Coef. (S.E.)
Intercept	−50.924*** (5.702)	−51.281*** (6.017)	−1.321*** (0.494)	1.463*** (0.524)	−48.896*** (5.662)	−53.633*** (5.969)
Resist	0.098*** (0.024)		0.011*** (0.002)		0.081*** (0.024)	
Sensitive		−0.008 (0.021)		0.001 (0.002)		−0.009 (0.021)
IC					1.534*** (0.251)	1.608*** (0.248)
L.LEV	0.118*** (0.013)	0.123*** (0.013)	−0.003** (0.001)	−0.002* (0.001)	0.122*** (0.013)	0.127*** (0.013)
L.Resist	0.137*** (0.005)		0.137*** (0.005)		0.137*** (0.005)	
L.Sensitive		0.390*** (0.016)		0.390*** (0.016)		0.390*** (0.016)
HS	0.353*** (0.089)	0.213*** (0.077)	0.353*** (0.089)	0.213*** (0.077)	0.353*** (0.089)	0.213*** (0.077)
IMR	0.028 (0.471)	−0.693 (0.472)	0.130*** (0.041)	0.033 (0.041)	−0.171 (0.468)	−0.746*** (0.468)
YEAR/IND	YES	YES	YES	YES	YES	YES
observations data	4249	4249	4249	4249	4249	4249
Wald_chi2	3528.81***	3293.92***	732.14***	642.74***	3628.87***	3400.49***

*** Significant at 1%; ** Significant at 5%; * Significant at 10%

Mode 6.

$$DResist_{i,t} = \theta_0 + \theta_1 LEV_{i,t-1} + \theta_2 TAT_{i,t-1} + \theta_3 GROWTH_{i,t-1} + \theta_4 DTL_{i,t-1} + \theta_5 ShrZ_{i,t} +$$
$$\theta_6 IN_{DIRECTOR_i,t} + \theta_7 AUDIT_{i,t-1} + \theta_8 LnASSET_{i,t} + \theta_9 LnSALARY_{i,t-1} + \theta_{10} STATE_{i,t} +$$
$$\theta_{11} Resist_{i,t-1} + \theta_{12} HS_{i,t} + \theta_{13} \sum_t YEAR \sum_t \sum_t IND_t + \varepsilon_{i,t}$$

$$(7)$$

Mode 7.

$$DSensitive_{i,t} = \zeta_0 + \zeta_1 LEV_{i,t-1} + \zeta_2 TAT_{i,t-1} +$$
$$\zeta_3 GROWTH_{i,t-1} + \zeta_4 DTL_{i,t-1} + \zeta_5 ShrZ_i, + \zeta_6 IN_{DIRECTOR_i,t} + \zeta_7 AUDIT_i, -1 + \zeta_8 LnAS -$$
$$\sum_t YEAR$$
$$SET_{i,t} + \zeta LnSALARY_{i,t-1} + \zeta_{10} STATE_{i,t} + \zeta_{11} Sensitive_{i,t-1} + \zeta_{12} HS_{i,t} - \zeta_{13}$$
$$\sum_{\zeta_{14}} \sum_t IND + \varepsilon_{i,t}$$

$$(8)$$

As shown in Table 6, the coefficients on L.Resist, L.Sensitive and HS are the first-stage results, which are statistically significant ($p < 0.01$), implying that the variables introduced in the sample selection regression are valid. The coefficients on the remaining variables are the results in the second stage. In column 4 and 7, the coefficients on IMR are statistically significant ($0.130, p < 0.01; -0.746, p < 0.01$), indicating that there is a certain degree of "self-selection" problem in the sample. The Heckman two-stage model can effectively weaken the regression bias caused by the "self-selection" problem.

For the second-stage regression, in Models 1, 2 and 3, the coefficients on Resist are positive and significant ($0.098, p < 0.01; 0.011, p < 0.01; 0.081, p < 0.01$); those on Sensitive are not statistically significant ($-0.008, p > 0.10; 0.001, p > 0.10; -0.009, p > 0.10$). In Model 3, the coefficients on IC are positive and significant ($1.534, p < 0.01; 1.608, p < 0.01$). Again, these results indicate that compared with Pressure-sensitive institutions, Pressure-resistant institutional shareholding improve CSR performance and IC effectiveness, and effective IC prestens a significant mediating effect between Pressure-resistant institutional ownership and CSR performance.

7 Conclusions and Suggestions

7.1 Conclusions

This study analyzes the impacts of heterogeneous institutional ownership on CSR performance and IC effectiveness, and the mediating effect of IC between institutional ownership and CSR performance, to provide empirical evidence for institutional investors to participate in corporate governance and improve CSR performance. The results show that Pressure-resistant institutional shareholding significantly improves CSR performance and IC effectiveness. However, Pressure-sensitive institutional ownership has no significant promoting effect on CSR performance and IC effectiveness. Effective IC has a significant mediating effect between Pressure-resistant institutional ownership and CSR performance, but this effect is not reflected between Pressure-sensitive institutional ownership and CSR performance. Compared with Pressure-sensitive institutions, Pressure-resistant institutions supervise corporate IC construction, to feed-back the expectations and demands of stakeholders in addition to economic interests, and improve CSR performance. This study provides new evidence for interpreting the role of heterogeneous institutional shareholding, and is helpful for the regulators to monitor the standardization of institutional shareholding behaviors.

7.2 Suggestions

While "developing institutional investors beyond normal conditions," the regulators should focus on promoting institutional investors to play the role of stabilizing the capital market. In order to better guide institutional investors to improve CSR performance, it is necessary to optimize the structure of institutional investors, expand the ranks of institutional investors engaged in long-term value investment, increase the shareholding ratio of Securities investment funds, QFII and Social security funds, and enhance their abilities to improve CSR performance and enhance IC effectiveness. Meanwhile, the regulatory authorities guide Insurance companies, Securities brokers, Financial companies and other Pressure-sensitive institutional investors to establish a long-term shareholding concept, to build an incentive mechanism for institutional investors to hold shares for a long time. A Reasonable incentive mechanism should be designed to guide listed companies to improve equity structure, to improve CSR performance, and promote the healthy and sustainable development of the national economy.

The regulators should take measures to encourage enterprises to further enhance IC effectiveness, and promote the positive effect of IC in improving CSR performance and stabilizing the capital market. Meanwhile, the regulators encourage institutional investors to take the initiative to participate in corporate business decisions, and enhance the transparency of internal business decisions and information disclosure. IC construction is a long-term systematic process. Institutional investors supervise enterprises to improve IC construction, optimize the quality of IC information disclosure, promote the design of IC to be more reasonable, more effective operation, and safeguard the legitimate rights and interests of stakeholders. By enhancing IC effectiveness, enterprises can reduce the risk expectation of stakeholders, promote the mediating effect of IC between institutional shareholding and CSR performance, and enhance the consciousness of improving CSR performance.

References

1. Wang, L., Juslin, H.: Corporate social responsibility in the Chinese forest industry: understanding multiple stakeholder perceptions. Corp. Soc. Responsib. Environ. Manag. **20**(3), 129–145 (2013)
2. Cheng, B., Ioannou, I., Serafeim, G.: Corporate social responsibility and access to finance. Strateg. Manag. J. **35**(1), 1–23 (2014)
3. Singh, K., Misra, M.: Linking corporate social responsibility (CSR) and organizational performance: the moderating effect of corporate reputation. Eur. Res. Manage. Bus. Econ. **27**, 100139 (2021)

4. Bhattacharya, A., Good, V., Sardashti, H., Peloza, J.: Beyond warm glow: the risk-mitigating effect of corporate social responsibility (CSR). J. Bus. Ethics **171**(2), 317–336 (2021)
5. Zhang, D.X., Li, Z.H.: Research on the impact of institutional investors on the performance of their holding companies – based on the perspective of institutional investors' self-protection. J. Manage. Sci. **20**(5), 82–101 (2017)
6. Commission, C.S.R.: Report on the Development of Corporate Governance in China. China Finance Press, Beijing (2010)
7. Brickley, J.A., Lease, R.C., Smith, C.W.: Ownership structure and voting on antitakeover amendments. J. Financ. Econ. **20**(1), 267–291 (1988)
8. Chen, X., Harford, J., Li, K.: Monitoring: which institutions matter? J. Financ. Econ. **86**(2), 279–305 (2007)
9. Puspa, M., George, T., Shireenjit, K. J.: Institutional investors in Australia: do they play a homogenous monitoring role? Pacific-Basin Finan. J. **40**(B), 266–288 (2007)
10. Liang, S.K.: Does institutional investor ownership affect the company & apos; cost stickiness? Manage. World **34**(12), 133–148 (2018)
11. Helwege, J., Intintoli, V.J., Zhang, A.: Voting with their feet or activism? Institutional investors' impact on CEO turnover. J. Corp. Finan. **18**(1), 22–37 (2012)
12. Tian, L.H., Wang, K.D.: The "cover-up effect" of social responsibility information disclosure and the risk of the collapse of listed companies: DID - PSM analysis from China stock market. Manage. World **33**(11), 146–157 (2017)
13. Jeffrey, L.C., Fang, X.H.: Institutional investor stability and crash risk: Monitoring versus short-termism. J. Bank. Finance **37**(8), 3047–3063 (2013)
14. Elyasiani, E., Jia, J.: Distribution of institutional ownership and corporate firm performance. J. Bank. Finance **34**(3), 606–620 (2010)
15. Bajo, E., Barbi, M., Bigelli, M., Hillier, D.: The role of institutional investors in public-to-private transactions. J. Bank. Finance **37**(11), 4327–4336 (2013)
16. Nofsinger, J.R., Sulaeman, J., Varma, A.: Institutional investors and corporate social responsibility. J. Corp. Finan. **58**, 700–725 (2019)
17. Dyck, A., Lins, K.V., Roth, L., Wagner, H.F.: Do institutional investors drive corporate social responsibility? International evidence. J. Financ. Econ. **131**(3), 693–714 (2019)
18. Bushee, B.J.: The influence of institutional investors on myopic r&d investment behavior. Account. Rev. **73**(3), 305–333 (1998)
19. Attig, N., Cleary, S., Ghoul, S.E., Guedhami, O.: Institutional investment horizons and the cost of equity capital. Financ. Manage. **42**(2), 441–477 (2013)
20. Hofman, P.S., Moon, J., Wu, B.: Corporate social responsibility under authoritarian capitalism: dynamics and prospects of state-led and society-driven CSR. Bus. Soc. **56**(5), 651–671 (2017)
21. McCahery, J. A., Sautner, Z., Starks, L.T.: Behind the scenes: the corporate governance preferences of institutional investors. J. Finan. **71**(6), 2905–2932 (2016).
22. Ward, C.W.R., Yin, C., Zeng, Y.Q.: Institutional investor monitoring motivation and the marginal value of cash. J. Corp. Finan. **48**(2), 49–75 (2018)
23. Lu, Y., Zhu, Y.J., Hu, X.Y.: Empirical study on institutional investors & apos; shareholding and listed companies & apos; violations. Nankai Manage. Rev. **21**(1), 13–23 (2012)
24. Bushee, B.J., Jung, M.J., Miller, G.S.: Do investors benefit from selective access to management? J. Finan. Rep. **2**(1), 31–61 (2017)
25. Deng, D.Q., Wen, S.B., Pan, L.N., Liu, H.T.: Quality of internal control, heterogeneity of institutional investors and shareholding decision: an empirical study based on self selection model. Manage. Rev. **26**(10), 76–89 (2014)
26. Niu, J.B., Wu, C., Li, S.N.: Types of institutional investors, equity characteristics and voluntary information disclosure. Manage. Rev. **25**(3), 48–59 (2013)
27. Altamuro, J., Beatty, A.: How does internal control regulation affect financial reporting? J. Account. Econ. **49**(1), 58–74 (2010)

28. Mitra, S., Jaggi, B., Hossain, M.: Internal control weaknesses and accounting conservatism: evidence from the post-Sarbanes-Oxley period. J. Acc. Audit. Financ. **28**(2), 152–191 (2013)
29. Hoitash, U., Hoitash, R., Bedard, J.C.: Corporate governance and internal control over financial reporting: a comparison of regulatory regimes. Acc. Rev. **84**(3), 839–867 (2009)
30. Goh, B.W.: Audit committees, board of directors, and remediation of material weaknesses in internal control. Contemp. Account. Res. **26**(2), 549–579 (2009)
31. Ntim, C.G., Soobaroyen, T.: Corporate governance and performance in socially responsible corporations: newempirical insights from a neo-institutional framework. Corp. Governance Int. Rev. **21**(5), 468–494 (2013)
32. Chen, Y.Q., Ma, L.L.: Empirical analysis on the market response of social responsibility accounting information of listed companies in China. Acc. Res. **26**(11), 18–25 (2005)
33. Li X, Zheng C M, Liu G, Muhammad S S. The Effectiveness of Internal Control and Corporate Social Responsibility: Evid. Chinese Capital Mark. Sustain. **10**(11), 4006 (2018).
34. Chen, H., Na, C.H., YuTian, M.Z., Han, X.F.: Internal control and R&D subsidy performance. Manage. World **34**(12), 149–164 (2018)
35. Wen, Z.L., Ye, B.J.: Mediating effect analysis: method and model development. Prog. Psychol. Sci. **22**(2), 731–745 (2014)
36. Chen, G.X., Tang, S.Y.: Research on the relationship between corporate internal governance and social responsibility – empirical experience from executive compensation and ownership structure. Hum. J. **42**(12), 32–41 (2016)
37. Li, B., Guo, J.E., Su, K.: Enterprise risk taking: is a daughter inferior to a man? Anal. Based CEO Gender. Forecast **36**(3), 21–27 (2017)
38. Dhaliwal, D.S., Li, O.Z., Tsang, A., Yang, Y.G.: Voluntary nonfinancial disclosure and the cost of equity capital: the initiation of corporate social responsibility reporting. Account. Rev. **86**(1), 59–100 (2011)
39. Dai, Y.H.: Institutional investors, ownership nature and cost of equity capital. Financ. Res. **40**(9), 143–159 (2018)
40. Hu, M., Yang, J.: Can analyst coverage reduce the incidence of fraud? Evid. China Appl. Econ. Lett. **21**(9), 605–608 (2014)
41. Li, C.T., Song, M., Zhang, X.: Analyst tracking and earnings management: evidence from Chinese listed companies. Finan. Res. **36**(7), 124–139 (2014)

SLA Negotiation and Renegotiation in Cloud SLA Management: Issue and Challenges

Saleh Alkhamees[✉]

College of Computers, Umm Al Qura University, Makkah, Saudi Arabia
Saalkhamees@uqu.edu.sa

Abstract. Service-level agreement (SLA) is the commitment between consumers and providers. Service providers commit the consumers to assure the quality, availability and responsibility. SLA renegotiation is negotiation between consumers and providers to improve the quality of service. Cloud computing service provided by providers can be guaranteed with SLA. Therefore, SLA renegotiation is vital to service and profit of both providers and consumers. This article presents some detailed analysis of previous papers and the comparison of components of theirs. In this paper, an improved framework is proposed to solve the existing problems of traditional SLA renegotiation process. In the end, limitation and future work are concluded.

Keywords: SLA · Cloud computing · SLA violation · Service level agreement · SLA renegotiation

1 Introduction

With technology getting advanced, more individuals and companies tend to use cloud services to help organise their files and data. Cloud computing offers a wide range of services from hardware, to readymade software and a platform to build customised software. These services classified into three main models: Infrastructure as a Service (IaaS), Platform as a Service (PaaS), and Software as a Service (SaaS). A consumer and a provider when agreed on services they form an agreement called as service level agreement (SLA). Before forming an SLA, both parties pass through multiple steps of negotiation [1].

SLA negotiation can be defined as the process of establishing a commitment between consumers and service providers by specifying the nature of the required service and the level of quality of service (QoS) which must be guaranteed to the customer [2]. SLA is playing an important role for the service provider as it controls the quality of provided services in the cloud-based system. The cloud environment is dynamic in nature, and the SLA parameters need to be reviewed frequently to fulfil requirements. Therefore, it is critical to adjust SLA during service operations so that there is a satisfactory level of service continuity for all parties [3]. When there are any discrepancies, then both parties get back to reconsider different service level objectives (SLOs), and the process

© ICST Institute for Computer Sciences, Social Informatics and Telecommunications Engineering 2022
Published by Springer Nature Switzerland AG 2022. All Rights Reserved
W. Hussain and M. A. Jan (Eds.): IoTaaS 2021, LNICST 421, pp. 159–170, 2022.
https://doi.org/10.1007/978-3-030-95987-6_11

of renegotiation started. Therefore, SLA negotiation and renegotiation are the processes that help to improve the quality of contracts between a consumer and a provider [4, 5]. Majority of the earlier studies presume that the SLA cannot be adjusted once it has been modified, but we suggested that the 'no-win' situation should be changed into a 'win–win' one with the help of an automated renegotiation method. The purpose of introducing the renegotiation method is to create an innovative SLA that restricts the losses on both sides.

In this paper, we analysed existing approaches to discuss SLA negotiation and renegotiation in the cloud environment. We have categorised existing approaches into three classes – trustable model-based framework, proactive detective SLA framework and QoS monitoring frameworks. We further critically evaluate existing approaches, identified gaps and proposed our framework. The rest of the paper is organised as follows. Section 2 discusses the related literature. In Sect. 3, we present a critical analysis of existing approaches. Section 4 highlights gaps in existing literature, Sect. 5 we present our proposed framework and Sect. 6 concludes the paper with future direction.

2   Related Work

Renegotiation is one of the most important things in SLA. Existing researches are very valuable to our study. These articles are reviewed and analyzed to comprehend the principle and frameworks about renegotiation of SLA. In this section the brief reviews of these papers are presented. After the studying and reviewing of several articles, we categorize them into three different forms as presented in Fig. 1:

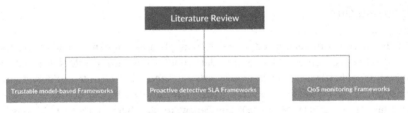

Fig. 1. Literature review

- Trustable Model-based Frameworks.
- Proactive Detective SLA Frameworks.
- QoS Monitoring Frameworks.

2.1   Trustable Model-based Frameworks.

It was asserted by the authors [4] that the in latest SLA, there is the need to have a greater number of trustworthy service providers, especially in the health and medical-related fields [6]. Service terms are one of the trusted factors that are usually described in the Service Level Agreement that the providers and their customers both have to follow. The authors proposed proactive SLA renegotiation while providing the service. This is to ensure that customers continue to trust cloud providers. The article discussed requirements and critical aspects for renegotiation, including determining SLA violation and examining service level limitations [7]. Certain properties are included in the renegotiation framework, for example, proactive actionability, the predetermined SLA and other related areas. This kind of negotiation framework can increase the trust levels, specifically in medicinal and health-related clouds. In addition, customers are also prevented from relocating their resources. The framework is also likely to play a part in research pertaining to resource optimisation, Autonomic Computing and SLA management. The authors in the article [8, 9] stated that managing service of quality in complex environment cloud service is a big challenge. The study introduced that there are three main components in rSLA framework: the rSLA language, the rSLA services and a set of Xlets. Authors proposed the rSLA language, which is designed and applied in the Ruby Language and Xlets configuration with a detailed description. Two scenarios presented to testify the performance of the rSLA model, the first one is tested by a PaaS application. The second scenario focuses on its usage at the IaaS level in the real pilot. The results show that the rSLA framework allows the dynamic setup of service quality management in a short period of time frame at a low cost. According to authors [10, 11], for an SLA to be successful and acceptable, it should be trusted and securely monitored. An SLA framework put forward in this article which includes negotiation and creates secure monitoring method that includes a third-party to improve the security and trust in the SLA. Implementation a case development of an SLA for cloud computing mechanisms presented in this article. Secure monitoring of the SLA is put forward through the involvement of a third party. The general theme of the WSLA has been adopted by the suggested SLA framework, which was initially designed for Web Services. The SLA between the consumer and the cloud provider created before the use of services. The provider determines the SLA parameters for any service, and the customer can negotiate them. Those SLA parameters signify the quality of service parameters. The main question the article talked about is that trust management in cloud computing is more significant than previously. Since cloud always acts dynamically, trust attributes need to be monitored continuously to assure SLA can work well. A trust model should be created to guarantee service-level agreement can work well in cloud computing. The authors in. attempted to build a cloud trust management model to evaluate the trust attributes of cloud service. The model should be user-side based and consider more of users' trustworthy. The model should have adaptability as well and can be used to make decisions. Statistics were used to analyses trust attributes and trustworthy attributes. Different kinds of calculation applied to the whole process of experiment [12]. Comparing is used as well to see the difference of performance among simple trust model, fuzzy trust model and cloud-trust data and fitting curve. Attributed based trust management is designed to assure SLA cloud services. Authors in [6] state that due to the possibility of the long term commercial relationship between consumers and providers, it is necessary to design a brokerage service level agreement (bSLA) to benefit all parties in the business, consumer and Cloud Anchor platform. This article introduced the basic concepts of service level agreement (SLA), brokerage service level agreement (bSLA), resource service level agreement (rSLA) and explained the typical relationship between these terms in a successful service scenario. The authors presented a new SLA renegotiation mechanism which ensures that the most trusted businesses get the lowermost resource prices and brokerage fees. To design a new approach to the issue, the authors analysed four other SLA renegotiation models from existing study and found the advantages and disadvantages of each of these models. This article focused on the financial perspective of the service level agreement instead of technical value, such as availability and bandwidth value. The authors only discussed the situation of services that providers delivers services via third party platform.

2.2 Proactive Detective SLA Frameworks.

Service level agreement. However, it is not possible to adjust such SLA during operations. A real-time and proactive SLA renegotiation framework discussed to facilitate the dynamic character of cloud-based systems [13]. Besides, a new method is put forward to determine and forecast service violation, which helps in guaranteeing proactive renegotiation. According to the authors [14], profit-recognising scheduling decisions should be made by the providers while allocating client requirements to virtual resources [15]. The SLA that has been decided should be adhered to during decision-making. Since the cloud environment is extremely dynamic, it is possible that due to unforeseen events, the preliminary scheduling plans may be affected, leading to unexpected SLA violations. Therefore, there may be a 'no-win' situation for the provider and the client. When there is an SLA violation, the possibly high penalty that has been decided in the original SLA to be paid by the provider. However, from the perspective of the customer, when there is an SLA violation, a business-critical job may be cancelled, and the loss faced by the client cannot be compensated by an SLA penalty alone. In addition, when there are increasing SLA violations, the provider's reputation may also deteriorate, leading to a decrease in the number of potential clients. The new method decreases the provider's loss in profit and reduces the number of cancelled jobs faced by the client, in contrast to implementing the original SLA. The degree of customer satisfaction in utility computing mechanisms is critical, because of which SLAs become extremely important. The main goal is to manage SLAs, including management of SLA autonomy or trade-off between various Quality of Service (QoS) parameters [16]. However, no classification exists on the whole for these extensive solutions [17]. The purpose of the article is to comprehensively analyses the way SLAs are developed, managed and implemented in utility computing settings. The key ideas of SLA and the two kinds of SLA lifecycle have been discussed in this article. The WS-Agreement signifies a language and a Web service protocol that is developed for establishing service-level agreements (SLAs) on the basis of preliminary offers, and for supervising those offers during runtime. This description of WS-Agreement is quite general and does not consider the view that an agreement may be altered at runtime [18]. The WS-Agreement is mainly used to generate the SLA between agreement parties, and it comprises of three sections: a plan for defining an agreement, a plan for defining an agreement template, and various kinds of ports and operations used to supervise the agreement life cycle from production to termination and supervising the agreement states between them. The key component of this WS-Agreement implementation is the negotiation manager (NegMgr), which performs negotiations between SLAs and system-external contractors. To be addressable by potential contractors, it needs to offer an interface to the neighbouring world. The implementation of the Negotiation Manager is done using a Globus Toolkit 4.0 service. This service permits the use of various mechanisms offered by the toolkit, including authorisation, authentication, GridFTP and supervisory services. The research [19] states that although cloud service platforms provide consumers convenient environment to deploy applications, service level agreement management is becoming more difficult because of the increasing dynamism of application environment and different vendors of service. The authors proposed the rSLA service and language, aiming to reduce the time of setting up SLA significantly [20]. According to the authors, this rSLA service and its language are both flexible enough to instrument virtually into any environment. Also, it is agile enough to scale and SLA management as needed. The researchers started their work by discussing the system model outlining how the rSLA service deal with interfaces of a heterogeneous environment. The approach addresses the efficient specification of SLAs in a formal language. Besides that, the Xlet architecture abstractions successfully overcome the issues of heterogeneity.

2.3 QoS Monitoring Frameworks

T t is essential to have a legal agreement for negotiating and renegotiating between the two cloud parties and to describe the Quality of Service (QoS) needs of crucial service-based procedures. According to the authors [16], there isn't any model, using which, the clients can assess cloud offering and rank them based on their interests. Therefore, a method requires for fulfilling these requirements of customers. A framework was put forward in this article that would enable customers to analyse and decide between the various cloud service offerings in the market. The purpose of the suggested framework is to shape the SLA with an accurate and unambiguous explanation of services key performance indicators (KPIs) to facilitate automated negotiation and renegotiation based on an agreement between customers and providers. The purpose of presenting the approach is mainly to present a method that suggests the Cloud providers' list of services and encourages the cloud users to choose the most reliable service by combining the automatic SLA negotiation with the measurement besides the service quality factors. An innovative automated negotiation framework for the cloud was presented by the authors [21] for providing a decision-support system for customers to accomplish the required service efficiently. The decision-making system considered the existing cloud market situation, time limitations and multiple QoS factors. Strategies and decision-making procedures can also be affected by the dynamic cloud market competitions among providers. There are two main aspects of the negotiation framework: 1) multiple QoS parameters are more stable using prioritisation and that regarding user preferences. 2) the most significant provider is determined to choose the best offer based on various objectives of the different parties involved in the negotiation. Besides, the system for decision-making takes into account the existing cloud market situation, multiple QoS parameters and time limitations [22, 23]. A QoS model considers different parameters such as - price, availability, process time and time. Those dimensions are using extensively and are domain-independent.

The authors [9] proposed SLA management approach Optimised Personalised Viable SLA (OPV-SLA) framework in clouding computing which can help service provider create a better SLA to deal with SLA violations [5]. The article not only has a detailed analysis about the existing data of SLA management in cloud computing but also provides a complete framework using three QoS parameters – throughput, availability and response time which can assist service providers in forming a better SLA.

3   Critical Analysis

In this section, we critically analysed existing SLA management approaches, as presented in Table 1. We analysed different approaches based on historical data, QoS monitoring approach, provider revenue, violation detection and multi-provider matching mechanism. The reason for selecting the mentioned parameters is because we believe that these parameters play an active role to assist cloud consumer during negotiation and renegotiation process. The critical analysis of these approaches describes below.

Table 1. Critical analysis of existing approaches

Author	Single provider cloud service				Multi-provider match module
	History of data analysis	QoS monitoring	Provider revenue	Violation detection	
[2]	Yes	Yes	No	No	No
[24]	No	No	Yes	No	No
[25]	Yes	No	No	Yes	No
[26]	Yes	Yes	No	No	No
[27]	No	Yes	No	Yes	No
[28]	Yes	No	Yes	Yes	No
[29]	No	Yes	No	Yes	No
[30]	Yes	Yes	No	Yes	No
[31]	Yes	No	No	Yes	No
[32]	Yes	No	No	Yes	No
[33]	Yes	Yes	No	Yes	No
[18]	Yes	Yes	Yes	Yes	No
[34]	Yes	Yes	No	Yes	No
[22]	No	No	Yes	No	No
[35]	No	Yes	No	No	No
[36]	Yes	Yes	No	No	No
[37]	Yes	Yes	Yes	Yes	No
[1]	Yes	Yes	No	Yes	No
[19]	Yes	No	Yes	No	No
[38]	Yes	Yes	No	Yes	No

(continued)

Table 1. (*continued*)

Author	Single provider cloud service				Multi-provider match module
	History of data analysis	QoS monitoring	Provider revenue	Violation detection	
[39]	Yes	No	No	Yes	No
[40]	Yes	Yes	Yes	Yes	No
[41]	No	Yes	No	No	No
[42]	No	No	Yes	Yes	No
[17]	Yes	Yes	No	Yes	No
[43]	No	No	Yes	No	No
[8]	No	Yes	No	Yes	No

After a thorough analysis, we found the following gaps:

- All existing researches do not consider that the consumers of cloud services can use service from more than one provider.
- Although some of these articles mentioned the revenue of cloud services providers, most of them do not present this perspective in the paper.
- Many articles consider violation monitoring function as an essential part of their models. However, none of them paying more attention to the same violations after the renegotiation agreements.

Although there are some existing frameworks focus on QoS in the process of SLA renegotiation, they did not consider the service that consumers are using. For example, consumer A uses cloud service for video meeting while consumer B uses cloud service for website server. Apparently, consumer needs a higher quality of QoS controlling and monitoring because of the higher demand for video meeting.

4 Proposed Framework

After comparing the related works from previous study [1, 3, 6, 16, 44–48] and digging out their research gaps, we designed the following framework to solve these problems. The proposed framework contains four functional modules- multi-provider match module, risk and cost management module, QoS management module and SLA violation detection module as presented in Fig. 2. The objective of this architecture is to build a high-efficiency and reliable SLA renegotiation system for cloud services users to solve their problems which exist in traditional SLA frameworks. The proposed framework gives a customer a flexible plan to choose best available option. In risk and cost management module the customers can decide which provider give them the best particular service, so customers can choose any service form different provider to reach their need and avoid risks. This step can be the first step. Multi-provider match module was created to help user to negotiate and re-negotiate to any service form different providers. QoS management module will store history data, when a customer need a new service, it may this as a parameter. SLA violation detection module care more to monitoring any violation. The penalty will be applied if there any violation, also is can store history of violation. Below will explain more about each module:

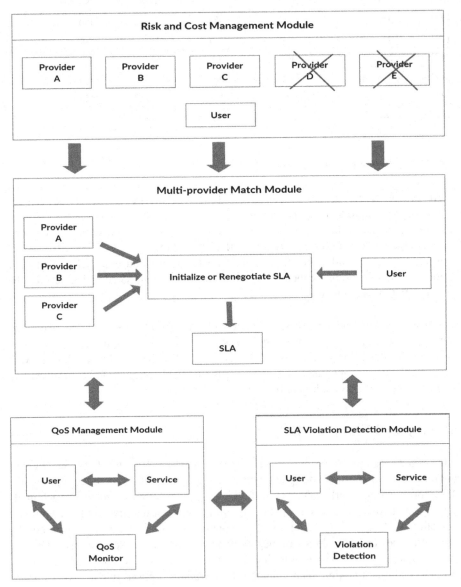

Fig. 2. Proposed framework for SLA management

1. Multi-provider match module
   Although some cloud service consumers only have one type of demand which need cloud service, many clients have more requirements on different types of business needs. For example, an international enterprise A need cloud services to support its online sale business and the need of online video meeting. In this case, one single cloud service might not be able to fulfil all the requirements due to many reasons. The multi-provider match module will present the clients a series of collocations of cloud services to meet the demands from different needs while initializing SLA or renegotiating SLA.
2. Risk and cost management module
   As mentioned in previous sections, some related study discussed about the revenue of service providers, however none of them consider the financial problem from the customer's perspective. The risk and cost management module will help cloud service users to choose the most cost-effective solution and weigh the risks with every choices by the performance of services from history.
3. QoS management module
   The reason why consumers and service providers sometimes might need to renegotiate new SLA is that because the cloud service providers updated the platform, or the consumers changed their requirements. The growing business needs of consumers is one of the most important and common reason they change their requirements. It might be lower latency and loss of packet. The QoS management module will keep monitoring the QoS performance of consumers' systems and inform the administrator while they have abnormal situations. It also could help consumers choose better service providers based on history performance when renegotiating SLA.
4. SLA violation detection module
   The SLA violation detection module is the key part of this framework. It helps cloud services users timely identify the violation and isolate the root cause. When there is a need of SLA renegotiation, this module could help decision makers analysis the advantage and risk of each services provider based on violations history and calculate the penalty.

5 Conclusion and Future Work

Recently, more and more people rely on Cloud. Most big companies offer different technical solutions over the internet. Most these services are considering about small and medium companies to help them to start their business easily and cheaper. SLA is the first step to in Cloud Computing, it is like the contract between two parties to define all rights for both parties. Most companies want to avoid any issue that may happen in the future. So, researches spend time to find a solution to negotiate and renegotiate between them to satisfy both. In this paper, we proposed a framework which contains four modules which are multi-provider match module, risk and cost management module, QoS management module and SLA violation detection module, to improve the process of SLA renegotiation for both consumers and services providers. However, the framework we proposed is mainly based on theory research. Therefore, to testify the efficiency of this frame work, we will try to take experiments in real scenarios. On the other hand, this framework is more from the perspective of consumers of cloud services; hence we will try to consider things more from cloud services providers' perspective in the future. In the future, there is no doubt that this topic, SLA renegotiation, will be mentioned and discussed more and more frequently. It can be predicted that more and more companies will use cloud services in the future.

References

1. Hussain, W., et al.: Formulating and managing viable SLAs in cloud computing from a small to medium service provider's viewpoint: a state-of-the-art review. Inf. Syst. **71**, 240–259 (2017)
2. Hani, A.F.M., Paputungan, I.V., Fadzil Hassan, M.: Service level agreement renegotiation framework for trusted cloud-based system. In: Park, J., Stojmenovic, I., Choi, M., Xhafa, F. (eds.) Future Information Technology. Lecture Notes in Electrical Engineering, vol. 276, pp. 55–61, Springer, Berlin (2014). https://doi.org/10.1007/978-3-642-40861-8_9
3. Alkalbani, A.M., Hussain, W.: Cloud service discovery method: a framework for automatic derivation of cloud marketplace and cloud intelligence to assist consumers in finding cloud services. Int. J. Commun. Syst. **34**(8), e4780 (2021)
4. Hussain, W., Hussain, F.K., Hussain, O.K.: Maintaining trust in cloud computing through SLA monitoring. In: Loo, C.K., Yap, K.S., Wong, K.W., Beng Jin, A.T., Huang, K. (eds.) Neural Information Processing. ICONIP 2014. Lecture Notes in Computer Science, vol. 8836, pp. 690–697. Springer, Cham (2014). https://doi.org/10.1007/978-3-319-12643-2_83
5. Hussain, W., et al.: Profile-based viable service level agreement (SLA) violation prediction model in the cloud. In: 10th International Conference on P2P, Parallel, Grid, Cloud and Internet Computing (3PGCIC), Krakow, Poland, IEEE (2015)
6. Hussain, W., et al.: Risk-based framework for SLA violation abatement from the cloud service provider's perspective. Comput. J. **61**(9), 1306–1322 (2018)
7. Hussain, W., et al.: Cloud marginal resource allocation: a decision support model. Mob. Netw. Appl. **25**, 1418–1433 (2020)
8. Ranaldo, N., Zimeo, E.: Capacity-driven utility model for service level agreement negotiation of cloud services. Futur. Gener. Comput. Syst. **55**, 186–199 (2016)
9. Hussain, W., et al.: Provider-based optimized personalized viable SLA (OPV-SLA) framework to prevent SLA violation. Comput. J. **59**(12), 1760–1783 (2016)
10. Hussain, W.: Optimized personalized viable SLA management framework for small and medium providers to avoid SLA violation in cloud (2016)
11. Alghamdi, A., et al.: The need of an optimal QoS repository and assessment framework in forming a trusted relationship in cloud: a systematic review. In: 2017 IEEE 14th International Conference on e-Business Engineering (ICEBE), IEEE (2017)
12. Hussain, W., Hussain, F.K., Hussain, O.K.: Towards soft computing approaches for formulating viable service level agreements in cloud. In: Arik, S., Huang, T., Lai, W., Liu, Q. (eds.) Neural Information Processing. ICONIP 2015. Lecture Notes in Computer Science(), vol. 9492, pp 639–646. Springer, Cham (2015). https://doi.org/10.1007/978-3-319-26561-2_75
13. Hussain, W., et al.: Comparing time series with machine learning-based prediction approaches for violation management in cloud SLAs. Futur. Gener. Comput. Syst. **89**, 464–477 (2018)
14. Alrashed, B.A., Hussain, W.: Managing SLA Violation in the cloud using Fuzzy re-SchdNeg Decision Model. In: 2020 15th IEEE Conference on Industrial Electronics and Applications (ICIEA), IEEE (2020)
15. Manzoor, S., Manzoor, M., Hussain, W.: An analysis of energy-efficient approaches used for virtual machines and data centres. In: 2017 IEEE 14th International Conference on e-Business Engineering (ICEBE), IEEE (2017)

16. Hussain, W., Sohaib, O.: Analysing cloud QoS prediction approaches and its control parameters: considering overall accuracy and freshness of a dataset. IEEE Access **7**, 82649–82671 (2019)
17. García García, A., Blanquer Espert, I., Hernández García, V.: SLA-driven dynamic cloud resource management. Future Gener. Comput. Syst.**31**, 1–11 (2014)
18. Wu, L., Buyya, R.: Service Level Agreement (SLA) in Utility Computing Systems (2010)
19. Deb, R.: The cloud computing with respect to provider and consumer. Int. J. Adv. Res. Comput. Sci. **5**(6), 4–8 (2014)
20. Hussain, W., Hussain, F.K., Hussain, O.K.: Comparative analysis of consumer profile-based methods to predict SLA violation. In: 2015 IEEE International Conference on Fuzzy Systems (FUZZ-IEEE), Istanbul, Turkey, IEEE (2015)
21. Hussain, W., Hussain, F., Hussain, O.: QoS prediction methods to avoid SLA violation in post-interaction time phase. In: 2016 IEEE 11th Conference on Industrial Electronics and Applications (ICIEA), Hefei, China, IEEE (2016)
22. Ludwig, H., et al.: rSLA: monitoring SLAs in dynamic service environments. In: Barros, A., Grigori, D., Narendra, N., Dam, H. (eds.) Service-Oriented Computing. ICSOC 2015. Lecture Notes in Computer Science(), vol. 9435, pp 139–153. Springer, Berlin (2015). https://doi.org/10.1007/978-3-662-48616-0_9
23. Alkalbani, A.M., Hussain, W., Kim, J.Y.: A centralised cloud services repository (CCSR) framework for optimal cloud service advertisement discovery from heterogenous web portals. IEEE Access **7**, 128213–128223 (2019)
24. Mohamed, M., et al.: The rSLA framework: monitoring and enforcement of service level agreements for cloud services. In: 2016 IEEE International Conference on Services Computing (SCC) (2016)
25. Binu, V., Gangadhar, N.D.: A cloud computing service level agreement framework with negotiation and secure monitoring. In: 2014 IEEE International Conference on Cloud Computing in Emerging Markets (CCEM) (2014)
26. Li, X., Du, J.: Adaptive and attribute-based trust model for service level agreement guarantee in cloud computing. IET Inf. Secur. **7**(1), 39–50 (2013)
27. Villano, U., De Benedictis, A., Rak, M.: SLAs for cloud applications: agreement protocol and REST-based implementation. Int. J. Grid Utility Comput. **8**, 120 (2017)
28. Cunha, R., Veloso, B., Malheiro, B.: Renegotiation of electronic brokerage contracts. In: Rocha, Á., Correia, A., Adeli, H., Reis, L., Costanzo, S. (eds.) Recent Advances in Information Systems and Technologies. WorldCIST 2017. Advances in Intelligent Systems and Computing, vol. 570, pp. 41–50. Springer, Cham (2017). https://doi.org/10.1007/978-3-319-56538-5_5
29. Goyal, S., Bawa, S., Singh, B.: Green service level agreement (GSLA) framework for cloud computing. Computing **98**(9), 949–963 (2016)
30. Aljoumah, E., et al.: SLA in cloud computing architectures: A comprehensive study. Int. J. Grid Distrib. Comput. **8**(5), 7–32 (2015)
31. Paputungan, I.V., et al.: Real-time and proactive SLA renegotiation for a cloud-based system. IEEE Syst. J. **13**(1), 400-41 1–13 (2018)
32. Omezzine, A., et al.: SLA and profit-aware SaaS provisioning through proactive renegotiation. In: 2016 IEEE 15th International Symposium on Network Computing and Applications (NCA) (2016)
33. Mohd Hani, A.F., Vitra Paputungan, I., Hassan, M.F.: Renegotiation in service level agreement management for a cloud-based system. ACM Comput. Surv. **47**, 1–21 (2015)
34. Sharaf, S., Djemame, K.: Enabling service-level agreement renegotiation through extending WS-Agreement specification. SOCA **9**(2), 177–191 (2015)
35. Gomes, R.: SLA renegotiation according to traffic demand (2013)

36. El-Awadi, R., Abu-Rizka, M.: A framework for negotiating service level agreement of cloud-based services. Procedia Comput. Sci. **65**, 940–949 (2015)
37. Wu, L., et al.: Automated SLA negotiation framework for cloud computing. In: 2013 13th IEEE/ACM International Symposium on Cluster, Cloud, and Grid Computing (2013)
38. Mehmood, S., Umar, A.: Scalable and flexible SLA management approach for cloud. Mehran Univ. Res. J. Eng. Technol. **36**, 87–96 (2017)
39. Peer, H., Bastian, K., Philipp, W.: Negotiation of service level agreements. In: Stephan, R.-M., Marcel, T. (eds.) Handbook of Research on Service-Oriented Systems and Non-Functional Properties: Future Directions, pp. 442–469. IGI Global, Hershey (2012)
40. Al-Ghuwairi, A.-R., et al.: A dynamic model for automatic updating cloud computing SLA (DSLA). In: Proceedings of the International Conference on Internet of things and Cloud Computing 2016, Cambridge, United Kingdom, pp. 1–7. ACM (2016)
41. Nandi, B.B., et al.: Dynamic SLA based elastic cloud service management: A SaaS perspective. In: 2013 IFIP/IEEE International Symposium on Integrated Network Management (IM 2013) (2013)
42. Uriarte, R.B., Tiezzi, F., De Nicola, R.: Dynamic SLAs for clouds. In: Aiello, M., Johnsen, E., Dustdar, S., Georgievski, I. (eds.) Service-Oriented and Cloud Computing. ESOCC 2016. Lecture Notes in Computer Science(), vol. 9846, pp. 34–49, Springer, Cham (2016). https://doi.org/10.1007/978-3-319-44482-6_3
43. Tata, S., et al.: rSLA: A Service Level Agreement Language for Cloud Services, pp. 415–422 (2016)
44. Hussain, W., Hussain, F.K., Hussain, O.K.: Risk Management framework to avoid SLA violation in cloud from a provider's perspective. In: Xhafa, F., Barolli, L., Amato, F. (eds) Advances on P2P, Parallel, Grid, Cloud and Internet Computing. 3PGCIC 2016. Lecture Notes on Data Engineering and Communications Technologies, vol. 1, pp. 233–241, Springer, Cham (2017). https://doi.org/10.1007/978-3-319-49109-7_22
45. Hussain, W., et al.: Integrated AHP-IOWA, POWA framework for ideal cloud provider selection and optimum resource management. IEEE Trans. Serv. Comput. **01**, 1–1 (2021)
46. Hussain, W., Merigó, J.M., Raza, M.R.: Predictive intelligence using ANFIS-induced OWAWA for complex stock market prediction. Int. J. Intell. Syst. (2021)
47. Hussain, W., et al.: A New QoS Prediction Model using Hybrid IOWA-ANFIS with Fuzzy C-Means, Subtractive Clustering and Grid Partitioning. Inf. Sci. (2021)
48. Hussain, W., et al.: Cloud marginal resource allocation: a decision support model. Mob. Netw. Appl. **25**(4), 1418–1433 (2020)

Machine Learning Predictions and Recommendations in IoT

Deep Learning Analysis of Australian Stock Market Price Prediction for Intelligent Service Oriented Architecture

Muhammad Raheel Raza[1](✉) and Saleh Alkhamees[2]

[1] Department of Software Engineering, Firat University, 23119 Elazig, Turkey
191137125@firat.edu.tr
[2] College of Computers in Al-Leith, Umm Al-Qura University, Makkah, Saudi Arabia
saalkhamees@uqu.edu.sa

Abstract. Stock exchanges are economic entities facilitating various trading assets like monetary values, activities, valuable metals, etc., among stockbroker participants. Prediction of Stock market rates and observing the behaviour of daily closing rates is a crucial task for many businesses and investment authorities. This acts as a precaution to know the suitable period for stakeholders to invest. Deep Learning, in this regard, is considered to perform forecasting tasks efficiently with better accuracy. For this purpose, our study performs forecasting of Australian Stock Market daily closing rates based on Deep Learning approaches of LSTM and GRU from January 4 2000, to January 17 2017. This work predicts the closing rates for the next 216 days. A comparative analysis of prediction accuracy between Deep Learning methods like Long Short-Term Memory (LSTM) along with Gated Recurrent Unit (GRU) is performed. Results reveal that the deep learning model LSTM performs better than the other approach based on the results obtained. Performance of the models is measured using metrics such as RMSE and R^2 scores, where LSTM achieved a comparatively less RMSE value of 0.072 and the largest R^2 score of 0.855.

Keywords: Stock market · Price prediction · LSTM · GRU · Service oriented architecture

1 Introduction

Stock market prediction is a difficult endeavour when it comes to predicting future stock prices. The stock market is too tough to determine because of its volatile nature. Every day, stock values fluctuate dramatically. Stock market forecasting is in high demand among stock consumers [1]. To forecast future stock costs with high accuracy, implementing all derived criteria at every time is a big challenge. Data regarding stock market prices are generated in large quantities and fluctuate per second [2]. The stock market is a complicated and difficult process through which people can make money or be

W. Hussain and M. A. Jan (Eds.): IoTaaS 2021, LNICST 421, pp. 173–184, 2022.
https://doi.org/10.1007/978-3-030-95987-6_12

deprived of their life savings [3]. Since the stock market is among the essential vital sectors wherein investors invest, predicting stock market prices has always been a popular subject for researchers regarding economic and technical fields [4, 5].

Stock exchanges are financial bodies that facilitate the trading of various assets like monetary values, activities, and valuable metals etc., among stock broker participants [6]. With a trading volume of thousands of billions of dollars, it piques people's interest in generating a profit. Goods are purchased and sold on the marketplace, and the subsequent value is used to assess if the transaction was profitable or not. The stock value is determined in general by its listing on a stock market and the number of its transactions [7–9]. The maximum a share is traded, the more valuable it becomes; on the other hand, if a share is traded in a low margin, it is less significant to some traders and thus, its value falls. Depending on the ability to estimate future values, this market anticipation might result in gains or losses [10]. As a result, the difficulty becomes determining the best time to buy/enter or sell/exit a company for profit based on stock market history [11].

Since predicting the stock market prices remains a challenging task for many company experts and researchers, estimating stock market values is both an intriguing and demanding field of study. Predicting the stock market with 100% accuracy is extremely difficult due to extrinsic factors. The most common characteristics of stock market data are temporal variation and nonlinearity. In the stock market, stock market forecasting is crucial [12]. If investors do not have enough information and knowledge, their investments risk losing the most money. To make high volume profits, investors need to estimate how much a company's stock will be worth in the future [13]. Various prediction systems have been created to make accurate stock market predictions [14]. Deep Learning methods are observed to implement prediction tasks achieving high accuracy and precision [15, 16]. The paper's primary purpose is to analyze the behaviour of stock rates by implementing deep learning approaches like LSTM and GRU. Each method predicts the daily closing prices of the stock market for the last 216 days.

The rest of this paper is as follows. In Sect. 2, we briefly explain the literature review. In Sect. 3, we present our proposed method and performance evaluation results. Section 4 presents the results of our LSTM and GRU models. Finally, Sect. 5 describes the conclusion part.

2 Literature Review

Many kinds of research have been conducted on Stock Market Price forecasting using Time Series Analysis Techniques, Machine Learning and Deep Learning Techniques [28]. This section contains a brief description of literature implementing deep learning approaches for Stock Market Price prediction analysis.

2.1 Frameworks with Deep Learning-Based Stock Market Prediction Approaches

To estimate future stock market value, a deep learning-based technique is used by Kalyoncu et al. [1] to analyze previous stock data. It employed Long-Short Term Memory

(LSTM) to estimate the stock price of five famous Turkish firms listed on the stock exchange. As a result, it helped establish a highly reliable stock prediction model for assisting investors in making better investing decisions. To present a novel deep learning-based prediction approach that incorporates typical stock financial index variables and media platforms text elements as model parameters, Ji et al. [4] use Doc2Vec to create lengthy text feature vectors from media platforms, which are subsequently reduced in size using a layered auto-encoder to equalize the dimensions of text feature variables and stock financial index variables. Moreover, the time-series data of stock price is decomposed using the wavelet transform to remove the random noise induced by stock market fluctuations. Finally, the stock price is predicted using a long short-term memory model. The experiment's findings reveal that the technique outperforms all three benchmark models in terms of all types of assessment parameters and can accurately predict share price.

Hu et al. [7] performed a survey of all manuscripts using all the neural network-based approaches, such as LSTM, CNN, RNN, and GRU, to classify stock prices. In addition, this study examines each article's dataset, parameter, methodology, and outcomes. It is discovered that newer models integrating LSTM with additional approaches, such as DNN, have received a lot of attention. Reinforcement learning and other DL algorithms produced excellent results. Hiransha et al. [17] utilize day-by-day closing prices from two separate stock exchanges: the National Stock Exchange of India (NSE) and the New York Stock Exchange (NYSE) (NYSE). The training is performed on the stock price of a single NSE business and forecasted for five distinct NSE and NYSE companies. CNN has been discovered to surpass the other models. Despite being trained on NSE data, the network remained capable of predicting for the NYSE. This was achievable because both stock markets had similar internal characteristics. When the findings were contrasted to the ARIMA model, it was shown that neural networks outperformed the current linear model.

Shen and Shafiq [14] gathered two years' worth of data from the Chinese stock market and provided a complete feature engineering and deep learning-based model that predicts stock market price trends. The suggested approach is comprehensive since it incorporates stock market dataset preprocessing, several feature engineering methods, and a proprietary deep learning-based approach to predict stock market price trends. To observe if there was a link between changes in a company's stock price and the general public expressed opinions or sentiments regarding it, Mehta et al. [6] devised and deployed a stock price forecast accuracy method that took public mood into account. To estimate future stock values, the suggested algorithm considers public mood, views, news, and past stock prices. SVM model, MNB classifier, linear regression, Naive Bayes, and LSTM were among the machine-learning and deep-learning approaches used for the research.

This research of Li and Pan [18] provides a revolutionary deep learning technique for forecasting stock behaviour in the future. Using a blended ensemble learning approach, the model integrates different recurrent neural networks connected to a neural network. For the test case, they used the S& P 500 Index in the analysis. The results reveal that the proposed deep learning blending ensemble model surpasses the other available price-prediction models. The paper [10] aids in effective forecasting and identifies the primary elements influencing stock price fluctuations. An adaptive neuro-fuzzy model is used to quantify the predictive potential of business performance measures and their relevance for 58 listed corporations from the Abu Dhabi Securities Exchange and the Dubai Financial Market for 2014–2018. According to the study [19], ROE is the most important predictor, whereas ROA is the least important. The most significant profitability metric is EPS, whereas the least effective is PM.

Table 1. Summary of the literature work.

Authors	Time period for datasets	Model utilized	Results obtained
Kalyoncu et al. [1]	2014 to 2019	LSTM	Accuracy = 90% for 5 different datasets of BIST 30
Ji et al. [4]	January 2010 to November 2019	Doc-word with LSTM LSTM	RMSE value of Doc-Word LSTM = 0.110 and R2 score = 0.957 RMSE value of LSTM = 0.579 and R2 score = 0.774
Hu et al. [7]	2015 to 2020	LSTM CNN DNN RNN RL	Accuracy of LSTM = 43% Accuracy of CNN = 48% Accuracy of DNN = 53% Accuracy of Reinforcement Learning = 50%
Hiransha et al. [17]	1 January 1996 to 30 June 2017	RNN LSTM CNN MLP	MAPE of RNN = 5.82 MAPE of LSTM = 6.03 MAPE of CNN = 4.05 MAPE of MLP = 4.81
Mehta et al. [6]	1 October 2014 to 31 December 2018	Naïve bayes LR Decision tree SVC LSTM	Accuracy of Naive = 86.72% Accuracy of LR = 86.75% Accuracy of DT = 81.43% Accuracy of SVC = 89.46% Accuracy of LSTM = 92.45%
Li and Pan [18]	December 2017 to June 2018	LSTM DP-LSTM GRU	MPA of LSTM = 99.29% MPA of DP-LSTM = 99.48% MPA of GRU = 99.57%

3 Methodology

3.1 Long Short-Term Memory (LSTM)

Long Short-Term Memory (LSTM) remembers long-term dependencies, which can help with sequence prediction. Because LSTM has feedback connections, it can interpret the entire data sequence [24]. Speech recognition, language processing, and other applications are some listed benefits [25]. The LSTM is an RNN-based neural network that remembers prior information and functions well on various gradient-related problems [20]. The input, forget, and output gates are the three gates that operate within an LSTM memory cell for data processing. Each fresh data entry is made through the cell's input gate. The forget gate eliminates the unneeded data from the cell by ignoring it [26]. The structure of the LSTM cell is explained in Fig. 1.

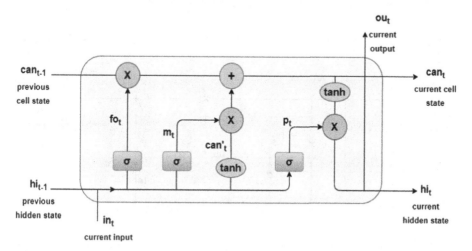

Fig. 1. Long short-term memory (LSTM) cell structure.

An input 'in' and the previous hidden state 'hi' are supplied to the sigmoid activation function to calculate the amount of data to forget for the forget gate 'fo' at a time 't'.

$$fo_t = \sigma\big[W_{fo} * (hi_{t-1}, in_t) + bias_{fo}\big] \tag{1}$$

Two equations determine the quantity of data to be kept in the memory cell. First, the sigmoid activation function is applied to the combination mentioned above. Second, using the identical inputs, the activation function has been substituted with tanh.

$$input_t = \sigma\big[W_{input} * (h_{t-1}, in_t) + bias_{input}\big] \tag{2}$$

$$can'_t = \tanh\big[W_{can'} * (hi_{t-1}, in_t) + bias_{can'}\big] \tag{3}$$

The previous cell state 'can(t-1)' is updated by using formula:

$$can_t = (can_{t-1} * fo_t) + (input_t * can'_t) \tag{4}$$

For the output gate, the equations are as follows:

$$ou_t = \sigma\,\big|[W_{ou} * (hi_{t-1}, in_t) + bias_{ou}\big] \tag{5}$$

$$hi_t = ou_t * can_t \tag{6}$$

3.2 Gated Recurrent Unit (GRU)

GRUs are a kind of RNN equivalent to LSTM but have two functional gates, the reset and update gates. These gates help to solve the vanishing gradient problem. GRU retains a hidden state in the place of cell state [21]. The reset gate is in charge of keeping the concealed state. As compared to LSTM, GRU is faster and requires minimum memory [27]. The structure of a GRU cell is shown in Fig. 2 as follows:

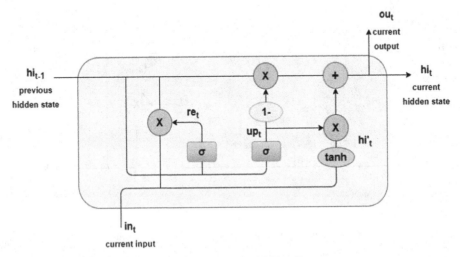

Fig. 2. Gated recurrent unit (GRU) cell structure.

The reset gate is responsible for maintaining a hidden state as follows:

$$re_t = \sigma\big[W_{re} * (hi_{t-1}, in_t)\big] \qquad (7)$$

The update gate handles the long-term memory of the cell as follows:

$$up_t = \sigma\big[W_{up} * (hi_{t-1}, in_t)\big] \qquad (8)$$

Hidden state 'hi' is determined by first calculating a candidate hidden state, as:

$$hi'_t = \tanh[\ W_{hi} * [\ (\ hi_{t-1}, re_t) + in_t\ ]] \qquad (9)$$

The candidate hidden state is then used to achieve the current hidden state value:

$$hi_t = (\ up_t * hi_{t-1}) + (1 - up_t) * hi'_t \qquad (10)$$

4 Proposed Model

This section explains the implementation performed for Stock Market Price Prediction using DL techniques. A description of the Stock Market dataset, the hyper-parameter configuration of DL models, experimentation and forecast accuracy measure are given in the section.

4.1 Dataset Description

Firstly, we have used a stock market data posted on Australian Stock Market price. Their records are updated on daily basis. We considered the closing rates of stock market data from January 4 2000, to January 17 2017. The dataset conatins five columns: Date, Opening rate, Low price, High price and Closing rate of the date. Then, we split the dataset into a training set and a test set with a ratio of 95:05. The training set has 4104 entries, and the test set has a total of 216 data. The stock market closing prices are to be predicted for the next 31 days. Table 2 shows the division of the dataset into training and testing sets. However, Table 3 describes the hyper-parameters configuration of deep learning models.

Table 2. Division of training and testing samples in australian stock market dataset.

Australian stock market dataset	Training sample	Testing sample	Total
Total records	4104	216	4320
Percentage	95%	5%	100%

Table 3. Overview of hyper-parameter configuration.

Hyper-parameters	Australian stock market dataset
Model	Sequential
Epochs	30
Hidden layer	4
No of neuron	100 (each layer)
Optimizer	Adam
Activation function	Linear
Batch size	32

4.2 Experimentation

Two prediction models have been used, the deep learning model as LSTM and GRU. Figure 3 explains the step-by-step procedure for Deep Learning methods of LSTM and GRU from extracting the dataset, splitting it into training and testing datasets and using models for prediction purposes to obtain results [22]. Firstly we have taken the dataset and checked whether there is any missing value or not. After confirming the absence of missing value in our dataset, we applied the deep learning algorithms of LSTM and GRU.

According to Fig. 2, before using LSTM and GRU model, we preprocessed data. All data is converted to float then normalized between 0 and 1. After preprocessing, we have fit the LSTM and GRU model by using many parameters. We have selected parameters that give us a small RMSE value and the highest R^2 score to forecast stock market closing rates from March 11, 2016, to January 17, 2017 (216 days).

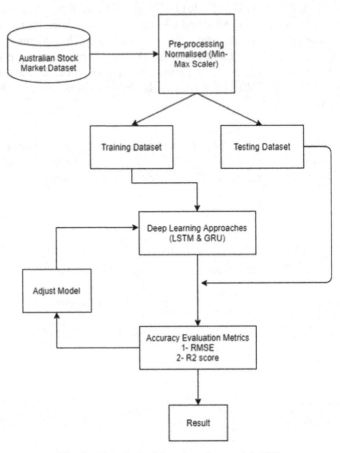

Fig. 3. Flowchart of deep learning models [23].

4.3   Forecast Accuracy Measures

We have used the root mean square error (RMSE) and R^2 score to forecast accuracy measures. The two accuracy measures can be expressed as follows:

$$RMSE = \sqrt{\frac{\sum_{i=1}^{N} (Q - P)^2}{N}} \tag{11}$$

In Eq. (11), where Q, P and N denotes actual value, predicted value and sample size.

$$R^2 \text{ score } = 1 - (RSS/TSS) \tag{12}$$

In Eq. (12), where RSS represents the sum of squares of residuals, TSS represents the total sum of squares.

5 Experimental Results

The main goal of this work has to predict stock market prices using deep learning techniques. We have also compared the results of both techniques and found the best model. For implementation, we have used Jupyter Notebook and python language. Many libraries were imported, such as pandas, Scikit-learn, Numpy, Keras, Tensorflow, Statsmodels etc. The dataset is loaded using pandas and then split into a 95% training and 5% testing set.

In the deep learning technique, we have used two algorithms such as LSTM and GRU. For LSTM and GRU model, first, we normalized all data between 0 and 1 using MinMaxScaler. We then divided the dataset into two parts training and testing set with a ratio of 95:05. Then fit LSTM and GRU model. For better results, we have done many times hyper-parameter tuning. According to Table 1, we have used different hyper-parameters such as epochs (30), hidden layer (4), number of neurons (100 each layer), batch_size (32), activation function (linear) and optimizer (Adam) for the best result. In Table 4, we performed a comparative analysis of two deep learning models- LSTM and GRU and observed their difference with the actual Closing rates of Stock market prices for the last 31 days of the test dataset. In Table 5, we calculated the RMSE and R^2 scores and concluded the LSTM model as the best model for forecasting stock market prices.

Table 4. Comparative analysis of actual and predicted closing stock market rates for the last 31 calendar days.

Dates	LSTM	GRU	Actual closing rates
12/1/2016	5436.258	5420.01	5500.2
12/2/2016	5438.539	5427.436	5444
12/5/2016	5434.315	5431.241	5400.4
12/6/2016	5419.95	5428.494	5428.7
12/7/2016	5408.714	5423.755	5478.1
12/8/2016	5410.544	5422.834	5543.6
12/9/2016	5430.789	5430.355	5560.6
12/12/2016	5459.278	5444.426	5562.8
12/13/2016	5486.307	5461.126	5545
12/14/2016	5503.566	5476.003	5584.6
12/15/2016	5519.718	5490.927	5538.6
12/16/2016	5523.638	5501.433	5532.9
12/19/2016	5519.909	5507.252	5562.1

(continued)

Table 4. (*continued*)

Dates	LSTM	GRU	Actual closing rates
12/20/2016	5518.818	5512.035	5591.1
12/21/2016	5524.979	5518.702	5613.5
12/22/2016	5537.93	5528.2	5643.9
12/23/2016	5557.398	5541.154	5627.9
12/28/2016	5573.169	5553.997	5685
12/29/2016	5594.502	5569.579	5699.1
12/30/2016	5616.89	5587.139	5665.8
1/3/2017	5629.156	5601.755	5733.2
1/4/2017	5646.611	5617.847	5736.4
1/5/2017	5663.838	5634.545	5753.3
1/6/2017	5680.89	5651.435	5755.6
1/9/2017	5695	5667.196	5807.4
1/10/2017	5714.672	5684.831	5760.7
1/11/2017	5724.523	5699.055	5771.5
1/12/2017	5729.8	5710.04	5766.9
1/13/2017	5731.046	5717.887	5721.1
1/16/2017	5721.773	5719.687	5748.4
1/17/2017	5714.559	5719.357	5699.4

Table 5. Comparison of RMSE, R^2 scores of applied deep approaches.

Model	LSTM	GRU
RMSE	**0.0724**	0.0855
R^2 Score	**0.8386**	0.7749

According to Table 5, LSTM and GRU model's RMSE values are 0.0724 and 0.0855, respectively, while the R^2 scores are 0.8386 and 0.7749. The smaller the RMSE value and larger the R^2 score of a model, the better the model performs prediction and achieves results [29].

6   Conclusion

This research collected the Australian Stock Market daily closing price dataset from January 4 2000, to January 17 2017. We forecasted the closing price of the last 216 days using two models LSTM and GRU. For deep learning models, we performed different hyper-parameter tuning to get the best results for prediction. Based on forecasting accuracy measures (RMSE and R^2 score), the LSTM model's performance is better than the GRU model. The RMSE and R^2 score of LSTM has obtained 0.0724 and 0.8386, respectively. This shows that LSTM performs best for long-time forecasting of Stock market prices.

References

1. Kalyoncu, S., et al.: Stock market value prediction using deep learning. Data Sci. Appl. **3**(2), 10–14 (2020)
2. Hussain, W., Merigo, J.M., Gao, H., Alkalbani, A.M., Rabhi, F.: Integrated AHP-IOWA, POWA framework for ideal cloud provider selection and optimum resource management. IEEE Trans. Serv. Comput. **01**, 1–1 (2021)https://doi.org/10.1109/TSC.2021.3124885
3. Alkalbani, A.M., Hussain, W.: Cloud service discovery method: a framework for automatic derivation of cloud marketplace and cloud intelligence to assist consumers in finding cloud services. Int. J. Commun. Syst. **34**(8), e4780 (2021)
4. Ji, X., Wang, J., Zhijun, Y.: A stock price prediction method based on deep learning technology. Int. J. Crowd Sci. **5**(1), 55–72 (2021)
5. Hussain, W., et al.: A new QoS prediction model using hybrid IOWA-ANFIS with fuzzy C-Means, subtractive clustering and grid partitioning. Inf. Sci. **584**, 280–300 (2021)
6. Mehta, P., Pandya, S. Kotecha, K.: Harvesting social media sentiment analysis to enhance stock market prediction using deep learning. PeerJ Comput. Sci. **7**, e476 (2021)
7. Hu, Z., Zhao, Y. Khushi, M.: A survey of forex and stock price prediction using deep learning. Appl. Syst. Innov. **4**(1), 9 (2021)
8. Hussain, W., et al.: Formulating and managing viable SLAs in cloud computing from a small to medium service provider's viewpoint: a state-of-the-art review. Inf. Syst. **2017**(71), 240–259 (2017)
9. Hussain, W., Hussain, F.K., Hussain, O.K.: Towards soft computing approaches for formulating viable service level agreements in cloud. In: Arik, S., Huang, T., Lai, W.K., Liu, Q. (eds.) ICONIP 2015. LNCS, vol. 9492, pp. 639–646. Springer, Cham (2015). https://doi.org/10.1007/978-3-319-26561-2_75
10. Mohamed, E.A., et al.: Impact of corporate performance on stock price predictions in the UAE markets: neuro-fuzzy model. Intell. Syst. Account. Finan. Manage. **28**(1), 52–71 (2021)
11. Hussain, W., Sohaib, O.: Analyzing cloud QoS prediction approaches and its control parameters: Considering overall accuracy and freshness of a dataset. IEEE Access **2019**(7), 82649–82671 (2019)
12. Raza, M.R., Varol, A., Hussain. W.: Blockchain-based IoT: an overview. In: 2021 9th International Symposium on Digital Forensics and Security (ISDFS), IEEE (2021)
13. Hussain, W., et al.: Cloud marginal resource allocation: a decision support model. Mob. Netw. Appl. **25**(4), 1418–1433 (2020)
14. Shen, J., Shafiq, M.O.: Short-term stock market price trend prediction using a comprehensive deep learning system. J. Big Data **7**(1), 1–33 (2020)
15. Raza, M.R., et al.: Sentiment analysis using deep learning in cloud. In: 2021 9th International Symposium on Digital Forensics and Security (ISDFS), IEEE (2021)
16. Hussain, W., Merigó, J.M., Raza, M.R.: Predictive intelligence using ANFIS-induced OWAWA for complex stock market prediction. Int. J. Intell. Syst. (2021). https://doi.org/10.1002/int.22732
17. Hiransha, M., et al.: NSE stock market prediction using deep-learning models. Procedia Comput. Sci. **132**, 1351–1362 (2018)

18. Li, Y., Pan, Y.: A novel ensemble deep learning model for stock prediction based on stock prices and news. Int. J. Data Sci. Anal. **13**(2), 1–11 (2021)
19. Hussain, W., et al.: Provider-based optimized personalized viable SLA (OPV-SLA) framework to prevent SLA violation. 2016, The Computer Journal (2016)
20. Raza, M.R., Hussain, W., Merigó, J.M.: Long short-term memory-based sentiment classification of cloud dataset. In: 2021 Innovations in Intelligent Systems and Applications Conference (ASYU), pp. 1–6 (2021). https://doi.org/10.1109/ASYU52992.2021.9598999
21. Raza, M.R., Hussain, W., Merigó, J.M.: Cloud sentiment accuracy comparison using RNN, LSTM and GRU. In: 2021 Innovations in Intelligent Systems and Applications Conference (ASYU), pp. 1–5 (2021). https://doi.org/10.1109/ASYU52992.2021.9599044
22. Hussain, W., Alkalbani, A.M., Gao, H.: Forecasting with machine learning techniques. Forecasting **2021**(3), 868–869 (2021). https://doi.org/10.3390/forecast3040052
23. Hussain, W., et al.: Comparing time series with machine learning-based prediction approaches for violation management in cloud SLAs. Futur. Gener. Comput. Syst. **2018**(89), 464–477 (2018)
24. Hussain, W., Gao, H., Raza, M.R. et al.: Assessing cloud QoS predictions using OWA in neural network methods. Neural Comput Applic (2022). https://doi.org/10.1007/s00521-022-07297-z
25. Raza, M.R., Hussain, W., Varol, A.: Performance analysis of deep approaches on airbnb sentiment reviews, In: 2022 10th International Symposium on Digital Forensics and Security (ISDFS), pp. 1–5 (2022). https://doi.org/10.1109/ISDFS55398.2022.9800816
26. Hussain, W., Raza, M.R., Jan, M.A., Merigo, J.M., Gao, H.: Cloud risk management with OWA- LSTM predictive intelligence and fuzzy linguistic decision making. IEEE Trans. Fuzzy Syst. 1 (2022). https://doi.org/10.1109/TFUZZ.2022.3157951
27. Hussain, W., Merigó, J.M.: Centralised quality of experience and service framework using PROMETHEE-II for cloud provider selection. In: Gao, H., Kim, J.Y., Hussain, W., Iqbal, M., Duan, Y. (eds.) Intelligent Processing Practices and Tools for E-Commerce Data, Information, and Knowledge, pp. 79–94. Springer Publishing, Cham (2022). https://doi.org/10.1007/978-3-030-78303-7_5
28. Raza, M.R., Varol, A.: Digital currency price analysis via deep forecasting approaches for business risk mitigation. In: 2021 2nd International Informatics and Software Engineering Conference (IISEC), pp. 1–5 (2021). https://doi.org/10.1109/IISEC54230.2021.9672381
29. Hussain, W., Merigó, J.M., Rabhi, F., Gao, H.: Aggregating fuzzy sentiments with customized qos parameters for cloud provider selection using fuzzy best worst and fuzzy TOPSIS. In: León-Castro, E., Blanco-Mesa, F., Alfaro-García, V., Gil-Lafuente, A.M., Merigó, J.M., Kacprzyk, J. (eds.) Soft Computing and Fuzzy Methodologies in Innovation Management and Sustainability. Lecture Notes in Networks and Systems, vol. 337. Springer, Cham (2022). https://doi.org/10.1007/978-3-030-96150-3_6

Machine Learning and Deep Learning for Predicting Indoor and Outdoor IoT Temperature Monitoring Systems

Nur Indah Lestari[1], Mahmoud Bekhit[2,3]([⊠])[iD], Mohamed Ali Mohamed[4],
Ahmed Fathalla[2][iD], and Ahmad Salah[5][iD]

[1] 2 Messiter Street, Campsie, NSW 2194, Australia
[2] Department of Mathematics, Faculty of Science, Suez Canal University,
Ismailia 41522, Egypt
{mahmoud_bakhit,fathalla_sci}@science.suez.edu.eg
[3] School of Electrical and Data Engineering, University of Technology Sydney,
Sydney 2007, Australia
[4] 2P Perfect Presentation, Riyadh 105523, Saudi Arabia
[5] Faculty of Computers and Informatics, Zagaizg University, Zagazig 44519, Egypt
ahmad@zu.edu.eg

Abstract. Nowadays, IoT monitoring systems are ubiquitous. These systems utilized sensors to measure the temperature indoors or outdoor. These sensors can be temporarily unavailable for several reasons, such as power outages. Thus, the server that collects the temperatures should find an alternative for predicting the temperature during the downtime of temperature sensors. In this context, there are several machine learning models for predicting temperature. This work is motivated to study the performance gap of predicting outdoor and indoor temperatures. In the proposed study, we utilized a deep learning recurrent neural network called Gated Recurrent Units (GRUs) and four machine learning models, namely, random forest (RF), decision trees (DT), support vector machines (SVM), and linear regression (LR) for predicting the temperature during the downtimes of the temperature sensors. Then, we evaluated the proposed models on a realistic dataset. The results show that predicting the indoor temperature is more predictable than the outdoor temperature. Moreover, the results revealed that the SVM model was the most accurate model for this task.

Keywords: Deep learning · Indoor · IoT · Machine learning temperature prediction · Outdoor

1 Introduction

Many natural disasters are tied to weather patterns. Predicting and monitoring climate occurrences are critical challenges for society and numerous economic

W. Hussain and M. A. Jan (Eds.): IoTaaS 2021, LNICST 421, pp. 185–197, 2022.
https://doi.org/10.1007/978-3-030-95987-6_13

sectors. Due to various reasons, such as a lack of region-specific parametrizations and data availability, numerical weather prediction models are currently unable to recreate precipitation patterns accurately. As machine learning models were reported to address various problems from different fields successfully [3,12,19], the machine learning models are compared to satellite-observed precipitation patterns for distinct climate seasons. These machine learning algorithms are capable of making exceptionally accurate climate predictions for the majority of the world's continents. [4,14].

Climate effect studies on ecological, agricultural, environmental, and industrial sectors have used air temperature estimations as a crucial component. Accurate temperature forecasting aids in the protection of life and property and the planning of operations for the government, industry, and the general public. Machine Learning approaches can aid in the precise prediction of temperatures based on a collection of input characteristics, such as radiation, rain, relative humidity, prior temperature, solar, and wind speed observations, to name a few [9].

Several works proposed to address the outdoor temperature prediction. In [32], an Internet of Things (IoT) stand-alone system has provided a dynamic datasheet on city climate metrics like as temperature, humidity, pressure, Carbon Monoxide (CO), and dangerous air contaminants. The method aids in the design of pollution control measures as well as raising public awareness about the issue. An IoT-based climate monitoring system for rural areas was proposed in [27]. Every five minutes, the system was able to submit monitoring data. Wind speed and direction, rainfall, temperature, barometric pressure, and humidity were all part of the monitoring data. The system was used to mitigate natural disasters. In order to detect fires in outdoor situations such as woods, an IoT prototype was created. The system used a low power wide area network as well as sensors to detect heat, chemical compounds, and flame. The technology was designed to ensure that temperature and gas measurements were accurate when a fire started [31]. The authors of [24] described a low-cost method of monitoring and forecasting outside temperature using single-board computers as temperature sensors. The method models the association between device CPU temperature at each device and external temperature using linear regression.

The authors in [29] had designed an IoT system to remotely monitor and collect the greenhouse parameters such as temperature, light, soil, carbon dioxide (CO2), and moisture. So, the system enabled controlling these parameters has led to good crops growth. Pressure and temperature were collected from a press machine in the industry's press shop assembly section using an IoT-based industrial monitoring and control system. The system was used to determine if a component was functional or not [30]. An IoT voltage management system linked with an Android smartphone was demonstrated to safeguard appliances and devices from overheating in a home or commercial setting. The system offered automated temperature ventilation and regulated the voltage of alternating current (AC)-supported equipment [16]. To acquire optimal clinker production, an industrial IoT based on an image processing system framework was built to measure and manage the temperature of rotary kilns in the cement sector. To generate high-quality clinker, precise temperature mapping of flame pictures was used to manage the temperature within the rotary kiln [7].

Despite these several efforts for predicting indoor and outdoor temperatures, to the best of the authors' knowledge, there is no work that studied which task is easier to predict (i.e., an indoor or outdoor temperature prediction). In other words, this work answers the question of whether indoor or outdoor temperatures are more predictable. The temperature readings are collected using IoT devices fixed within rooms and outside these rooms. In addition to answering this question, this work investigates the performance gap between four machine learning-based temperature prediction methods against the well-known GRU architecture. The machine learning-based models and the deep learning-based models under comparison are evaluated on a real-life dataset on five different performance metrics. Besides, this study was conducted on tuning the models' hyperparameters and the lag value of the data which achieved the best results. The main contributions of this work can be summarized as follows:

- To our knowledge, this is the first study to compare the indoor against the outdoor prediction temperature prediction. We evaluated the performance of the predictive model on five different accuracy metrics.
- The proposed models are utilized to predict the temperature during the down times of the sensor.

The rest of the paper is organized as follows. Section 2 exposes the background of this work. In Sect. 3 the existing methods are discussed. Then, the utilized models are discussed in Sect. 4. Section 5 exposed the evaluation and results of the proposed system. Finally, the paper is concluded in Sect. 6.

2   Background

In the following, we will explain the basic ideas of the utilized machine learning models.

2.1   Random Forest

Random forest (RF) is described as a collection of tree predictors and a mechanism for aggregating the results of the individual tree predictors. Every tree predictor with a random subsample of the dataset, either in terms of observations or features. The RF algorithm used in this study develops a tree by picking or mixing characteristics at each node in a random manner. To generate a training dataset for each characteristic chosen, we used a strategy that included randomly picking replacement samples from the original training set, where N is the number of samples in the training set. The most often used aggregation methods are average probability and most common class, with the latter serving as an extension of the previous.

2.2   Decision Trees

The Decision trees (DT) model is one of the most frequently applied methods for predictive modeling in various applications, including classification and regression. The decision tree technique performs excellently and indefinitely well when discontinuous data is used, even when noise arises. Numerous strategies were explored to discover the optimal method for splitting the input data. One of the primary purposes of the decision tree approach is to locate the most critical splits between the tree's nodes, hence improving the categorization of the data. To do this, we must apply the appropriate decision rules to the given data, which substantially impacts the algorithm's performance.

The DT model takes advantage of Information Gain (IG); because a decision tree model's objective is to discover the optimal split node that ensures high accuracy. The IG approach looks for the most appropriate nodes that yield the greatest amount of information, which may be quantified using an Entropy factor. The Entropy factor is used to quantify the degree of disorder in a system. The following formula may be used to compute the entropy of the output:

$$E(s) = \sum_{i=1}^{c} -p_i \log_2 p_i. \tag{1}$$

2.3   Support Vector Machine

Support vector machine (SVM) is built on a statistical learning theory to determine the best decision boundaries for class separation. SVMs choose the linear decision boundary that leaves the most margin between the two classes in a two-class pattern recognition task. The margin is the sum of the distances from the two classes' nearest locations to the hyperplane. The margin is calculated using the data nearest to the hyperplane. These data points are called 'support vectors' and are always few. Initially, SVMs were developed to solve two-class (binary) issues. When numerous classes are involved, a multiclass method is required. Techniques such as 'one versus one' and 'one against the others' are frequently used for multiclass situations.

2.4   Linear Regression

Linear regression (LR) is considered the basic regressor. Its basic idea is to find a function to map the input to the output. The term linear comes from that the coefficients maintain the linear property. Meanwhile, the feature can be of non-linear order. The linear regression model is nothing but a linear line when the features in the equation are linear. The function curvature can be increased to fit the data shape by increasing the order of the feature from linear to non-linear. Thus, linear regression can be seen as a curve fitting method. The data should be split into two sets in linear regression, namely, training and test sets. The training data determine the shape of the curve, while the model accuracy is measured by computing the distance between the data points of the test set and the curve. The linear regression can be applied when its assumptions are held. The assumptions are linearity, homoscedasticity, Independence, and normality.

3   Literature Review

Numerous comfort management techniques have been developed to use indoor and outdoor environmental conditions and maintain a specific comfort level for building occupants and managing to the optimal resources in the cloud [17, 18, 21, 22]. The ambient outdoor temperature has a considerable effect on the indoor temperature, as well as on the amount of energy consumed for cooling and heating.

Energy consumption is critical in remaining buildings, as most buildings use energy to maintain a particular level of comfort for inhabitants. Temperature control in a resident's area is a critical function of occupant buildings. The modeling approaches utilized in the literature have gotten increasingly complex over time to enhance prediction model performance [23]. According to previous research, such as in [2], the heating, ventilation, and air conditioning (HVAC) systems consume the most energy in a structure. As a result, controlling HVAC systems in existing buildings should be considered in order to increase energy efficiency through better energy strategies. Designing a model that takes environmental conditions into account is critical for configuring the optimal HVAC system settings. Literature has taken into account a variety of comfort factors, the most prominent of which are indoor air quality, visual comfort, and thermal comfort. These factors both affect user comfort, and energy consumption [11].

For forecasting, several machine learning methods have been suggested, including the artificial neural network (ANN), the support vector machine (SVM), the hidden Markov model (HMM), and several more as presented in [20, 33]. Nivine et al. [5] developed a novel method for forecasting the inside temperature up to four hours in advance using Artificial Neural Network (ANN) and considering the outdoor parameters. Additionally, the authors of [25] regulated the cooling load in a smart building by adding a Neural Network (NN) into an intelligent system that allows examination and prediction of the building's energy need as well as identification of essential elements affecting energy usage. The study demonstrates that the building's capacity is critical in predicting the HVAC system's cooling demand.

The authors of [28] examined the influence of users' behaviors and practices on the potential for energy savings in smart buildings. The authors identified the user as the primary element affecting energy demand and categorized the user's effect on energy needs into three major components: HVAC, plugging loading systems, and lighting. Additionally, Varick et al. [13] examined building occupancy and its effect on energy savings using real-time data. They suggested an occupancy model that could be incorporated effectively into the building's HVAC system through Markov Chains.

In [26], a novel model for predicting the hourly cooling load in office buildings was created using Support Vector Regression (SVR). The hyper-parameters of the model were adjusted to obtain the most accurate temperature forecast. Additionally, authors of [10] investigated the possibility of forecasting building energy consumption using SVR and the effect of different SVR settings on prediction accuracy. According to the study, SVR achieved the best accuracy when compared to other comparable research techniques, including genetic programming and neural networks.

Researchers in [23] utilized deep learning to predict the ideal indoor temperature and then automatically regulate the air conditioner based on that forecast. In order to maximize the HVAC's thermal energy storage, Abdullatif et al. [6] developed a cooling load forecasting model that uses the generalized regression neural network (GRNN) and takes into account the building's orientational features and occupancy. With the use of neural networks and polynomial regression models, Catalina accurately forecasted the monthly heating demand for residential buildings based on the structure of the structures [8].

4   Methodology

4.1   Overview

Figure 1 shows that the prediction model requires a set of historical data for indoor and outdoor temperatures to forecast future temperatures for both cases. The model used these historical data as input to be trained for the prediction model. The prediction model is used to forecast indoor and outdoor environments considering many environmental surroundings and characteristics. The settings are subject to vary over time. As a result, the data must be continuous for both training and prediction. The input data is used to anticipate the next time, which might be a single data point or a data sequence from a previous point to the present point in time. The prediction model's output is a dataset containing the projected indoor and outdoor temperatures and environmental parameters. The main goal is to determine the forecasting indoor and outdoor temperatures value for the building, which can be used to determine the least amount of energy required to maintain a pleasant atmosphere. As a result, the actuators must provide a pleasant environment for the user while consuming the least amount of energy possible.

4.2   Feature Engineering and Model Building

We proposed applying the data differencing to the raw input temperature. Time series forecasting issues are traditionally turned into supervised learning problems using lag characteristics. The lag value of the proposed models is set by searching for the value that yields the best prediction accuracy. This happened through utilizing the grid search approach. Thus, the problem is framed as a time series analysis problem. The data is split into training, validation, and test sets.

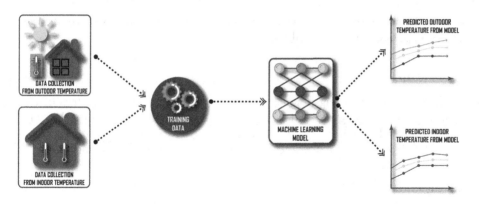

Fig. 1. The proposed temperature prediction system.

Regarding building the models, we proposed tuning the models' hyperparameters using the grid search method for the GRU model. A custom architecture is proposed to fit the nature of the data. The overfitting was checked by comparing the difference between the validation and training losses.

5 Experimental Results

5.1 Dataset

The dataset includes the temperature measurements from IoT sensors deployed outside and within a business building room (admin) that were randomly recorded in the dataset. At random intervals, this was recorded. The recording was accomplished at a rate of one second. The dataset contains different attributes, namely, room_id, noted_date, temperature, and IoT sensing device place (i.e., out/in), as listed in Table 1. These temperature measurements were

Table 1. Dataset features description.

No	Feature	Description
1	id	Unique ID for each reading
2	room_id	The room id at where the sensor was placed, inside and outside
3	noted_date	Date and time of temperature reading
4	temp	Temperature readings
5	out/in	Determine if the reading came from a source sensor within or outside the room

collected by IoT sensors that were placed outside and inside a private room. The dataset is publicly available online[1].

5.2   Setup

The utilized programming language was Python. The hyperparameters of the models are tuned using the grid search approach to obtain the best results. The proposed models used 10,000 observations for each indoor and outdoor data, where data are split into 80% and 20% for training and testing, respectively.

5.3   Evaluation Metrics

In order to assess the performance of the proposed models, we used five evaluation metrics used in various time series and regression applications [1,15]. Evaluation metrics' equations (i.e., Eqs. 2–6) define the utilized evaluation metrics where different patterns of error values are measured.

$$MAE = \frac{1}{N} \sum_{i=1}^{N} \left| Y_i - \hat{Y}_i \right| \tag{2}$$

$$MSE = \frac{1}{N} \sum_{i=1}^{N} \left(Y_i - \hat{Y}_i \right)^2 \tag{3}$$

$$RMSE = \sqrt{\frac{1}{N} \sum_{i=1}^{N} \left(Y_i - \hat{Y}_i \right)^2} \tag{4}$$

$$MAPE = \frac{1}{n} \sum_{i=1}^{N} \left| \frac{Y_i - \hat{Y}_i}{Y_i} \right| \times 100\% \tag{5}$$

$$R^2 = 1 - \frac{\sum_{i=1}^{N} (y_i - \hat{y}_i)^2}{\sum_{i=1}^{N} (y_i - \bar{y})^2} \tag{6}$$

where y_i represents the true values, N indicates the number of observations, $\bar{y}$ represents the mean true values, and $\hat{y}_i$ represents the predicted values.

5.4   Results and Discussion

Figure 2 depicts the MAE of the proposed five models for the indoor and outdoor temperature prediction. Apparently, for the five models, the prediction errors for the indoor temperature are less than the prediction errors for the outdoor temperature. Moreover, the best model for the temperature prediction was SVM and LR, where the former was slightly better than the latter. The deep learning model (i.e., GRU) performance was an average, while the worst prediction rates

---

[1] https://www.kaggle.com/atulanandjha/temperature-readings-iot-devices.

were achieved by DT and RF models. In the same context, Table 2 lists the performance metrics for the five models on five different accuracy metrics. The listed results emphasize that the indoor temperature is more predictable than the outdoor temperature. The accuracy gap varies based on the utilized model. One can conclude that the more accurate the model is, the less the accuracy gap between the indoor and outdoor temperature prediction model and vice versa.

Table 2. The accuracy rates for the proposed models on five different metrics.

Model	Data	MAE	MSE	RMSE	R^2	MAPE
GRU	Indoor	0.44174	0.55045	0.73987	0.88591	1.40952
	Outdoor	0.69523	0.99453	0.99461	0.95875	2.39551
RF	Indoor	0.65144	0.96432	0.982	0.80029	2.03945
	Outdoor	0.89171	1.79257	1.33887	0.92599	3.12289
DT	Indoor	0.65007	0.96055	0.98007	0.80107	2.0354
	Outdoor	0.89182	1.81794	1.34831	0.92494	3.12271
SVM	Indoor	0.41856	0.53633	0.73234	0.88892	1.35239
	Outdoor	0.47891	0.62716	0.79193	0.97411	1.59394
LR	Indoor	0.42409	0.53252	0.72974	0.88971	1.37103
	Outdoor	0.47076	0.62528	0.79075	0.97418	1.56435

The task of tuning machine learning models' hyperparameters is straightforward. On the contrary, the deep learning model architecture selection and hyperparameter is a relatively more sophisticated task. Thus, understanding the effect of parameter tuning on the proposed GRU model is vital. Figure 3 depicts the MEA values against the number of feature lags. Figure 3 can help select the lag value that achieves the highest accuracy rates. The best lag value for the indoor and outdoor temperatures prediction was 2 and 4, respectively. In Fig. 4, the overfitting of the GRU model was examined. As the difference between the training and validation losses is small, the proposed GRU model does not suffer from the overfitting problem. Finally, the variance of the proposed GRU model was examined in Fig. 5 for five runs of each model. The indoor and outdoor prediction models have the same behavior, except the overall performance of the former is better than the latter. The results revealed that predicting the outdoor temperature is less accurate to the indoor temperature. This can be linked to the fact the outdoor temperature is affected by more factors than the indoor temperature.

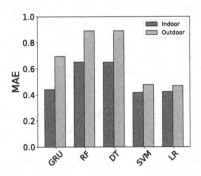

Fig. 2. MAE of the proposed models for indoor and outdoor temperature prediction.

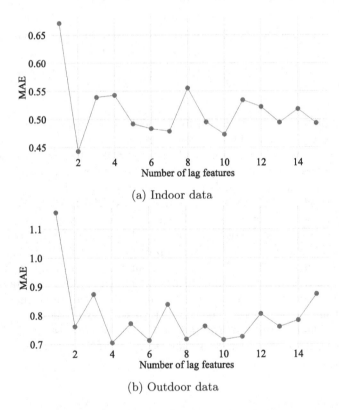

Fig. 3. Grid search results for obtaining optimal number of lags for the GRU model.

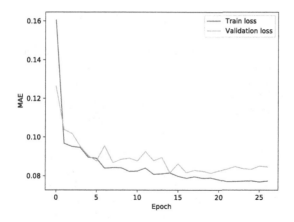

Fig. 4. Training and validation loss for the GRU model.

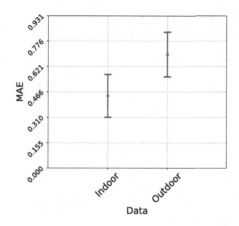

Fig. 5. Error-bar for running GRU models for 5 times.

6   Conclusion

Temperature monitoring through IoT-based systems is commonplace. These systems can help in making decisions that control power consumption. In this work, we utilized four machine learning models and one deep learning model for predicting indoor and outdoor temperature based on the historical temperature data collected by an IoT system. This study aims to know which type of temperature is more predictable and to figure out the performance gap of the five utilized models. Based on a real-life dataset, the utilized models are evaluated on five accuracy metrics: MAE, MSE, RMSE, MAPE, and R^2. The obtained results revealed that the indoor temperature prediction is more predictable than the outdoor temperature. Moreover, the SVM and LR models achieved the best performance, while the worst performance was obtained from the RF and DT models. The results outlined that the more accurate the model is, the less the difference of the prediction error between the indoor and outdoor models. Finally, the proposed model can be utilized to predict the future temperature when the sensor goes down temporarily. The future direction includes comparing the machine learning and deep learning models to the statistical models such as ARIMA.

References

1. Alameer, Z., Fathalla, A., Li, K., Ye, H., Jianhua, Z.: Multistep-ahead forecasting of coal prices using a hybrid deep learning model. Resour. Policy **65**, 101588 (2020)
2. Alawadi, S., Mera, D., Fernández-Delgado, M., Alkhabbas, F., Olsson, C.M., Davidsson, P.: A comparison of machine learning algorithms for forecasting indoor temperature in smart buildings. Energy Syst., 1–17 (2020)
3. Aldahiri, A., Alrashed, B., Hussain, W.: Trends in using IoT with machine learning in health prediction system. Forecasting **3**(1), 181–206 (2021)
4. Anochi, J.A., de Almeida, V.A., de Campos Velho, H.F.: Machine learning for climate precipitation prediction modeling over south America. Remote Sens. **13**(13), 2468 (2021)
5. Attoue, N., Shahrour, I., Younes, R.: Smart building: use of the artificial neural network approach for indoor temperature forecasting. Energies **11**(2), 395 (2018)
6. Ben-Nakhi, A.E., Mahmoud, M.A.: Cooling load prediction for buildings using general regression neural networks. Energy Convers. Manage. **45**(13–14), 2127–2141 (2004)
7. Bojja, P., Prasanna, N.M., Kumari, P.R., Bhuvanendhiran, T., Kumar, P.J.: Development of conventional controller based on image processing for monitoring and controlling burning zone temperature in a cement plant in rotary kiln process through IoT. Instrum. Mesures Métrologies **20**(4) (2021)
8. Catalina, T., Virgone, J., Blanco, E.: Development and validation of regression models to predict monthly heating demand for residential buildings. Energy Buildings **40**(10), 1825–1832 (2008)
9. Cifuentes, J., Marulanda, G., Bello, A., Reneses, J.: Air temperature forecasting using machine learning techniques: a review. Energies **13**(16), 4215 (2020)
10. Dong, B., Cao, C., Lee, S.E.: Applying support vector machines to predict building energy consumption in tropical region. Energy Buildings **37**(5), 545–553 (2005)
11. Dounis, A.I., Caraiscos, C.: Advanced control systems engineering for energy and comfort management in a building environment-a review. Renew. Sustain. Energy Rev. **13**(6–7), 1246–1261 (2009)
12. Eldesouky, E., Bekhit, M., Fathalla, A., Salah, A., Ali, A.: A robust UWSN handover prediction system using ensemble learning. Sensors **21**(17), 5777 (2021)
13. Erickson, V., Cerpa, O.: Occupancy-based system for efficient reduction of HVAC energy. In: Proceedings of the 10th International Conference on Information Processing in Sensor Networks (IPSN 2011) (2010)
14. Fathalla, A., Li, K., Salah, A., Mohamed, M.F.: An LSTM-based distributed scheme for data transmission reduction of IoT systems. Neurocomputing **485**, 166-180 (2021)
15. Fathalla, A., Salah, A., Li, K., Li, K., Francesco, P.: Deep end-to-end learning for price prediction of second-hand items. Knowl. Inf. Syst. **62**(12), 4541–4568 (2020). https://doi.org/10.1007/s10115-020-01495-8

16. Foysal, M.R., Hossain, R.A., Islam, M.M., Sharmin, S., Moon, N.N.: IoT based temperature control system of home by using an android device. In: 2021 1st International Conference on Emerging Smart Technologies and Applications (eSmarTA), pp. 1–8. IEEE (2021)

17. Gamal, M., Abolhasan, M., Lipman, J., Liu, R.P., Ni, W.: Multi objective resource optimisation for network function virtualisation requests. In: 2018 26th International Conference on Systems Engineering (ICSEng), pp. 1–7. IEEE (2018)

18. Gamal, M., Jafarizadeh, S., Abolhasan, M., Lipman, J., Ni, W.: Mapping and scheduling for non-uniform arrival of virtual network function (VNF) requests. In: 2019 IEEE 90th Vehicular Technology Conference (VTC2019-Fall), pp. 1–6. IEEE (2019)

19. Hosny, K.M., Darwish, M.M., Li, K., Salah, A.: Covid-19 diagnosis from CT scans and chest X-ray images using low-cost raspberry PI. PLoS ONE 16(5), e0250688 (2021)

20. Hussain, W., Merigó, J.M., Raza, M.R.: Predictive intelligence using ANFIS-induced OWAWA for complex stock market prediction. Int. J. Intell. Syst. (2021)

21. Hussain, W., Merigo, J.M., Gao, H., Alkalbani, A.M., Rabhi, F.A.: Integrated AHP-IOWA, POWA framework for ideal cloud provider selection and optimum resource management. IEEE Trans. Serv. Comput. (2021)

22. Hussain, W., Sohaib, O., Naderpour, M., Gao, H.: Cloud marginal resource allocation: a decision support model. Mob. Netw. Appl. 25(4), 1418–1433 (2020)

23. Jin, W., Ullah, I., Ahmad, S., Kim, D.: Occupant comfort management based on energy optimization using an environment prediction model in smart homes. Sustainability 11(4), 997 (2019)

24. Krintz, C., Wolski, R., Golubovic, N., Bakir, F.: Estimating outdoor temperature from CPU temperature for IoT applications in agriculture. In: Proceedings of the 8th International Conference on the Internet of Things, pp. 1–8 (2018)

25. Kwok, S.S., Yuen, R.K., Lee, E.W.: An intelligent approach to assessing the effect of building occupancy on building cooling load prediction. Build. Environ. 46(8), 1681–1690 (2011)

26. Li, Q., Meng, Q., Cai, J., Yoshino, H., Mochida, A.: Applying support vector machine to predict hourly cooling load in the building. Appl. Energy 86(10), 2249–2256 (2009)

27. Muslim, M.A., Setyawan, R.A., Basuki, A., Razak, A.A., Hario, F.P., Fernando, E.: IoT based climate monitoring system. In: IOP Conference Series: Earth and Environmental Science, vol. 746, p. 012044. IOP Publishing (2021)

28. Nguyen, T.A., Aiello, M.: Energy intelligent buildings based on user activity: a survey. Energy Buildings 56, 244–257 (2013)

29. Pallavi, S., Mallapur, J.D., Bendigeri, K.Y.: Remote sensing and controlling of greenhouse agriculture parameters based on IoT. In: 2017 International Conference on Big Data, IoT and Data Science (BID), pp. 44–48. IEEE (2017)

30. Priyanka, E., Maheswari, C., Thangavel, S.: IoT based field parameters monitoring and control in press shop assembly. Internet Things 3, 1–11 (2018)

31. Roque, G., Padilla, V.S.: LPWAN based IoT surveillance system for outdoor fire detection. IEEE Access 8, 114900–114909 (2020)

32. Shete, R., Agrawal, S.: IoT based urban climate monitoring using raspberry PI. In: 2016 International Conference on Communication and Signal Processing (ICCSP), pp. 2008–2012. IEEE (2016)

33. Ullah, I., Ahmad, R., Kim, D.: A prediction mechanism of energy consumption in residential buildings using hidden Markov model. Energies 11(2), 358 (2018)

Introducing the BrewAI AutoML Tool

Siu Lung Ng[1]([✉]), Fethi A. Rabhi[1], Gavin Whyte[2], and Andy Zeng[2]

[1] School of Computer Science and Engineering, University of New South Wales, Sydney 2052, Australia
{siu_lung.ng,f.rabhi}@unsw.edu.au
[2] BrewAI, Head Office, Suite 03, level 22, 56 Pitt Street, Sydney 2000, Australia
{gavin.whyte,andy.zeng}@brewai.com

Abstract. AutoML tools provide an automation service for data scientists and software engineers to save time from data preprocessing and modeling building. Existing AutoML tools usually require users to have data science knowledge and programming skills to use the services, however, most non-expert and business users do not have such skills to use these AutoML tools. In addition, many AutoML tools require a special infrastructure or cloud provider. In this paper, we introduce BrewAI: a commercial-grade tool that provides an easy-to-use AutoML service for business users. The paper describes how the use of service-oriented computing design principles gives BrewAI flexibility, scalability and performance at a reasonable cost. The paper also describes a case study that shows how BrewAI enables business users to outperform more than three-quarters of Kaggle competitors in an NLP classification task.

Keywords: AutoML · Web application · ML pipeline · ML for business

1 Introduction

The application of Machine Learning (ML) techniques in industry presents many challenges. Although there are many libraries and technologies that provide ML functionalities "out of the box", many challenges remain such as deciding which technique works with which problem, transforming datasets into the right format expected by each software product, ensuring they are of sufficient quality, fine-tuning the ML parameters and validating the models. Once a model needs to be made operational, constructing complete "ML pipelines" that fit with an organisation's internal IT systems and that can be operated and maintained by non-specialised staff also presents many challenges. In addition, the performance of such ML pipelines is very sensitive to a number of design decisions, which constitutes a high entry barrier for new users.

The demand for simple solutions that work without the need to be operated by ML-experts has given rise to the field of automated machine learning (AutoML). The goal of AutoML is to make ML more systematic and efficient by automating several human-extensive activities. It enables domain scientists to apply ML without the need to understand and learn the underlying technologies in detail.

© ICST Institute for Computer Sciences, Social Informatics and Telecommunications Engineering 2022
Published by Springer Nature Switzerland AG 2022. All Rights Reserved
W. Hussain and M. A. Jan (Eds.): IoTaaS 2021, LNICST 421, pp. 198–207, 2022.
https://doi.org/10.1007/978-3-030-95987-6_14

Whilst the goal of scientific research is to create AutoML tools that aim for full automation, several companies are now developing their own AutoML systems that aim to offer some form of "semi-automation" in assisting organisations to deploy ML pipelines at lower costs. However, many existing solutions are still expensive or require expert staff to operate them. This paper presents an alternative solution called BrewAI which is designed for providing a care-free user experience and explainability combined with a scalable technological infrastructure at a modest cost.

The rest of the paper is structured as follows. Section 2 defines some basic AutoMl concepts. Section 3 describes BrewAI and Sect. 4 a case study of applying the system. Section 5 concludes this paper.

2 Background

AutoML refers to the automation of several activities related to ML such as experiment design, data collection, data cleanup, missing data imputation, feature selection, model discovery, model explanation, hyperparameter optimization (HPO), model monitoring and anomaly detection. A recent survey [1] describes the AutoML pipeline as consisting of several processes: data preparation, feature engineering, model generation, and model evaluation (see Fig. 1).

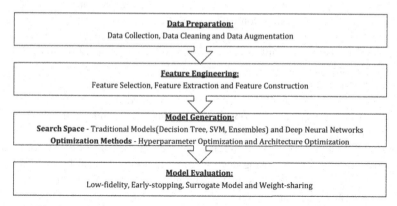

Fig. 1. An overview of AutoML pipeline (adapted from He et al. [1]).

There is a huge diversity in the tools available to support AutoML. Auto-WEKA [2] is one of the first AutoML systems based on the well-known WEKA machine learning toolkit. TPOT [3] automatically constructs and optimizes tree-based machine learning pipelines from a small set of fixed ML components that are connected in predefined ways. Auto-sklearn [4] is similar but adds several improvements such as meta-learning for warm starting the optimization and automatic ensembling. Inspired by Auto-sklearn, Auto-PyTorch [5] uses an ensembling method to implement an automated post-hoc ensemble model selection [6] for efficient optimization.

As mentioned earlier, several companies are now developing their own AutoML systems that aim to assist organisations to deploy ML pipelines with minimal effort and costs. Big tech companies are offering AutoML products such as Azure Machine Learning [7] and Amazon SageMaker Autopilot [8] and Google's AutoML [9]. Other offerings exist from other large companies such as SAS and IBM (Automated Artificial Intelligence or AutoAI[1]).

One of the problems with these solutions is that they are tied to a particular platform or cloud infrastructure or installed on a user's desktop. Some solutions are more specialised and can work in different environments. They include H2O Driverless AI [10, 11] which supports fully- or semi-automated feature engineering and selection, model tuning and training of predictive models and DataRobot[2] which has recently acquired Algorithmia.[3] Still, these solutions may be tied to specific infrastructures that bring high costs to SMEs and government organisations and may not be easy to deploy and operate by non-expert staff. In this paper, we investigate new opportunities for addressing these issues via alternative AutoML tools such as BrewAI.

3   Introduction to BrewAI

3.1   General overview

BrewAI[4] is designed to be a simple and cost-effective solution that delivers ML functionalities for organisations that don't have a specialised staff or alternatively used by specialized staff with the intention of reducing time to market with AI models. Like other AutoML systems, BrewAI simplifies the creation and deployment of ML models. Starting from just a simple spreadsheet, a user can train, build and deploy a commercial-grade ML model within an IT infrastructure with minimal efforts [12].

Its software architecture is based on service-oriented design principles in which autonomous software services can operate and communicate independently from each other. This architecture is illustrated in Fig. 2.

The BrewAI engine which is at the heart of the system is responsible for tackling supervised learning problems using deep learning methods. Driven by feature Importance, the business user has a say in fine-tuning, can deal with different data types including numerical, text, categorical and binary. New data types such as images will be released on the roadmap. The engine is built over several other systems. Its code base relies on the PyTorch library. Hyperparameter optimization is automatically conducted using Optuna [13] and HyperOpt [14]. Feature importance is developed utilising Optuna so a user can dynamically construct the search spaces for the hyperparameters.

BrewAI has the ability to aggregate data from different sources, each data source can be independently serviced by an API that can operate autonomously to encode and feed data into the model. All BrewAI software components are virtualised in containers using Kubernetes [15]. This allows them to be deployed on a scalable cloud platform (e.g.,

---

[1] https://dataplatform.cloud.ibm.com/docs/content/wsj/analyze-data/autoai-overview.html.

[2] https://www.datarobot.com/.

[3] https://algorithmia.com/.

[4] www.brewai.com.

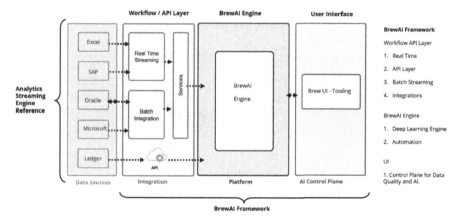

Fig. 2. Components of the BrewAI architecture (adapted from Rabhi et al. [12]).

Amazon's EC2). The use of an elastic cloud means the system can adapt to different data sizes and loads.

An important component is the BrewAI User Interface which displays results at different stages of the ML pipeline in a way that is easily comprehended by the user. The user can also direct the different stages like training via simple button clicks.

3.2 BrewAI Model Building Process

To use BrewAI, users should firstly log in to the web server and the software will automatically go through five stages to compute the prediction results from the AutoML model. Figure 3 illustrates the five stages in the BrewAI model building process. There is no restriction in the order to follow when performing these five stages, users can jump into any stage to check the previous actions in that specific stage [12].

Fig. 3. BrewAI's five stages for AutoML.

Stage 1 - Train. In this stage, users can upload the tabular data file to the BrewAI webpage through the interface. Figure 4 shows BrewAI's interfaces for training data upload (top) and model training submission (bottom). After clicking the "Load Data" button (see Fig. 4 Top), a dataset preview will be shown, users will then select the target column for prediction. The model will be built after clicking the "Submit Model" button (see Fig. 4 Bottom). BrewAI will automatically define the type of machine learning tasks (regression or classification), handle the data pre-processing, and build the AutoML model.

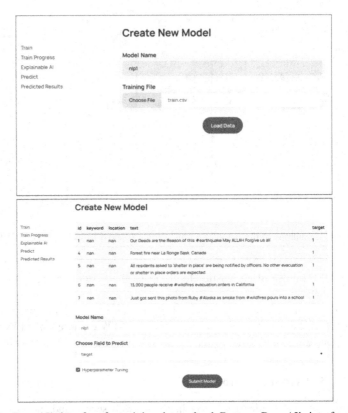

Fig. 4. Top: BrewAI's interface for training data upload. Bottom: BrewAI's interface for loaded dataset review and model training submission.

Stage 2 – Train Progress. Users can see the status of data processing and model building. No action is required from the users in this stage.

Stage 3 – Explainable AI. This stage is to show explainable details of the data and model after model training is completed. The explainable data shows the details of data quality and data type for each input feature. The explainable model shows the details of the class distribution, model performance, confusion matrix, performance by class, and feature importance. Figure 5 shows BrewAI's interface for data and model explanation.

BrewAI also provides intuitive visulization (see Fig. 6) for prediction results such as different charts for confusion matrix and feature importance.

Stage 4 – Predict (Model Inference). In this stage, users can select a specific model trained in stage 2 to predict the test dataset. All previously trained models will be saved in BrewAI's server for future inference, users are allowed to come back to this page anytime and select a trained model to do predictions for test datasets.

Model Explanation

Train
Train Progress
Explainable AI
Predict
Predicted Results

Summary

Model Name: NaturalLanguageProcessingwithDisasterTweets	Training Data: train.csv	Target Variable: target
Problem Type: classification	Accuracy: 80.18%	Submitted: 2021-09-20-15-41-40

1. Training Data Information

1.1. Basic Infomation

Number of rows: 7613	Number of columns: 5
Number of cells with inf/-inf values : 0	Number of cells with Null values : 2595

1.2. Data Quality

Issue	Count	Action
Empty Columns	0	N/A
Rows with empty target variable values	0	N/A
Duplicate Rows	0	N/A

1.3. Column Type Deduction

Column Name	Data Type	Sub Type	Empty Values
id	Numeric	Int	0 / 0.00%
keyword	Categorical	Category	61 / 0.80%
location	Text	Short Text	2534 / 33.30%
text	Text	Rich Text	0 / 0.00%
target	Categorical	Binary Category	0 / 0.00%

Fig. 5. BrewAI's interface for data and model explanation.

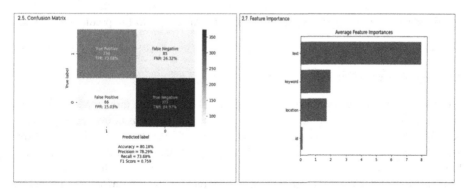

Fig. 6. Left: interface for confusion matrix. Right: interface for feature importance.

Stage 5 – Predicted Results. After finishing the prediction in stage 4, users can explore the prediction results in this stage. BrewAI also allows users to preview and download previously predicted results to csv files by clicking buttons (see Fig. 7).

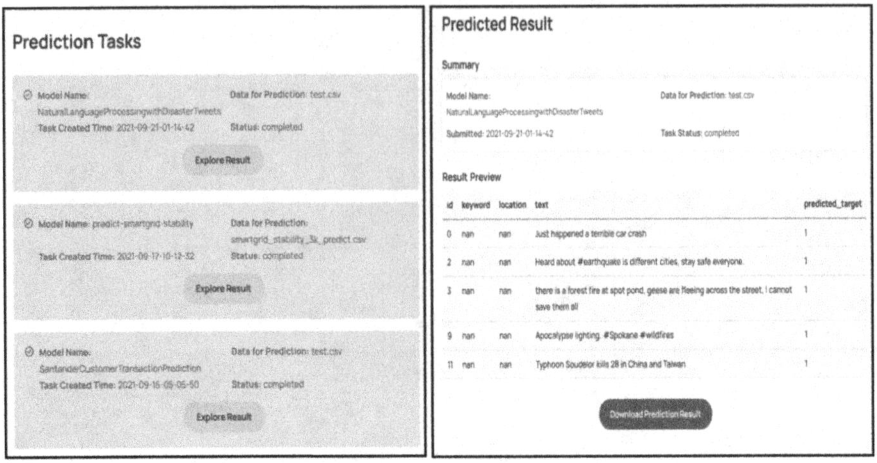

Fig. 7. Left: interface for result exploration. Right: interface for result preview and download.

4 Case Study of Using BrewAI

In this case study, we went through the model-building process in the BrewAI web application and applied the BrewAI service to a selected dataset from the Kaggle competition [16]. The purpose of this case study is to show how BrewAI enables non-expert and business users to apply the machine learning model to do the prediction through AutoML.

4.1 Experimental Setting

Kaggle competitions include various types of machine learning tasks made by Kaggle or other companies like Google and Microsoft. The competitions allow people to compete for machine learning predictions based on the given datasets. In our case study, we selected the dataset from the "Natural Language Processing with Disaster Tweets" Kaggle competition for the experiment. This dataset is a csv file which consists of a table of 4 columns (features) and 7613 rows (samples) in the training dataset including integers, strings, and random empty values. The competition task is to classify whether a given tweet is about a real disaster or not for the test dataset with 3263 samples.

Solving such a natural-language-processing (NLP) problem requires advanced data-preprocessing and model-building techniques. The input features of this dataset are mixed with a column of integers, a column of a single word, a column of short text, and a column of long text, some features include a small number of empty values and the prediction target is a column of Boolean type data. Without AutoML, data scientists usually apply multiple data pre-processing strategies for this kind of machine learning task, such as normalization, one-hot encoding, lemmatization, tokenization, word embedding, etc. Also, designing good a NLP model requires advanced machine learning knowledge. Unfortunately, business analysts or non-expert users usually do not have such skills for NLP machine learning tasks. In this case study, we want to demonstrate how BrewAI enables business users to apply machine learning models to solve NLP classification tasks.

We simply uploaded the training dataset (the csv file) to the BrewAI webpage and then went through the five stages mentioned earlier. The predicted result for the test dataset was downloaded from another BrewAI server and then submitted to the Kaggle "leaderboard" for comparison among other competitors. The Kaggle system shows that our BrewAI model achieved an F1 score of 0.80937 and ranked 295 out of 1241 competitors (tested on Sep23 2021). This means without any effort in environment setup, data pre-processing and model building, our BrewAI AutoML model beat more than three quarters (76.2%) of Kaggle competitors in this NLP classification task.

4.2 Evaluation

The evaluation is based on the usability, data/model explainability, and performance for non-expert and business users.

- For the usability aspect, BrewAI does not require any data pre-processing and modeling skills to apply machine learning models. The interface consists of only dropdown selection controls and confirm buttons which are easy enough for anyone with a basic level of computer proficiency to use. The model building processing is fully automatic without worrying about parameter settings. The only requirement for using BrewAI is users need to understand which is the target they want the AutoML model to learn. Although BrewAI only works with tabular/structural data and does not work with non-tabular data, users can still transform any form of data into a tabular format for classification and regression tasks.
- For the model explainability aspect, BrewAI can show necessary details about the data and model that business users can understand. The users can have a summary of their datasets without any programming skills or manual data analysis. There has no explanation about the model parameters or model generation process in BrewAI. Nevertheless, most business users only focus on the data and results such as data quality, performance, and feature importance that BrewAI can provide.
- For the model performance aspect, although the result did not shine in this Kaggle competition, non-expert users with the BrewAI model still beat more than three quarters (>900) of competitors and ranked top 25% with simple button clicks, and with no data pre-processing and model building efforts.

5 Conclusions and Future Work

Recent years have witnessed the rise in using AutoML tools in industry as they provide automation facilities for data preprocessing and modeling building tasks associated with the use of machine learning methods. Despite the availability of a wide range of tools and the promise of costs savings, these advantages have not necessarily materialised in practice as there are hidden staff and infrastructure costs associated with many solutions.

Some AutoML tools such as H2O and Auto-Pytorch require users to have programming skills for setting up the python environment, which business users usually do not have. On the other hand, paid AutoML services by big technology companies such as Google AutoML and AWS SageMaker have better usability than open-source products, but they are usually bundled with other related cloud services and that could cost more than just an AutoML service. These cloud services also require tedious cloud-platform setup by cloud engineers before enabling AutoML services.

Owing to its architectural design based on service-oriented principles, BrewAI can be deployed and configured in different ways and thus able to satisfy different needs, including a low-cost solution for Small and Medium Enterprises (SMEs). It does not have a huge panoply of ML techniques, focusing on regression and classification using deep learning techniques. This is because it is primarily targeting business users with a good understanding of the data but without programming skills and advanced data science knowledge, such as business analysts.

Research work that facilitates the application of AutoML tools in industry is expected to intensify in the near future addressing many remaining challenges. Amongst them, BrewAI is expected to deal with those that contribute to enhancing the user experience and the quality of the underlying software services:

- **Inclusion of business objectives**: non-technical users usually want business insights from the machine learning model instead of accuracy and training time that most technical users are concerned about.
- **Need for transparency**: non-technical users do not understand the black-box nature of deep learning. Current explainable AI is still lacking the capability to explain business decision-making.
- **Data quality**: most progress has been done on the model building side, the bottleneck in many AutoML tools is on the data side to ensure high data quality during the acquisition.
- **Performance**: to achieve good performance and avoid input pipeline stalls, businesses need more control over how to achieve the best balance between accuracy and cost considerations (making optimum use of resources available).
- **Data security**: provide data protection or encryption solutions for data uploading and result downloading.
- **Cost-effectiveness**: optimize the utilization of cloud resources and provide more flexible usage plans for the users.

References

1. He, X., Zhao, K., Chu, X.: AutoML: a survey of the state-of-the-art. knowledge-based systems. **212** (2021). https://doi.org/10.1016/j.knosys.2020.106622
2. Kotthoff, L., Thornton, C., Hoos, H.H., Hutter, F., Leyton-Brown, K.: Auto-WEKA: automatic model selection and hyperparameter optimization in WEKA. In: Hutter, F., Kotthoff, L., Vanschoren, J. (eds.) Automated Machine Learning: Methods, Systems, Challenges, pp. 81–95. Springer, Cham (2019). https://doi.org/10.1007/978-3-030-05318-5_4
3. Olson, R.S., Moore, J.H.: TPOT: a tree-based pipeline optimization tool for automating machine learning. In: Hutter, F., Kotthoff, L., Vanschoren, J. (eds.) Automated Machine Learning: Methods, Systems, Challenges, pp. 151–160. Springer, Cham (2019). https://doi. org/10.1007/978-3-030-05318-5_8.

4. Feurer, M., Klein, A., Eggensperger, K., Springenberg, .J.T., Blum, M., Hutter, F.: Auto-sklearn: efficient and robust automated machine learning. In: Hutter, F., Kotthoff, L., Vanschoren, J. (eds.) Automated Machine Learning: Methods, Systems, Challenges, pp. 113–134. Springer, Cham (2019). https://doi.org/10.1007/978-3-030-05318-5_6
5. Zimmer, L., Lindauer, M., Hutter, F.: Auto-pytorch: multi-fidelity MetaLearning for efficient and robust AutoDL. IEEE Trans. Pattern Anal. Mach. Intell. **43**, 3079–3090 (2021). https://doi.org/10.1109/TPAMI.2021.3067763
6. Caruana, R., Niculescu-Mizil, A., Crew, G., Ksikes, A.: Ensemble selection from libraries of models (2004)
7. Barga, R.: Predictive Analytics with Microsoft Azure Machine Learning. Apress, Berkeley (2015)
8. Das, P., et al.: Amazon sagemaker autopilot: a white box AutoML solution at scale. In: Proceedings of the 4th Workshop on Data Management for End-To-End Machine Learning, DEEM 2020 - In conjunction with the 2020 ACM SIGMOD/PODS Conference. Association for Computing Machinery, Inc (2020). https://doi.org/10.1145/3399579.3399870.
9. Wong, C., Houlsby, N., Lu, Y., Gesmundo, A.: Transfer Learning with Neural AutoML. (2018)
10. H2O.ai | AI Cloud Platform, https://www.h2o.ai/. Accessed 22 Sep 2021
11. Cook, D.: Practical Machine Learning with H2O. O'Reilly Media, Newton (2016)
12. Rabhi, F., Ng, A., Mehandjiev, N.: AutoML applications in business: a case study using BrewAI. FinanceIT@UNSW Research Group Internal report, Sydney (2021)
13. Akiba, T., Sano, S., Yanase, T., Ohta, T., Koyama, M.: Optuna: a next-generation hyperparameter optimization framework. In: Proceedings of the ACM SIGKDD International Conference on Knowledge Discovery and Data Mining, pp. 2623–2631. Association for Computing Machinery (2019). https://doi.org/10.1145/3292500.3330701
14. Bergstra, J., Komer, B., Eliasmith, C., Yamins, D., Cox, D.D.: Hyperopt: a python library for model selection and hyperparameter optimization. Comput. Sci. Discov. **8**, 14008 (2015)
15. Kubernetes. https://kubernetes.io/. Accessed 22 Sep 2021
16. Kaggle: Your Machine Learning and Data Science Community https://www.kaggle.com/. Accessed 23 Sep 2021

A Novel Dual Prediction Scheme for Data Communication Reduction in IoT-Based Monitoring Systems

Ahmed Fathalla[1], Ahmad Salah[2], Mohamed Ali Mohamed[3], Nur Indah Lestari[4], and Mahmoud Bekhit[1,5(✉)]

[1] Department of Mathematics, Faculty of Science, Suez Canal University, Ismailia 41522, Egypt
{fathalla_sci,mahmoud_bakhit}@science.suez.edu.eg
[2] Faculty of Computers and Informatics, Zagaizg University, Zagazig 44519, Egypt
ahmad@zu.edu.eg
[3] 2P Perfect Presentation, Riyadh 105523, Saudi Arabia
[4] 2 Messiter Street, Campsie, NSW 2194, Australia
[5] School of Electrical and Data Engineering, University of Technology Sydney, Sydney 2007, Australia

Abstract. Internet of things (IoT) based monitoring systems became commonplace. These systems are built upon a large number of devices and sensors. The data collection task of a large number of sensors and devices in an IoT system includes a massive number of data communications. The more the number of devices, the critical is the network bottleneck. In this context, the dual prediction scheme was proposed as a solution for mitigating the large size of communication volumes. The dual prediction scheme consists of a model for predicting future measurements based on historical data. This model is duplicated on both sides, the edge side (i.e., sensor) and the data collection device (i.e., cluster head). The literature includes several works which proposed many dual prediction schemes based on several techniques such as filters and moving average. The literature does not include utilizing the ensemble learning models. This motivates this work to investigate the gradient boosting regression model's performance compared to the existing solutions. The proposed and state-of-the-art models are evaluated on a realistic dataset. The obtained results show that the proposed model outperforms the existing dual prediction schemes in terms of communication reduction.

Keywords: Dual prediction scheme · Gradient boosting · IoT · Monitoring system · Regression

1 Introduction

The Internet of Things (IoT) is a term used to enable the interconnection and communication of various network-enabled devices (e.g., things) that generate

W. Hussain and M. A. Jan (Eds.): IoTaaS 2021, LNICST 421, pp. 208–220, 2022.
https://doi.org/10.1007/978-3-030-95987-6_15

and share data about their surroundings through a network [10, 24]. The IoT network is frequently comprised of many sensing devices (*i.e.*, nodes) that are deployed and dispersed across a vast geographical region [13].

Wireless Sensor Networks (WSNs) enable the creation of a diverse variety of possible IoT applications, such as environmental monitoring (e.g., smoke, humidity, temperature, and gas). Sensor devices in the IoT networks capture massive amounts of real-world observation and measurement data. Continuous data transfer between end devices (nodes) results in a massive communication overhead over networks. As a result, the overall energy consumption of IoT applications increases significantly. Reduced data transmission between IoT devices decreases significantly energy consumption and extends the network's lifetime, particularly in battery-powered nodes/networks [4]. Additionally, when identifying a target of interest inside a monitoring surveillance region, it is important to reduce the number of transmissions between sensors and the Fusion Center (FC) in order to maximize network bandwidth efficiency [5]. In such techniques, the FC makes a global determination about the target based on the sensor-transmitted local determination of the target's presence/absence [4].

Data transmission is a significant source of high communication procedures and energy consumption in IoT networks. Additionally, data transmission between end devices utilizes energy than data sensing [12, 14, 15, 22]. In general, network longevity and dependability are critical criteria for many IoT monitoring application scenarios and ensuring that the cloud's resources are utilized to their full potential [19].

While these techniques can considerably reduce transmissions, they suffer from performance degradation to increase the accuracy, necessitating the constant updating of prediction models to include fine-grained changes [22]. Dual prediction techniques [3, 23, 29] have been developed to overcome this issue. In dual prediction schemes, the prediction model are deployed at the end point nodes. That is, the same prediction model with the same parameters are running on the sensing device and the other device (*e.g.*, cluster head) so that both devices are predicting the same values using historical data of previous data obtained from sensor nodes. Sensor nodes choose whether or not to broadcast their observations to a central server based on the discrepancy between the predicted and real values (e.g., a gateway or a base station).

Dual prediction reduces the number of data transfers between the sensor and the sink nodes to the possible minor level, requiring sensor nodes to communicate just a subset of their felt values without compromising the accuracy of the actual measurement results [8].

Several present research focuses on dual prediction models as proposed in [6, 25, 26]. Optimizing the communication route between sensors is critical for IoT networks to consume fewer energy [26]. To this aim, IoT networks are shifting their focus to creating local techniques for data transmission reduction and delay avoidance. Numerous publications, such as [4, 6, 22], used data reduction methods to data gathered by sensor nodes in order to reduce data transmission in sensor networks [25]. Data reduction is frequently accomplished by using predictive models that attempt to anticipate the present measured values of sensor nodes based on the data they have already provided to a Base Station (BS) or a Cluster Head (CH). In this scenario, measurements that may be anticipated are omitted based on specific criteria such as accuracy, resulting in less data transfer between nodes and a central server.

The same scenario applies between sensor nodes and CH; in principle, it is determined by the network topology or its architecture. Interested readers may study the influence of data prediction systems on the decrease of WSN transmissions by consulting Dias et al. [8]. Kalman filters are used by Jain et al. [20] to build a dual prediction method that anticipates future sensor data. As an alternative to pre-existing information about sensor data approaches, Kalman filters depend on a priori assumptions about statistical data characteristics (e.g., data distribution).

To the best of the authors' knowledge, evaluation of ensemble learning models and their performance are not investigated yet. In this context, we proposed the first ensemble learning model to be utilized in dual prediction schemes for communication reduction. We framed the problem of sensors measurement prediction as a time series problem. The historical measurements are used to train the proposed model, and then the proposed gradient boost model is used to predict the future sensors' measurements. The main contributions of this paper can be summarized as follows.

- To our knowledge, we proposed the first dual prediction scheme based on an ensemble learning model.
- We evaluated the performance of the proposed scheme on a real-life dataset. The results outlined that the proposed scheme outperformed the existing methods.

The rest of this paper is organized as follows. Section 2 discusses the related work of dual prediction schemes in the field of IoT. In Sect. 3, the proposed system is exposed. The evaluation and expire mental results of the proposed model are discussed in Sect. 4. Finally, the paper is concluded in Sect. 5.

2   Related Work

In this section, we discuss the existing methods for communication reduction in IoT systems. These utilized methods can be classified based on the prediction approach, such as adaptive filter and deep learning. Besides, the data reduction task can be achieved by combining an additional task, e.g., data compression.

An architecture that combined both edge computing and online learning was proposed to predict the future data for IoT search accurately. This architecture was used to reduce the communication time between the layers of IoT search architecture. Besides, minimize the continuous data queries and the upload operations done by the massively distributed sensors. To selectively report genuine data, edge computing was done at the edge sensors to determine the overall transmission value of all data in the reporting cycle. The cloud layer was primarily in charge of collecting the characteristics of reported data and adapting the related prediction model in real-time [28].

In [16], a cost-aware dual prediction scheme model (CA-DPS) was presented to cut down on data transmission between IoT sensor nodes and the fusion center. The suggested CA-DPS technique selects the strategy that delivers the lowest projected transmission cost from various options within a certain prediction horizon. The future transmission cost was calculated by bootstrapping the model residuals associated with each approach. The suggested technique yields a substantial decrease in the communication required for a given error restriction, according to simulation findings using both synthetic and actual measurement data.

IoT applications consume a high amount of energy because huge data are collected, measured, and transmitted. To reduce the giant consumption of energy and extra load on communication, an adaptive method for data reduction (AM-DR) was presented. The AM-DR approach used a convex combination of two decoupled Least-Mean-Square (LMS) windowed filters with different sizes to predict the next measured values at the source and CHs. Hence, sensor nodes only have to transmit their instant sensed values that differ significantly from the predicted values based on a pre-defined threshold [12].

As machine learning methods are successful utilized in different problem [1, 2,9,11,17,18], the authors of [21] employed both approaches as part of a two-tier data reduction architecture. The DP method was used to minimize traffic between CHs and sink nodes, whereas the DC scheme was used to reduce traffic between cluster nodes and CHs. NNs, LSTMs, and OSSLMS machine learning algorithms were used for the DP approach. Many DC techniques were used, such as PCA, T-SVD, and NMF. For both DP and DC schemes, efficient methods were constructed and compared in transmission reduction and accuracy. The ultimate goal of this work is to conserve energy and bandwidth. Dual Prediction (DP) and Data Compression (DC) techniques are employed to reduce the transmission burden across WSNs.

A self-managing WSN architecture was proposed to aid sensor network optimization at the application layer, combining cloud computing, data analysis, and sensor networks. Additional processing should be avoided since sensor nodes have limited resources. Using the Reinforcement Learning (RL) technique QLearning, in reaction to changes in the environment, a new approach was devised to alter the sample intervals of the sensor nodes. It allowed for the optimization of WSNs by calculating the prediction methods (single or dual) and cloud service requirements for the applications. Business models might now focus on sensor data due to the suggested self-managing architecture [7].

For WSNs, a two-stage dual prediction data reduction method was developed. The initial stage was data reduction, which attempted to reduce the number of transfers between the sensor and sink nodes. If the gathered data is redundant, predictable, or incorrect, it will be deleted for transmission. To ensure data dependability, incorrect data at the sensor nodes is deleted and replaced with predicted values at the sink node. The Kalman Filter prediction algorithm was used at the sink node to forecast non-transmitted data from end nodes in the second stage [27].

This discussion outlined that there are several methods proposed for communication reduction using dual prediction schemes. While there are several machine learning models utilized in dual prediction schemes, but to our knowledge, none of these methods utilized the ensemble learning predictive models.

3   The Proposed System

In a Dual Prediction Scheme (DPS), sensing devices/nodes send environmental monitoring data collected to the Gateways (GWs) during an initiation phase in order to pick a prediction model [22]. The GW and sensor nodes may pick their own prediction models; on the other hand, sensing nodes may choose their own prediction method and send the predictive model's parameters values to the GW; or, alternatively, the GW may grant the decision to select the prediction method for the group of sensors. Making a decision regarding which prediction model to use can be made at run-time, and it is not essential to commit to a strategy for the whole lifespan of the WSN.

Sensor nodes can take advantage of their closeness to the data source after selecting (and distributing) the prediction models. When it comes to transmitting actual measurements, they can only do so if their forecasts are incorrect. Sensor nodes and GW may start a new initialization phase and pick new prediction models if the accuracy of predictions is compromised from time to time.

The proposed dual prediction scheme is composed of successive phases where phases' transitions are based on a predefined parameters which represents the number of miss-predicted observations. By the end of each phase, the model parameters are updated to fit final data pattern to start a new phase. Then, the updated model parameters are sent to the sensor node to resume the prediction task.

Before any prediction model is adopted, the startup step guarantees that the GW has comprehensive environmental knowledge. As a result, following this phase, the GW may use the same prediction models as the sensor nodes without transmitting anything new. The sensor nodes' and GW's activities are depicted in Fig. 1. Different prediction methods can be selected frequently depending on the information that is concurrently accessible to sensor nodes and the GW. As a disadvantage, the diversity of prediction models is limited by the sensor nodes' memory and processing capacity constraints. The Least Mean Squares (LMS) technique has produced accurate predictions in simulations in which sensor nodes and GW created their prediction models separately [22,25]. For instance, in one situation, just 10% of the data would be required to monitor room temperature correctly [22].

In the proposed dual prediction scheme, we proposed using a gradient boosting on decision trees (i.e., Catboost[1]) as the predictive model. The

---

[1] https://catboost.ai/.

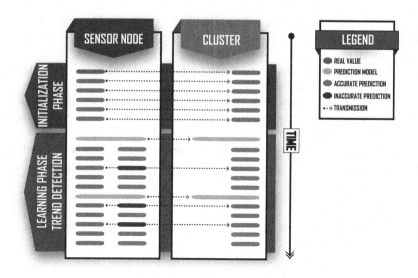

Fig. 1. The proposed dual prediction scheme.

ensemble learning model trains on the historical sensor measurements, and then the trained model is used to predict future measurements. We proposed training the catboost system on lagged data. The lag value in the proposed model is tunable. Thus, the best value can be determined based on the nature of the data patterns. Besides, the update mechanism of the proposed dual prediction scheme depends on the number of predicted measurements. In other words, the user of the proposed scheme can decide when the predictive model is updated/retrained after a tunable number of mispredicted values.

4 Results and Discussion

4.1 Dataset

The dataset is publicly available online[2]. The data are collected from three sensing devices. The collected data are measurements for carbon monoxide (CO), humidity, liquid petroleum gas (LPG), smoke, and temperature. We examined the proposed method performance using $10,000$ observations of the smoke values as representative for the other features. In other words, the data transmission reduction rates for the smoke values should be the same for the other features.

4.2 Setup

All the experiments framework are developed in the Python Programming language. We compared the proposed system against two well-known state-of-the-art methods, namely LMS [22], and AM-DR [12]. We used a lag value equal to

---

[2] https://www.kaggle.com/garystafford/environmental-sensor-data-132k.

three for all methods of comparison. Besides, we set the filter weights for the LMS as the default reported values, and we used the weight of 4 and 8 for the AM-DR method.

Experiments are conducted using three IoT sensing devices to evaluate the proposed model performance when data from different devices are used. The proposed approach and the comparative methods of comparison are evaluated in terms of transmission reduction percentage of the environmental data when different error-thresholds are used, the number of experiment's phases, and the number of miss-predictions. Data reduction percentage metric is defined in the base of Eq. 1.

$$data\_reduction\_ratio = \frac{NT}{S} \times 100 \tag{1}$$

where NT denotes the not transmitted observations (miss-predictions) count, and S is the total number of sensed observation.

4.3   Experimental Results

The first experiment examines the data reduction percentages when various error-threshold values are employed. For that purpose, we tested a wide range of error-threshold for three different sensors (i.e., sensing devices), as shown in Fig. 2. The Figure depicts the data reduction percentages for forecasting smoking values. In this experiment, the model is trained using 1, 000 observations and is tested using 10, 000 observations. Obviously, the higher the tolerance (i.e., threshold value), the higher the obtained data reduction rates. The proposed predictive model achieved the highest reduction rates compared to the other comparison methods for the three devices. Figure 2 clarifies that the proposed scheme has a significant performance gap compared to the LMS methods. On the other hand, the performance gap between the proposed and AM-DR methods varies for the different utilized devices. However, the overall performance of the proposed method outperformed the AM-DR method.

The second part of the results is about the performance of the proposed predictive model under different parameter values. We studied the effect of selecting a different number of mispredicted measurements on the data reduction and the number of model updates (i.e., phases) in Fig. 3. In Fig. 3(a), when the predictive model is updated after one mispredicted value, the data reduction was about 94.4%. Similarly, when the experiment was run with updating the predictive model after each five mispredicted values, the data reduction rate increased to almost 95%. Then, the data reduction rate decreased kept fluctuating as the number of mispredictions to update the model parameter increased. Thus, there is no clear relationship to decide the optimal number of mispredicted values to update the model. The user should examine this value to pick the optimal value based on the nature of the data at hand. In Fig. 3(b), the relationship between the number of times the model needed to be updated (i.e., phases), the y-axis, in correspondence to the number of mispredicted values needed to update the model, the x-axis. It is clear from Fig. 3 that the higher is the allowed number

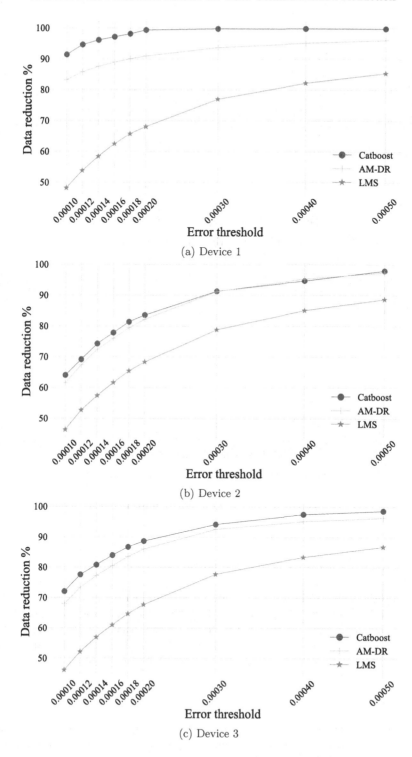

Fig. 2. Comparison of the proposed method, AR-DR, and LMS filters on data reduction rates.

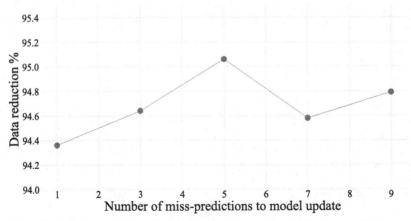

(a) Number of mispredictions for updating the model vs. the data reduction rate

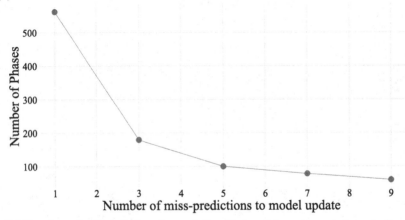

(b) Number of misprediction for updating the model vs. the number of phases

Fig. 3. The effect of different number of misprediction for updating the model on the performance.

of mispredicted values, the less is the number of required times to update the model.

In addition, we validated the accuracy of the model under different volumes of the training dataset in Fig. 4. In Fig. 4(a), the data reduction increases as the training data increases; This is linked to the model accuracy. The more is the data; the better is the model accuracy. Similarly, in Fig. 4(b), the number of mispredicted readings decreases as the training data increases.

4.4   Limitations

The proposed scheme has certain restrictions and underlying assumptions that must be considered. As a starting point, we present the scheme's assumptions.

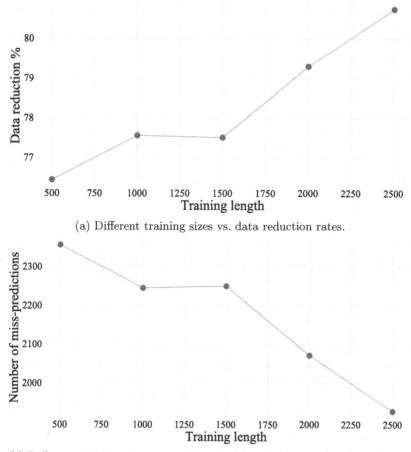

(a) Different training sizes vs. data reduction rates.

(b) Different training sizes vs. number of mispredictions for model updating.

Fig. 4. The effect of training size on the model accuracy.

Fog and edge computing architectures are suggested as WSN devices have limited processing power and energy. For that purpose, We take into account an IoT system in which data is exchanged between a cluster head and a sensing node. Generally, the proposed scheme considers similar situations where communication takes place between two end nodes communicating together with such comparable fog or edge computing architectures. One of the main limitations is that we suggest that the cluster head endpoint has an active and direct connection to a powerful and battery-powered device (i.e., fog device) to process the data and develop the required machine learning model. Meanwhile, the other endpoint has a the ability to process data, or is connected to an external edge device (e.g., Raspberry Pi).

The second limitation is that with the assumptions mentioned above are met, the training and updating procedures of the model might resume for few seconds.

Thus, that may result in a few or ten/hundred missed observations for specific time windows. Another issue is that the machine learning model must be sent from the fog device to the edge device, which takes kilobytes of data to simulate the energy use during this procedure.

5   Conclusion

The communication volumes in IoT-based monitoring systems are massive. One possible solution for this bottleneck in these monitoring systems is the dual prediction scheme. In this scheme, the sensors and CH predict the sensor's future measurements using the same predictive model. Only miss-predicted measurements are transferred from the sensing device to the CH if the difference between the real and predicted measurements is higher than a predefined threshold. In this vein, we proposed an ensemble learning model (i.e., gradient boost) as the predictive model in this scheme. The proposed predictive model performance is evaluated against state-of-the-art methods on a real-life environmental data of various attributes. The proposed model achieved a communication reduction reached 99%, which outperformed the existing methods.

References

1. Alameer, Z., Fathalla, A., Li, K., Ye, H., Jianhua, Z.: Multistep-ahead forecasting of coal prices using a hybrid deep learning model. Resour. Policy **65**, 101588 (2020)
2. Ali, A., Fathalla, A., Salah, A., Bekhit, M., Eldesouky, E.: Marine data prediction: an evaluation of machine learning, deep learning, and statistical predictive models. Comput. Intell. Neurosci. **2021** (2021)
3. Almalki, F.A., Ben Othman, S., Almalki, F.A., Sakli, H.: EERP-DPM: energy efficient routing protocol using dual prediction model for healthcare using IoT. J. Healthcare Eng. **2021** (2021)
4. Babcock, B., Olston, C.: Distributed top-K monitoring. In: Proceedings of the 2003 ACM SIGMOD International Conference on Management of Data, pp. 28–39 (2003)
5. Ciuonzo, D., Rossi, P.S.: Quantizer design for generalized locally optimum detectors in wireless sensor networks. IEEE Wireless Commun. Lett. **7**(2), 162–165 (2017)
6. Deshpande, A., Guestrin, C., Madden, S.R., Hellerstein, J.M., Hong, W.: Model-driven data acquisition in sensor networks. In: Proceedings of the Thirtieth International Conference on Very Large Data Bases, vol. 30, pp. 588–599 (2004)
7. Dias, G.M., Bellalta, B., Oechsner, S.: Using data prediction techniques to reduce data transmissions in the IoT. In: 2016 IEEE 3rd World Forum on Internet of Things (WF-IoT), pp. 331–335. IEEE (2016)
8. Dias, G.M., Bellalta, B., Oechsner, S.: The impact of dual prediction schemes on the reduction of the number of transmissions in sensor networks. Comput. Commun. **112**, 58–72 (2017)
9. Eldesouky, E., Bekhit, M., Fathalla, A., Salah, A., Ali, A.: A robust UWSN handover prediction system using ensemble learning. Sensors **21**(17), 5777 (2021)

10. Fathalla, A., Li, K., Salah, A., Mohamed, M.F.: An LSTM-based distributed scheme for data transmission reduction of IoT systems. Neurocomputing **485**, 166–180 (2021)
11. Fathalla, A., Salah, A., Li, K., Li, K., Francesco, P.: Deep end-to-end learning for price prediction of second-hand items. Knowl. Inf. Syst. **62**(12), 4541–4568 (2020). https://doi.org/10.1007/s10115-020-01495-8
12. Fathy, Y., Barnaghi, P., Tafazolli, R.: An adaptive method for data reduction in the internet of things. In: 2018 IEEE 4th World Forum on Internet of things (WF-IoT), pp. 729–735. IEEE (2018)
13. Fathy, Y., Barnaghi, P., Tafazolli, R.: Large-scale indexing, discovery, and ranking for the internet of things (IoT). ACM Comput. Surv. (CSUR) **51**(2), 1–53 (2018)
14. Gamal, M., Abolhasan, M., Lipman, J., Liu, R.P., Ni, W.: Multi objective resource optimisation for network function virtualisation requests. In: 2018 26th International Conference on Systems Engineering (ICSEng), pp. 1–7. IEEE (2018)
15. Gamal, M., Morsy, E., Fathy, A.: Multi-objective transmitters placement problem in wireless networks. In: Proceedings of the Sixth International Symposium on Information and Communication Technology, pp. 156–162 (2015)
16. Håkansson, V.W., Venkategowda, N.K., Kraemer, F.A., Werner, S.: Cost-aware dual prediction scheme for reducing transmissions at IoT sensor nodes. In: 2019 27th European Signal Processing Conference (EUSIPCO), pp. 1–5. IEEE (2019)
17. Hussain, W., Hussain, F.K., Saberi, M., Hussain, O.K., Chang, E.: Comparing time series with machine learning-based prediction approaches for violation management in cloud SLAS. Futur. Gener. Comput. Syst. **89**, 464–477 (2018)
18. Hussain, W., Merigó, J.M., Raza, M.R.: Predictive intelligence using ANFIS-induced OWAWA for complex stock market prediction. Int. J. Intell. Syst. (2021)
19. Hussain, W., Merigo, J.M., Gao, H., Alkalbani, A.M., Rabhi, F.A.: Integrated AHP-IOWA, POWA framework for ideal cloud provider selection and optimum resource management. IEEE Trans. Serv. Comput. (2021)
20. Jain, A., Chang, E.Y., Wang, Y.F.: Adaptive stream resource management using Kalman filters. In: Proceedings of the 2004 ACM SIGMOD International Conference on Management of Data, pp. 11–22 (2004)
21. Jarwan, A., Sabbah, A., Ibnkahla, M.: Data transmission reduction schemes in WSNs for efficient IoT systems. IEEE J. Sel. Areas Commun. **37**(6), 1307–1324 (2019)
22. Santini, S., Romer, K.: An adaptive strategy for quality-based data reduction in wireless sensor networks. In: Proceedings of the 3rd International Conference on Networked Sensing Systems (INSS 2006), pp. 29–36. TRF, Chicago (2006)
23. Shu, T., Chen, J., Bhargava, V.K., de Silva, C.W.: An energy-efficient dual prediction scheme using LMS filter and LSTM in wireless sensor networks for environment monitoring. IEEE Internet Things J. **6**(4), 6736–6747 (2019)
24. Sohaib, O., Lu, H., Hussain, W.: Internet of things (IoT) in e-commerce: for people with disabilities. In: 2017 12th IEEE Conference on Industrial Electronics and Applications (ICIEA), pp. 419–423. IEEE (2017)
25. Stojkoska, B., Solev, D., Davcev, D.: Data prediction in WSN using variable step size LMS algorithm. In: Proceedings of the 5th International Conference on Sensor Technologies and Applications, pp. 191–196. Citeseer (2011)
26. Stojkoska, B.L.R., Trivodaliev, K.V.: A review of internet of things for smart home: challenges and solutions. J. Clean. Prod. **140**, 1454–1464 (2017)
27. Wang, H., Yemeni, Z., Ismael, W.M., Hawbani, A., Alsamhi, S.H.: A reliable and energy efficient dual prediction data reduction approach to WSNs based on Kalman filter. IET Commun. **15**, 2285–2299 (2021)

28. Wu, F., Chen, Y., Chen, X., Fan, W., Liu, Y.: An adaptive dual prediction scheme based on edge intelligence. IEEE Internet Things J. **7**(10), 9481–9493 (2020)
29. Yu, T., Wang, X., Shami, A.: A novel fog computing enabled temporal data reduction scheme in IoT systems. In: GLOBECOM 2017–2017 IEEE Global Communications Conference, pp. 1–5. IEEE (2017)

Review-Based Recommender System for Hedonic and Utilitarian Products in IoT Framework

Anum Tahira[1], Walayat Hussain[1,2](✉) (iD), and Arif Ali[3]

[1] School of Computer Science, Faculty of Engineering and IT,
University of Technology Sydney, Ultimo 2007, Australia
anum.tahira@student.uts.edu.au, walayat.hussain@uts.edu.au,
walayat.hussain@vu.edu.au
[2] Victoria University Business School, Victoria University, Melbourne 3000, Australia
[3] Wellington Institute of Technology, Wellington, New Zealand
Arif.ali@weltec.ac.nz

Abstract. With the tremendous increase in product alternatives these days, many businesses rely heavily on recommender systems to limit the number of options they display to their customers on the front end. Many companies use the collaborative filtering algorithm and provide suggestions based on other consumers' choices, like the active user. However, this approach faces a cold start problem and is not suitable for one-time transactions. Thus, this research aims to create a recommender system that uses online customer reviews in the IoT framework to match the attributes of a product important to the shopper. The algorithm makes recommendations by first identifying the product's features essential to a customer. It then performs aspect-based sentiment analysis to identify those features in customer reviews and give them a sentiment score. Each customer review is weighted based on its creditably. As the impact of the recommender systems varies with the product type, an experimental study will be carried out to study the effect of the proposed algorithm differs with hedonic and utilitarian products.

Keywords: Aspect-based sentiment analysis · Recommender systems · Product reviews · Review characteristics · Hedonic product · Utilitarian product

1 Introduction

Due to the current COVID-19 pandemic, lockdown and social distancing laws have pushed a substantial portion of economic activity online. A report by Australian Post showed that in the year 2020, online sales increased up to 57%, with 1.36 million Australians purchasing online for the first time. The emergence of eCommerce as a primary mode of shopping has increased consumers' dependence on product reviews to supplement their knowledge of the product or service being sold (Gao et al. 2022). Several studies have confirmed the importance of customer review on the purchase intention (Jalilvand and Samiei 2012).

© ICST Institute for Computer Sciences, Social Informatics and Telecommunications Engineering 2022
Published by Springer Nature Switzerland AG 2022. All Rights Reserved
W. Hussain and M. A. Jan (Eds.): IoTaaS 2021, LNICST 421, pp. 221–232, 2022.
https://doi.org/10.1007/978-3-030-95987-6_16

These reviews are often in an unstructured textual format, explaining consumers' opinions on different aspects of products based on their own experience (Hussain and Merigó 2022). It offers fine-grained sentiment preferences of various facets of a single object that cannot be extracted from average ratings (Zhang et al. 2015). However, they are in a massive volume making it impossible for an average human reader to monitor and comprehend consumer feedback to find the right product that fits the user's preference. An automated sentiment analysis approach could be used to find what the previous customers have written about the features that the active user is looking for to overcome this issue.

Sentiment analysis uses Natural Language Possessing (NLP) and text analytics to extract attributes and components of the item to assess the polarity of consumers' comments (positive, negative, or neutral). Sentiment analysis is divided into three levels, document, sentence, and aspect. However, sentence and document level consider only one topic is expressed in the text, which is not always the case. For example, the sentence "I love all the shades of this eyeshadow palette although I think the pigmentation can be improved." However, it sounds positive, but we cannot evaluate the sentence to be entirely positive as the sentence is optimistic about the palette's shades but pessimistic about the pigmentation of the shades. Aspect based sentiment analysis can help to address the problem. The technique analyzes the user review by categorizing it by aspect and identifying the sentiment associated with them.

Sentiments associated with aspects of the product, unstructured data is converted to structured data, which can be used for qualitative and quantitative assessments.

Nevertheless, the content of the review is not the only variable that influences customers' purchase intention. Several studies have demonstrated how features such as review recency, quality, length, platform, and reviewer characteristics impact the consumer decision-making process (Jia and Lu 2018; Shah and Jha 2021).

The goal of the RS is to filter, prioritize, and effectively deliver personalized content to the user using techniques such as machine learning (Shoja and Tabrizi 2019). Many studies have found that recommender systems significantly affect buyer choice and lead to increased purchase volume. Different organizations use different algorithms to search through a vast amount of dynamically generated data to provide consumers, products that might interest them. However, the collaborative filtering technique is the most successful algorithm (Osman et al. 2019), which generates suggestions based on inter-user comparisons by locating other users who have seen or bought similar products to the user (Hosanagar and Lee 2015; Hussain et al. 2017a; Hussain et al. 2017b). While collaborative filtering is the most promising recommendation technique, its use in e-commerce has revealed well-known shortcomings, sparsity, and cold start (Chen et al. 2015). These problems are caused when customer ratings are insufficient in number to identify similarities in customer interest.

To overcome the sparsity problem, researchers have suggested using the valuable information from customer feedback to improve the performance of the current RS (Chen et al. 2015; Osman et al. 2019). They believe that the rich information embedded in the reviews can enhance the overall recommendation quality. Thus, having a more significant impact on the customer's decision-making process. Nonetheless, many studies have shown that the product's attribute (Utilitarian vs. Hedonic) moderates the impact of the recommender system (Lee and Hosanagar 2016).

By considering the importance of product attributes in the recommender systems, in this research, we will study the impact of RS developed using the output of aspect-based sentiment analysis on customer feedback and other characteristics of product reviews on purchase intentions. We also aim to investigate how the effect of user review-based recommender systems varies with different product types, such as utilitarian vs. hedonic.

2 Background and Relevant Work

In this section we will discuss the literature that is related to the framework. The section has been divided into seven sub-sections:

- Electronic word of mouth
- Sentiment analysis
- Characteristics of review
- Recommender systems
- Applications of recommender systems in IoT
- Utilitarian and hedonic product selection
- Recommender based on Sentiment Analysis and Review Characteristic.

A comparative analysis of all approaches are presented at the end of the section to analyze and compare all approaches based on different parameters. The discussion of each approaches are discussed as follows:

2.1 Electronic Word of Mouth

The emergence of social and eCommerce media has promoted consumers to share their experiences of specific products or services. These electronic words of mouth (eWOM) have become an integral part of eCommerce. They significantly impact the potential consumer's attitude and behaviour towards the product and other information on the website. Unlike traditional word of mouth (WOM), they are not restricted to the inner consumer circle but target a wider audience. Electronic WOM may be thought of as a social marketing and promotion tool that boosts retailers' knowledge-sharing practices at no expense.

Numerous studies have studied the importance of eWOM in eCommerce and its effect on purchase intention and sales. For instance, Hussain et al. in 2017 found that eWOM tends to reduce perceived risk. According to Jalilvand and Samiei (2012), e-WOM is one of the most potent factors affecting brand image and purchasing intention in the automobile industry. A study by Baber et al. in 2016 showed the effect of online word-of-mouth by a reliable and knowledgeable source on the buying intentions of the recipient is influenced by purchasing attitude. Similarly, another study in 2019 revealed that positive sentiment has a significant impact on sales. When investigating the impact on performance, sales of tablets vary with sentiments expressed in the review and their study (Li et al. 2019).

2.2 Sentiment Analysis

Sentiment Analysis (SA) uses Natural Language Processing technique to detect and extract sentiment from textual data (Hussain et al. 2022). Its application has expanded to nearly every possible domain, from consumer goods, utilities, hospitals, and financial services to social events and political campaigns. A system was proposed with an accuracy of 90% that utilized SA on product reviews to classify the comments into different categories, good or bad (Grabner et al. 2012).

Sentiment Analysis is studied at three levels: Document, Sentence, and Aspect. Document-level and sentence level determine that each document or sentence respectively expresses opinion for a single entity. However, this is not always the case. Aspect-based sentiment analysis techniques consist of two steps: aspect extraction and sentiment classification.

Many studies have previously highlighted that implementing aspect-based sentiment analysis (ABSA) on customer reviews is an effective technique to understand people's preferences about the product. Another study used SA to analyze movie reviews on discussion boards to identify different sentiments associated with movies, such as cast, story, director. (Thet et al. 2010).

2.3 Characteristics of Review

Different product review characteristics have a different impact on purchase intention. Features such as time of review, content related to product durability and quality (Zhang et al. 2011), reviewer's profile picture, characteristics, and reputation (Xu 2014) and valence of review, conflicting rating, and product-related attributes (Qiu et al. 2012) affect review credibility. Alkalbani et al. (Alkalbani and Hussain 2021; Alkalbani et al. 2019) proposed Harvesting as a Service (HaaS) crawler that intelligently extract real time consumer reviews from the internet and make it available in different format.

An experimental study by Qiu et al. in 2012 showed how positive reviews have a more significant impact on purchase decisions than negative reviews. The result of this study was confirmed by another experimental study by Jia and Lu in 2018. Thus, customer feedback characteristics and content can be used in a Recommender System (RS) to produce good quality recommendations (Chen et al. 2015; Osman et al. 2019).

2.4 Recommender System

A recommender system is a decision-making strategy; it alleviates information overload by suggesting a list of items that may interest a particular user. They are employed in various websites such as Netflix, YouTube, and Spotify, to provide video and music recommendations; Amazon and Alibaba to suggest a product to buy; Yahoo and Google news to help users decide what to read. In 2014, Hong and Pavlou found that simple acts of recommendation can reduce the perceived risk of buying online and increase purchase probability. Recommenders work by lowering product uncertainty and search cost barriers, as they might hinder purchase decisions Hussain et al. 2022. Literature by Gao et al. 2022 indicated, when a recommender proposes a product, it provides a social presence by saying 'people like you preferred X,' which positively impacts purchase intention.

Recommenders are built using various filtering techniques; each differs from identifying similarities between consumers and objects to identifying well-matched pairs (Osman et al. 2019). These techniques are divided into three categories collaborative filtering, content-based filtering, or hybrid filtering. The collaborative filtering approach is the most successful and commonly implemented. It suggests things by finding other people with similar tastes to the active user and relying on their recommendations. In contrast to collaborative filtering, content-based filtering uses similarities in features of the product to make recommendations. However, the effectiveness of both algorithms is limited when insufficient rating information is available to identify similarities in consumer interest or when a user has little historical data (Chen et al. 2015). The most common type elevates the strengths of collaborative and content-based filtering by merging the results obtained from both types of filtering and presenting a recommendation list. However, these algorithms fail to respond to the disparity of user context, continuously changing user preferences and delivering cross-domain suggestions (Hussain et al. 2018; Hussain et al. 2021a; Hussain et al. 2021b; Hussain et al. 2022).

2.5 Application of Recommender System in IoT

The Internet of Things (IoT) is a new paradigm that envisions a networked infrastructure that allows various devices to communicate with one another at any time and from any location. (Kiraly et al. 2019). It generates diverse artifacts such as services and applications making it difficult for consumers to identify the most relevant ones. Therefore, recommender systems are crucial components of IoT solutions (Cui et al. 2020; Kiraly et al. 2019), making finding relevant applications and services easier.

Examples of recommendations in IoT scenarios include installing apps, relevant data transfer to be deployed and hardware, and software components to complete specific tasks on a gateway. Some domain-specific examples in this context include food suggestions, customized shopping, health and animal monitoring, and smart homes (Kiraly et al. 2019). However, there are some challenges in using traditional recommendation systems in the IoT arena. The data in the IoT service system is enormous, complicated, and growing (Hussain and Sohaib 2019). Thus, it requires users to go through a lot of unnecessary information, leaving them exhausted and unsatisfied. Another issue is that users' interest varies with time. Traditional recommendation systems presume that users' interests remain constant, neglecting the intrinsic relationship between time and user choice. Therefore, it is important to design a personalized recommendation system that considers user preferences' real-time patterns and manages big data reliably and efficiently (Cui et al. 2020).

2.6 Utilitarian vs Hedonic

A product is often classified as utilitarian or hedonic. Hedonic products are fun, entertaining, and enjoyable, whereas utilitarian products are goal-oriented, helpful, functional, and essential. Furthermore, when looking for these items in an e-store, utilitarian products have quantitative characteristics such as memory capacity or screen resolution. In contrast, hedonic products have subjective attributes, such as fragrance or taste. As a result, when looking for a utilitarian product, the consumer is focused on the goal they hope to achieve with the product, so consumers are more concerned with the possibility of the product failing to meet the goal (Chiu et al. 2014). Hedonic goods, on the other hand, are bought solely for pleasure. Thus, the cost of getting the wrong hedonic product is less than the utilitarian product. Therefore, the increased perceived risk of not finding the right item, a buyer could compare more products suggested by the system to find the perfect utilitarian product. A study by Moon et al. (2017) suggested utilitarian and hedonic products have different influences on consumers' attitudes and purchase decisions. Thus, a recommender system needs to consider the type of product before making suggestions. Research by Park et al. (2011) explored those consumers tend to buy hedonic products when suggested to them in the same way they would buy when advised by people more like them.

2.7   Recommender Based on Sentiment Analysis and Review Characteristics

Sentiment Analysis can be used to detect sentiment from textual reviews with great accuracy (Raza et al. 2021a, 2021b, 2021). This technique can also convert the degree of negativity and positivity of preferences into a numerical rating to integrate with the filtering algorithm (Ricci et al. 2015; Hussain et al. 2020) (Raza et al. 2021). Kumar et al. in 2020, used SA of reviews on Twitter, movie metadata, and social graphs to suggest movies. They found out their proposed system recommended movies more precisely than other models. In another study, sentiment classification was performed on reviews to derive ratings. This rating was incorporated in item-based and user-based Collaborative Filtering algorithms to infer the User-Item Rating Matrix to enhance the working of the recommender (Zhang et al. 2013). Gao et al. (Gao et al. 2020) introduced an implicit knowledge using collaborative learning techniques for an optimal API recommendation in IoT environment. Rosa et al. (2015) proposed a framework for music suggestions for mobile devices, in which songs were recommended based on the user's mood. User's sentiments were extracted using SA of sentences posted on Social Networking Sites (SNS).

The suggested model demonstrated a 91% of customer satisfaction rate. There have been many pieces of research focused on how aspect-based sentiment analysis can improve the impact of the recommender system. A study showed recommendations that using ABSA on customer reviews performs better than traditional Collaborative algorithms (Zhang et al. 2015). In another study, Bauman et al. (2017) suggested a recommendation algorithm that used ABSA to make recommendations and suggest facets of the item to improve consumer's experience further. Osman et al. (2019) merged the numerical rating and rating gathered from ABSA of textual review to optimize the traditional Collaborative Filtering algorithm. However, very few efforts have been made to integrate review characteristics in the recommender system to make more valid and high-quality suggestions.

2.8 Comparative Analysis of Existing Approaches

Table 1 shows how each research is different from the other. From the comparative analysis, we found that none of the studies has studied the varying impact of the review-based recommender system on different product types, which is very important for the decision-making process. Moreover, none of the approaches has considered review characteristics in the decision-making process.

The comparative analysis of different approaches is presented in below table:

Table 1. Analysis of different previous studies

References	Aspect-based sentiment analysis	Review characteristics	Social data	Utilitarian VS hedonic	Recommendation provided
Bauman et al. (2017)	✓	✗	✓	✗	✓
Kumar et al. (2020)	✗	✗	✓	✗	✓
Zhang et al. (2013)	✗	✗	✗	✗	✓
Rosa et al. (2015)	✗	✗	✓	✗	✓
Zhang et al. (2015)	✓	✗	✗	✗	✓
Osman et al. (2019)	✓	✗	✗	✗	✓
Hussain et al. (2022)	✓	✗	✓	✗	✓
Thet et al. (2010)	✓	✗	✗	✗	✗

3 Proposed Approach

The study aims to incorporate aspect-based sentiment analysis (ABSA) of customer reviews and product characteristics in a recommender system. The study analyses the impact of review-based recommender systems on utilitarian and hedonic product purchase intention in an e-commerce setting.

The approach helps to improve the quality and validity of recommendations. Moreover, it has overcome problems like data sparsity and other issues highlighted earlier. However, to utilize customer's opinions and product characteristics in the context of the recommenders, it is important to translate user's textual preferences, not only in terms of negative and positive but to what extent they are pessimistic or an optimist. The proposed approach is comprised of the following steps, as presented in Fig. 1.

3.1 Extraction of Product Feature in Customer Reviews

The initial step in this process is to analyze the credibility of different product reviews on the social media website. This will help us to discard fake reviews by dishonest sellers and spammers and get more accurate product ratings. Reviews will be filtered out based on specified rules stated below.

– They have a lot of grammatical and spelling mistakes
– They are very short
– The same user has more than one review for the same product
– They were posted more than a year ago
– The reviews are not in English

After filtering the reviews, Aspect-based sentiment analysis will be performed using spaCy and TextBolb on the credible product reviews to extract product attributes from reviews. spaCy and TextBlob is a Python library for natural language processing used for sentiment analysis and text processing. The first goal in the extraction will be to split

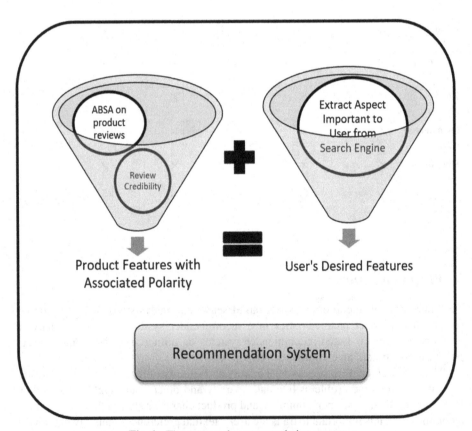

Fig. 1. The proposed recommendation system

sentences and extract product aspects and sentiment descriptions associated with them. Once this is done, we will classify them as positive or negative and associate a score.

3.2 Obtaining user Inputs Regarding Desired Features

User's preferred product features will be obtained by extracting the keywords that have been clearly specified by the user on the eCommerce's websites search engine.

3.3 Acquiring Matching Scores between Preferences and Reviews

The user will achieve a similarity score between a review and the desired attributes using a Natural Language Processing text analysis technique Word Embedding algorithm, word2vec and its pre-trained word vector.

3.4 Testing the Impact of the Review-Based Recommender on Hedonic and Utilitarian Products

Lastly, we will test this approach in an experimental study to explore its impact on different product attributes in the context of this study, Hedonic and Utilitarian. We will incorporate this recommender system in a functional eCommerce website simulation with Hedonic and Utilitarian types of products. And test what kind of product a user is most likely to put in a cart. We will also measure users' satisfaction with the recommendation provided to test the reliability of the recommender system proposed in this research.

This recommender framework will reduce issues associated with traditional models such as data sparsity and domain sensitivity and enhance suggestions' quality. The varying impact of this recommender approach will then be used to study its effect on Utilitarian and Hedonic product purchase decisions. This approach is novel as we will be studying the impact of the Review Based Recommender System on different product types (Utilitarian VS Hedonic).

4 Conclusion

The proposed study depicts how reviews on social media influence customers purchase decisions. Online retailers can leverage the result of this study to determine the most effective social media strategies for targeting and satisfying their target audiences. It enables them to optimize revenues on an e-commerce site. The research presented a novel approach integrating customer review information on social media and customer's interest in different aspects of the product gathered. The study analyzes keywords in the search engine in recommenders to enhance the suggestions compared to other traditional algorithms. This study also aids in determining which product types - hedonic or utilitarian- best serve a customer. The approach overcomes issues related to changing user preferences, changing data, lack of data, and domain sensitivity. In future, we will evaluate the approach in different complex nonlinear decision problems.

References

Alkalbani, A.M., Hussain, W.: Cloud service discovery method: a framework for automatic derivation of cloud marketplace and cloud intelligence to assist consumers in finding cloud services. Int. J. Commun. Syst. **34**(8), e4780 (2021). https://doi.org/10.1002/dac.4780

Alkalbani, A.M., Hussain, W., Kim, J.Y.: A centralised cloud services repository (CCSR) framework for optimal cloud service advertisement discovery from heterogenous web portals. IEEE Access **7**, 128213–128223 (2019)

Australia Post. Inside Australian Online Shopping, Australia, April 2021 (2021). https://auspost.com.au/content/dam/auspost_corp/media/documents/ecommerce-industry-report-2021.pdf

Baber, A., Thurasamy, R., Malik, M.I., Sadiq, B., Islam, S., Sajjad, M.: Online word-of-mouth antecedents, attitude and intention-to-purchase electronic products in Pakistan. Telematics Inform. **33**(2), 388–400 (2016). https://doi.org/10.1016/j.tele.2015.09.004

Bauman, K., Liu, B., Tuzhilin, A.: Aspect-based recommendations: recommending items with the most valuable aspects based on user reviews. In: Proceedings of KDD 2017, Halifax (2017). https://doi.org/10.1145/3097983.3098170

Chen, L., Chen, G., Wang, F.: Recommender systems based on user reviews: state of the art. User Model. User-Adap. Inter. **25**(2), 99–154 (2015). https://doi.org/10.1007/s11257-015-9155-5

Chiu, C.-M., Wang, E.T., Fang, Y.-H., Huang, H.-Y.: Understanding customers' repeat purchase intentions in B2C e-commerce: the roles of utilitarian value, hedonic value and perceived risk. Inf. Syst. J. **24**, 85–114 (2014). https://doi.org/10.1111/j.1365-2575.2012.00407.x

Cui, Z., Xu, X., Xue, F., Cai, X., Cao, Y., Zhang, W., Chen, J.: Personalized recommendation system based on collaborative filtering for IoT scenarios. IEEE Trans. Serv. Comput. **13**(4), 685–695 (2020)

Felfernig, A., Polat-Erdeniz, S., Uran, C., Reiterer, S., Atas, M., Tran, T.N.T., Dolui, K.: An overview of recommender systems in the internet of things. J. Intell. Inf. Syst. **52**(2), 285–309 (2019)

Gao, H., Huang, J., Tao, Y., Hussain, W., Huang, Y.: The joint method of triple attention and novel loss function for entity relation extraction in small data-driven computational social systems. IEEE Trans. Comput. Soc. Syst. (2022)

Gao, H.K., Jung, Y., Hussain, W., Iqbal, M., Duan, Y.: Intelligent Processing Practices and Tools for E-Commerce Data, Information, and Knowledge, Springer, Cham (2022). https://doi.org/10.1007/978-3-030-78303-7

Gao, H., Qin, X., Barroso, R.J.D., Hussain, W., Xu, Y., Yin, Y.: Collaborative learning-based industrial IoT API recommendation for software-defined devices: The implicit knowledge discovery perspective. IEEE Trans. Emerg. Top. Comput. Intell. (2020). https://doi.org/10.1109/TETCI.2020.3023155

Gräbner, D., Zanker, M., Fliedl, G., & Fuchs, M.: Classification of customer reviews based on sentiment analysis. In: Fuchs, M., Ricci, F., Cantoni, L. (eds.) Information and Communication Technologies in Tourism 2012, Springer, Vienna, pp. 460–470, January 2012, https://doi.org/10.1007/978-3-7091-1142-0_40

Hong, Y., Pavlou, P.A.: Product fit uncertainty in online markets: Nature, effects, and antecedents. Inf. Syst. Res. **25**(2), 328–344 (2014). https://doi.org/10.1287/isre.2014.0520

Hussain, S., Ahmed, W., Jafar, R.M.S., Rabnawaz, A., Jianzhou, Y.: eWOM source credibility, perceived risk and food product customer's information adoption. Comput. Hum. Behav. **66**, 96–102 (2017a). https://doi.org/10.1016/j.chb.2016.09.034

Hussain, W., Sohaib, O.: Analysing cloud QoS prediction approaches and its control parameters: considering overall accuracy and freshness of a dataset. IEEE Access **7**, 82649–82671 (2019). https://doi.org/10.1109/ACCESS.2019.2923706

Hussain, W., Hussain, F.K., Hussain, O.K., Damiani, E., Chang, E.: Formulating and managing viable SLAs in cloud computing from a small to medium service provider's viewpoint: a state-of-the-art review. Inf. Syst. **71**, 240–259 (2017b). https://doi.org/10.1016/j.is.2017.08.007

Hussain, W., Hussain, F.K., Hussain, O., Bagia, R., Chang, E.: Risk-based framework for SLA violation abatement from the cloud service provider's perspective. Comput. J. **61**(9), 1306–1322 (2018). https://doi.org/10.1093/comjnl/bxx118

Hussain, W., Merigó, J.M.: Centralised quality of experience and service framework using PROMETHEE-II for cloud provider selection. In: Gao, H., Kim, J.Y., Hussain, W., Iqbal, M., Duan, Y. (eds.) Intelligent Processing Practices and Tools for E-Commerce Data, Information, and Knowledge, pp. 79–94. Springer Publishing, Cham (2022)

Hussain, W., Merigó, J.M., Rabhi, F., Gao, H.: Aggregating fuzzy sentiments with customized QoS parameters for cloud provider selection using fuzzy best worst and fuzzy TOPSIS. In: León-Castro, E., Blanco-Mesa, F., Alfaro-García, V., Gil-Lafuente, A.M., Merigó, J.M., Kacprzyk, J. (eds.) Soft Computing and Fuzzy Methodologies in Innovation Management and Sustainability, LNCS, vol. 337, pp. 81–92. Springer, Cham (2022). https://doi.org/10.1007/978-3-030-96150-3_6

Hussain, W., Merigó, J.M., Raza, M.R.: Predictive intelligence using ANFIS-induced OWAWA for complex stock market prediction. Int. J. Intell. Syst. (2021a). https://doi.org/10.1002/int.22732

Hussain, W., Merigo, J.M., Gao, H., Alkalbani, A.M., Rabhi, F.: Integrated AHP-IOWA, POWA framework for ideal cloud provider selection and optimum resource management. IEEE Trans. Serv. Comput. **01**, 1–1 (2021b). https://doi.org/10.1109/TSC.2021.3124885

Hussain, W., Merigó, J.M., Raza, M.R., Gao, H.: A new QoS prediction model using hybrid IOWA-ANFIS with fuzzy c-means, subtractive clustering and grid partitioning. Inf. Sci. (2022). https://doi.org/10.1016/j.ins.2021.10.054

Hussain, W., Raza, M.R., Jan, M.A., Merigo, J.M., Gao, H.: Cloud risk management with OWA-LSTM predictive intelligence and fuzzy linguistic decision making. IEEE Trans. Fuzzy Syst (2022)

Hussain, W., Sohaib, O., Naderpour, M., Gao, H.: Cloud marginal resource allocation: a decision support model. Mob. Netw. Appl. **25**(4), 1418–1433 (2020). https://doi.org/10.1007/s11036-019-01457-7

Jalilvand, M.R., Samiei, N.: The effect of electronic word of mouth on brand image and purchase intention: an empirical study in the automobile industry in Iran. Market. Intell. Plan (2012). https://doi.org/10.1108/02634501211231946

Jha, A., Shah, S.: Disconfirmation effect on online review credibility: an experimental analysis. Decis. Support Syst. **145**, 113519 (2021). https://doi.org/10.1016/j.dss.2021.113519

Jia, Y., Lu, I.: Do consumers always follow "useful" reviews? The interaction effect of review valence and review usefulness on consumers' purchase decisions. JASIST **69**(11), 1304–1317 (2018). https://doi.org/10.1002/asi.24050

Kumar, S., De, K., Roy, P.P.: Movie recommendation system using sentiment analysis from microblogging data. IEEE Trans. Comput. Soc. Syst. **7**(4), 915–923 (2020). https://doi.org/10.1109/TCSS.2020.2993585

Lee, D., Hosanagar, K., Nair, H.: When do recommender systems work the best? The moderating effects of product attributes and consumer reviews on recommender performance. In: International World Wide Web Conference Committee (IW3C2), pp. 85–97 (2015). https://doi.org/10.1145/2872427.2882976

Li, S., Zhou, L., Li, Y.: Improving aspect extraction by augmenting a frequency-based method with web-based similarity measures. Inf. Process. Manage. **51**(1), 58–67 (2015). https://doi.org/10.1016/j.ipm.2014.08.005

Li, X., Wu, C., Mai, F.: The effect of online reviews on product sales: a joint sentiment-topic analysis. Inf. Manage. **56**(2), 172–184 (2019). https://doi.org/10.1016/j.im.2018.04.007

Liu, Q., Gao, Z., Liu, B., Zhang, Y.: Automated rule selection for aspect extraction in opinion mining. In: Twenty-Fourth International Joint Conference on Artificial Intelligence, pp. 1291–1297 (2015). https://www.ijcai.org/Proceedings/15/Papers/186.pdf

Moon, M.A., Khalid, M.J., Awan, H.M., Attiq, S., Rasool, H., Kiran, M.: Consumer's perceptions of website's utilitarian and hedonic attributes and online purchase intentions: a cognitive–affective attitude approach. Spanish J. Market.-ESIC **21**(2), 73–88 (2017). https://doi.org/10.1016/j.sjme.2017.07.001

Osman, N.A., Noah, S.A.M., Darwich, M.: Contextual sentiment-based recommender system to provide recommendation in the electronic products domain. Int. J. Mach. Learn. Comput. **9**(4), 425–431 (2019). https://doi.org/10.18178/ijmlc.2019.9.4.821

Park, D.H., Kim, H K., Choi, I.Y., Kim, J.K.: A literature review and classification of recommender systems on academic journals. J. Intell. Inf. Syst. **17**(1), 139–152 (2011). https://doi.org/10.13088/jiis.2011.17.1.139

Qiu, L., Pang, J., Lim, K.H.: Effects of conflicting aggregated rating on eWOM review credibility and diagnosticity: the moderating role of review valence. Decis. Support Syst. **54**(1), 631–643 (2012). https://doi.org/10.1016/j.dss.2012.08.020

Raza, M R., Hussain, W., Merigó, J.M.: cloud sentiment accuracy comparison using RNN, LSTM and GRU. In: 2021 Innovations in Intelligent Systems and Applications Conference (ASYU) (2021a)

Raza, M.R., Hussain, W., Merigó, J.M.: *Long* short-term memory-based sentiment classification of cloud dataset. In: 2021 Innovations in Intelligent Systems and Applications Conference (ASYU) (2021b)

Raza, M.R., Hussain, W., Tanyıldızı, E., Varol, A.: Sentiment analysis using deep learning in cloud. In: 9th International Symposium on Digital Forensics and Security (ISDFS), Elazig, Turkey (2021)

Raza, M.R., Varol, A., Hussain, W.: Blockchain-based IoT: An Overview. In: 2021 9th International Symposium on Digital Forensics and Security (ISDFS) (2021)

Ricci, F., Rokach, L., Shapira, B.: Recommender systems: introduction and challenges. In: Ricci, F., Rokach, L., Shapira, B. (eds.) Recommender Systems Handbook, pp. 1–34. Springer, Boston (2015). https://doi.org/10.1007/978-1-4899-7637-6_1

Rosa, R.L., Rodriguez, D.Z., Bressan, G.: Music recommendation system based on user's sentiments extracted from social networks. IEEE Trans. Consum. Electron. **61**(3), 359–367 (2015). https://doi.org/10.1109/TCE.2015.7298296

Shoja, B., Tabrizi, N.: Customer reviews analysis with deep neural networks for e-commerce recommender systems. IEEE Access. 1 (2019). https://doi.org/10.1109/ACCESS.2019.2937518.

Thet, T.T., Na, J.C., Khoo, C.S.: Aspect-based sentiment analysis of movie reviews on discussion boards. J. Inf. Sci. **36**(6), 823–848 (2010). https://doi.org/10.1177/0165551510388123

Xu, Q.: Should I trust him? The effects of reviewer profile characteristics on eWOM credibility. Comput. Hum. Behav. **33**, 136–144 (2014). https://doi.org/10.1016/j.chb.2014.01.027

Zhang, K., Cheng, Y., Liao, W.K., Choudhary, A.: Mining millions of reviews: a technique to rank products based on importance of reviews. In Proceedings of the 13th International Conference on Electronic Commerce, pp. 1–8, August 2011. https://doi.org/10.1145/2378104.2378116

Zhang, W., Ding, G., Chen, L., Li, C., Zhang, C.: Generating virtual ratings from Chinese reviews to augment online recommendations. ACM Trans. Intell. Syst. Technol. (TIST) **4**(1), 1–17 (2013). https://doi.org/10.1145/2414425.2414434

Zhang, Y., Liu, R., Li, A.: A novel approach to recommender system based on aspect-level sentiment analysis. In 2015 4th National Conference on Electrical, Electronics and Computer Engineering, pp. 1453–1458. Atlantis Press, December 2015. https://doi.org/10.2991/nceece-15.2016.259

IoT-Based Data Driven Prediction of Offshore Wind Power in a Short-Term Interval Span

Muhammad Khalid[1]([⊠]), Mir Bilal Khan[2], Imam Dad[3], and Shayhaq Fateh[4]

[1] Jacobs University Bremen, Campus Ring 1, 28759 Bremen, Germany
Khalid.csd.uob@gmail.com
[2] University of Hertfordshire Collage Lane, Hatfield AL10 9AB, UK
[3] University of Balochistan, Saryab Road, Quetta 87300, Pakistan
[4] University of Gwadar Balochistan, Gwadar, Pakistan

Abstract. Wind energy is becoming one of the most important suppliers of renewable energy but due to its reliance on weather conditions it is highly inconsistent and its integration into electricity grids is a challenge. In this research we present a comparative analysis of the performance of several prominent data mining techniques in prediction of wind energy generation. Data from the Big Data Challenge Bremen 2018 was used for short term forecasting. Of basic models, a decision tree produced the best performing model. It performed marginally better than SGD, OLS, LASSO and Bayesian ridge regression. Whereas, SVM, nearest neighbor and Gaussian NB performed very poorly. A further analysis using ensemble methods was performed where a Gradient Boosting was the best model. Further improvements of the IoT model are performed and limitations of this are discussed in detail.

Keywords: Big data · Wind power · SGD · SVM

1 Introduction

Wind energy is a major contributor towards renewable energy. Europe is a leader in producing wind power, lowering its bids on wind power more and more. This decrease comes from installing offshore wind parks, which can produce more with lower costs. The McKinsey institute is calling offshore wind even "the next big thing". In their research it is stated that European countries offer record low bids starting with The Netherlands who offered 54.50 euro per megawatt-hour, which was then lowered by the Danish by 49.90 euro per megawatt-hour. The bid then further decreased, beyond expectations, in the 2017 German action (de Pee et al. 2017). Other parts of the world have also noticed this and have made plans accordingly, such as the five-year offshore plan of China. Similar plans are made by Korea, Poland, Taiwan and the United States (de Pee et al. 2017).

Although offshore wind energy has many advantages, such as it can be located near densely populated coastlines, it has its challenges too. Besides being reliable on many

W. Hussain and M. A. Jan (Eds.): IoTaaS 2021, LNICST 421, pp. 233–243, 2022.
https://doi.org/10.1007/978-3-030-95987-6_17

factors outside the industry, like interest rates and steel prices, the most important factor is stabilizing the grid. Wind energy is very irregular since it relies heavily on weather conditions, therefore integration into the electricity grid becomes a challenge (de Pee et al. 2017).

Research in forecasting offshore wind energy is a relative new area but with the ever-increasing use of renewable energy it is becoming more important. Several different methods have been used for forecasting wind power in wind parks. In the past mostly physics-based modeling has been used to understand the nature of forecasting wind power. However, since many data is being produced about the turbines and weather conditions, a data driven approach could predict wind energy more precisely. Research is done in different time frames using different models. Models such as ARMA (Hussain et al. 2021) make no use of data that could contribute to the wind power but focus on a moving average, such a model was used in (Zhao et al. 2016). A common approach however is using meteorological data with a time series. In (Soman et al. 2010) a numeric weather prediction (NWP) model is compared to statistical approaches, artificial neural network (ANN) and also a combination of these. The results show that different methods work better in different time frames and therefore one should test several methods on data to find a specific fit for the specific time resolution (Hussain et al. 2015; Hussain et al. 2018; Hussain and Sohaib 2019). Landberg (Landberg 1999) used a different meterological model as NWP, a high resolution limited area model together with a wind atlas analysis and application approach, to predict up to 36 h ahead. Although these models make good predictions, neural networks outperform these in general. Data driven research using neural networks has therefore become very popular, for example in (Mohandes et al. 1998) and long term prediction in (Barbounis et al. 2006). Other popular models include fuzzy models that have proven to be rather useful in very short-term prediction. Damousis et al. (Damousis et al. 2004) use an improved fuzzy model for prediction between 0.5 and 2 h ahead. An example of more complex models is by Zhao et al. (Zhao et al. 2016) a extreme learning machine was used together with backward time series analysis to forecast ultra-short-term wind power of a time frame of up to 6 h. In some of the recent approaches Hussain et al. (Hussain et al. 2021; Hussain et al. 2021; Hussain et al. 2022) proposed a new prediction model by introducing ordered weighted averaging (OWA) operator in prediction model (Hussain et al. 2021a; Hussain et al. 2021b). The proposed approach has the capability to handle complex nonlinear prediction (Hussain et al. 2022).

All the models discussed are considered to be rather complex. This is also a representation of the research available today. However, using more simple models would increase insights that could be taken from the analysis. Also, research done on specifically offshore wind parks is sparse.

In this research data from a offshore wind park is used in order to predict short term wind energy. This research is done by competing in the competition "Big Data Challenge Bremen 2018" made available by the University of Bremen (Ciodaro et al. 2019). This challenge lasted the entire month of March 2018 and one could hand in proposed solutions 15 times. In the following sections the data and model will be described, then the results will be presented followed by a extensive discussion.

2 Model and Data

In this section the data used will be described as well as the preprocessing steps and the set up for training and finding the best model. All tasks were conducted using the Python 3 environment and making use of its data mining packages numpy, pandas, and Scikit learn.

2.1 Description of Dataset

The data used for predicting wind power was obtained from the Big Data Challenge Bremen (Ciodaro et al. 2019). This data included a training set with the power included and a testing set without the power. The goal was therefore to predict the wind power of the test set. The dimensions of the training data are (52508, 19) and the dimensions of the testing set are (17668, 19), which corresponds roughly to 75% training data and 25% testing data. This data is time series and the training set was 15 minutely data of January 2016 till June 2017, the test set had the remaining months of 2017.

The variables that are provided in the dataset are several wind measurements, installed capacity and an interpolation indicator. The target variable wind power was measured every 15 min and was also expected to be predicted in this time interval. However, the wind measurements were only hourly, and to determine the missing values for every 15 min a linear interpolation was already performed. The variable "Interpolation" distinguishes the "real" values from the interpolated ones, having a 0 for every real value. All provided variables are shown in Table 1 with a description.

Table 1. Features with their description

Feature	Description
Datum	Start date of a 15 min interval (YYYY-MM-DD hh:mm:ss) in local time ME(S)Z
Windgeschwindigkeit 48 M, Windgeschwindigkeit 100 M, Windgeschwindigkeit 152 M	The wind speed at heights: 48 m, 100 m and 152 m (measured in m/s)
Windgeschwindigkeit 100 MP10, Windgeschwindigkeit 100 MP90	Probabilistic wind speeds at 100 m (percentile 10–90) in the 15-min section (measured in m/s)
Interpoliert	The wind measurements are only available for the full hours and were therefore interpolated for the 15-min intervals. This field identifies such interpolated values
Verfügbare Kapazität	The maximum possible power of the wind farm at the current time, measured in kW
Output	The produced wind energy (measured in kWh/h)

2.2 Preprocessing

The data does not require a big amount of preprocessing since there are no missing values and all variables (except interpolation) are numerical. The preprocessing that was performed included feature scaling, making sure that big values are not necessarily more important than small ones. This was necessary because for example the variable of installed capacity has very big values compared to the other variables. Further, since the data was linearly interpolated, a cubic interpolation was performed. The result of using linear interpolation is shown in Fig. 1, left the original data of Windgeschwindigkeit48M and on the right a black-dotted line of the linear interpolation. To make the effect of interpolation clearer, Fig. 2 shows Windgeschwindigkeit48M zoomed in for the first 10 values. The left figure shows the linear interpolation and the right the cubic interpolation. From these figures it is not clear whether cubic interpolation will have a big effect on the prediction of the wind power. The results of using this will be shown in the next section.

Since the date variable as it is, is not usable in a regression, new features were made. From this date variable, the following new features were extracted: hour number (indicating which hour of the day it is), day number (Indicating which day of the year it is), week number (indicating which week of the year it is) and month number (indicating which month of the year it is).

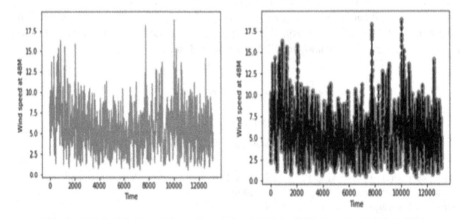

Fig. 1. Original (left) and linear interpolated (right) of Windgeschwindigkeit48M

2.3 Process of Modeling

The next step is using the data to predict the wind power of the test dataset. Since the provided test set does not have the target variable of wind power, a extra test set is created. A new training and test set were obtained by splitting the provided training dataset into a separate training and test set, according to the dimensions of the original split that is 75% training and 25% testing. These test and training sets were made keeping in mind that the data is time series and therefore no random sampling was involved. The method making a new test and training set was used because there was a limited number of submissions

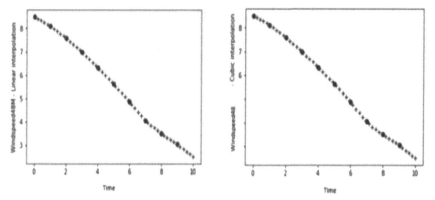

Fig. 2. First ten values of Windgeschwindigkeit48M using linear (left) and cubic (right)

for the competition and with this it was easier to see directly what models were working better. The process of finding the right model was done by simply applying several basic models to the data and then improving the model that turned out to be best.

3   Results

In this section the results of finding the best classifier will be shown. The results of using (and not using) interpolation, outlier removal, different loss functions and tuning parameters will be shown.

3.1   Finding the Model

First of all, the data was applied to a number of "basic" classifiers, in order to have an idea of the data and find what kind of classifier would work best. Table 2 shows these results, where "score" is the score provided by scikit learn and corresponds to R2, where 1 is the best value. From Table 2 it can be seen that a Decision tree works best in this case, it has a score of 0.7768. This means that a Decision tree model explains about 77.7% variability of the data around the mean.

In order to improve this score, the data was applied to several ensemble regressors that are mostly based on decision trees and would therefore improve the result. Table 3 shows that this is indeed the case, all ensemble methods improve the simple decision tree model by roughly 10%. Although the scores lie very close, Gradient Boosting (GBM) is chosen as the best classifier with a score of 0.8730. Meaning that the explained variability of the data increased by 9.62%, from decision tree to GBM.

3.2   Improving the Model

With regard to further improving the model, the parameters need to be tuned. The tuning is done by a so called GridSearchCV using cross validation. Before the tuning starts, it was found that using a loss function of "huber" gives better results than the default

Table 2. Results of applying different basic regressors

Regressor	Score
Decision tree	0.7768
SGD	0.7564
Baysian ridge	0.7525
OLS	0.7439
Lasso	0.7689
SVM	0.0468
Nearest neighbour centroid	0.0002
GaussianNB	0.0026

Table 3. Results of applying different ensemble regressors

Regressor	Score
Random forrest	0.8684
Extra Treesregressor	0.8711
Adaboost	0.8676
Bagging	0.8680
GBM	0.8730

used in scikit learn, which was least squares regression. Using this the score improved by 1.71% and was used in all further improvements.

As mentioned before the tuning was done by using a GridSearchCV. The cross validation in such a grid search was done by TimeSeriesSplit provided by scikit learn. This method is especially for time series data, such that samples are made with regards to the time series. Using a random state, the scores of the model without tuning and with tuning can be seen in Table 4. This table indicates that tuning the parameters increases the model score slightly by almost 1%, also one can observe that the mean increases and the standard deviation decreases indicating that the model improves.

The resulting model from the grid search has the following parameters: maximum depth of 5, minimal samples split of 700, minimal samples leaf of 60, subsample 0.75 and maximum number of features 9. Further decreasing the learning rate and increasing number of features does not improve the model any more. Initially the optimal number of features was 50, but the best result was found to be 100 with a learning rate of 0.05. The exact meaning of all of these parameters will not be discussed here, but can be found in the documentation of Scikit learn.

In order to further improve the results, cubic interpolation was applied to the data. Originally, a linear interpolation was used but this could indicate that not all data was correct. The results of this are also shown in Table 4. The importance of all features

Table 4. Results of tuning parameters, showing R^2 score and cross validation scores for linear and cubic interpolation

Models	R2	CV: Mean	CV: std	CV: Min	CV: Max
No tuning	0.8890	0.8567	0.0155	0.8406	0.8717
With Tuning	0.8899	0.8576	0.0147	0.8429	0.8723
With cubic interpolation					
No tuning	0.8893	0.8563	0.0148	0.8415	0.8711
With tuning	0.8847	0.8562	0.0137	0.8425	0.8687

according to this grid search was also plotted in Fig. 3 for linear interpolation and in Fig. 4 for cubic interpolation. The most interesting from these graphs is that the importance changes slightly with different interpolation, indicating that these models are actually different. Looking however back into the results in Table 4: Although the no-tuning model of cubic interpolation is slightly better than the no-tuning linear interpolation, it shows that linear interpolation is after all still the best option since tuning really improves the model.

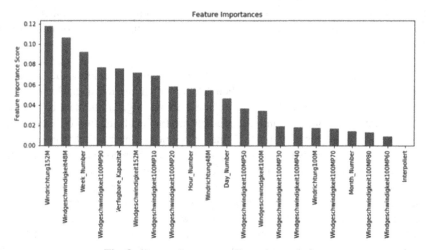

Fig. 3. Feature Importance linear interpolation

In order to eliminate effects of overfitting it was decided to test all of these models by handing them in on the challenge website. The result was that all the tuning and cubic interpolation actually decreased the performance of the model on the challenge data, which was not expected. The final technique applied to improve the score was removing outliers. However, removing outliers did not improve the score and also not the challenge score. Therefore, the final model that gave the best result on the test data for the challenge was a "simple" Gradient Boosting Regressor with Huber loss. In the next section these results will be discussed in more detail.

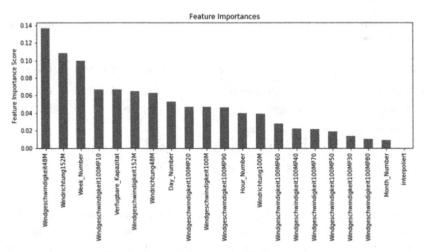

Fig. 4. Feature Importance cubic interpolation

4 Discussion

The idea behind a challenge such as this is not only to arrive at the best results, but to understand why certain methods seem to work significantly better than others. In this context, there were certain interesting observations made in the course of this project. They are as follows:

1. Conventionally, interpolation and outlier removal are considered the important approaches to take on immediately when dealing with numerical data. However, here this seems to be rather tricky. As it is shown above (Fig. 2), the data is generated through interpolation itself and the intervals are too small for further interpolation to make any significant difference. Hence, attempting linear or cubic interpolation did not seem to have any remarkable increase in model performance. Further, outlier removal is usually irrelevant to time series data, as every prediction is dependent on the data points that came before. Therefore, there are no outliers as such, and yet again, another conventionally popular approach seemed to be quite useless. The idea behind attempting outlier removal, however, was to prevent overfitting.
2. Another interesting observation has been that using Huber loss function instead of squared error loss seems to improve the model. A possible explanation for this points to the first observation again; due to lack of outliers Huber loss function works very effectively in comparison to a mean- squared loss.
3. The observation that may take one for surprise is the varied behavior of tuning parameters. In the model devised from the training data, tuning seemed to work rather effectively, prompting its use on the test data. However, due to overfitting, it had quite the reverse effect on the test data.
4. The final observation is that when linear and cubic interpolation was applied on the nine final features, (Fig. 3 and Fig. 4), it did seem make a difference considering that it caused certain features to change. However, the difference did not seem to improve model performance much.

The challenges faced in this project seemed to be rather different from conventional challenges that one faces while handling data. Pre-processing data to eliminate irrelevant information and handle missing values is usually a rather tricky and complex part of data analysis. However, the dataset provided for this project could be termed rather'clean'. Moreover, conventional methods seemed to adversely effect the results, which made the modeling rather tricky. Therefore, it must be considered that despite some methods churning out excellent results for some datasets, uninformed use of such methods may prove detrimental to model performance.

5 Conclusion

Due to limited time and a spirit of competition, only a number of methods were used. However, there may be more scope of improvement given that numerical, time-series data has always been very popular in research. Some methods that are used for such datasets have been discussed in this section.

Several classifiers such as Naive Bayes and Support Vector machines have enjoyed a lot of popularity in the field. Classifiers such as Naive Bayes have an advantage here as they may be straightforwardly extended into a semi-supervised learning algorithm, while SVM needs to be altered to transductive SVMs (Joachims 1999) in order to be fed into such an algorithm. There is remarkable research going on in the field of active learning (Hosein 2018) that also allows us to do so. The main idea behind active learning is that is a learning algorithm may choose the data it wants to learn from, it may perform better with conventional methods with substantially less data for training. Multiple stochastic and machine learning prediction methods [13–14] are applied to predict the behavior of the dataset. The approaches alert the service provider in case of any violation to mitigate the risk of violation and to take immediate remedial action.

The data handled in this project is numerical by large. Hence, without delving into assumptions and hypotheses, it may be simply pointed out that Decision Tree and SGD appear to work best for the model, in comparison to other basic regressors. Decision Trees have been considered somewhat reliable, its big advantage being the ability to find odd interactions. To use a simple example to explain this, in the prediction of voting behavior, if income only matters for people who are highly educated, trees can find that. In a linear regression, all interactions are made visible, which may turn out to be quite resource-consuming for large data sets; even with four variables and two-way interactions, there are six possible interactions, all of which are not mostly relevant.

Based on the type of data is provided, conventional validation or cross-validation may be applied. Conventional validation primarily involves partitioning the data set into two sets of seventy percent for training and thirty percent for test. This works with reliable accuracy when the data set is considerably large. However, when the data set in comparably smaller, conventional validation may not be very helpful. In recent studies, cross-validation has been proven to perform far better for data sets with poorly populated values. The basic idea is to not use the entire data set while training the learner, some of the data is removed before the training begins. After the learner has been trained, the data that was'left out' can be used to test the performance of the devised learner. However, it is interesting to note that cross-validation would be rather futile for this study as the dataset is time-series data, which cannot be sampled randomly. This, however, is the broad explanation for a whole class of model evaluation methods called cross-validation (Schneider 1997); the details, however, is beyond the scope of this paper.

An interesting approach to analyzing this data would be to further further interpolate between the intervals and generate more data. Given the time, it would be interesting the observe if the new model would be any different from the given model. The quality of interpolation, however, may be measured from two different viewpoints; prediction and characterization (Caruso 1999). Prediction implies that good-quality interpolation is when prediction error of an unknown point is minimized. Characterization states that the surface that results from good interpolation must, in most ways, resemble the original surface. However, it is not necessarily a trade-off.

Logically, the next approach would be to analyze the time-series data for trends; in this case, seasonal, etc. Autocorrelation and partial autocorrelation seem to be rather popular methods of doing so. Autocorrelation, sometimes known as 'serial correlation', is the correlation of a time series with its own past and future values. This helps identify patterns in long term data. The given dataset would be particularly relevant for using such methods as the data is generated in short intervals, over a long period of time.

Another possible approach would be to derive the features using Principal Component Analysis instead of using 'real' features. PCA is essentially a dimension-reduction tool that is used to reduce a large set of data to a significantly smaller set, while preserving the valuable information. This method may prove rather efficient when handling 'big' data.

Using neural networks and machine learning also seems like obvious ways of improving a given model. Given the dataset, a method that should work efficiently is Multilater Perceptron. An MLP can be viewed as a logistic regression classifier where, at first, the input is transformed using a learned non-linear transformation. This transformation projects the input data into a space where it becomes linearly separable, while this intermediate layer is referred to as a hidden layer. A single hidden layer is sufficient to make MLPs a universal approximator. However, there are substantial benefits to using many such hidden layers, i.e., the very premise of deep learning (Raza et al. 2021); this however, is largely beyond the scope of this paper.

Any, or a combination, of the above-mentioned approaches could further improve the performance of the model. With the increasing use of renewable energy (and therefore the demand of understanding such energies) and the many possibilities to further increase a forecasting model, there is a high motivation and potential for future research in this area.

References

de Pee, A., Küster, F., Schlosser, A.: Winds of change? Why offshore wind might be the next big thing (2017)

Barbounis, T.G., Theocharis, J.B., Alexiadis, M.C., Dokopoulos, P.S.: Long-term wind speed and power forecasting using local recurrent neural network models. IEEE Trans. Energy Convers. **21**, 273–284 (2006). https://doi.org/10.1109/TEC.2005.847954

Caruso, C.: Interpolation methods comparison. Comput. Math. Appl. **35**(12), 109–126 (1999)

Ciodaro, G., Cosin, D., Florent, R.: Project report bremen big data challenge-edition 2019 (2019)

Damousis, I.G., Alexiadis, M.C., Theocharis, J.B., Dokopoulos, P.S.: A fuzzy model for wind speed prediction and power generation in wind parks using spatial correlation. IEEE Trans. Energy Convers. **19**, 352–361 (2004). https://doi.org/10.1109/TEC.2003.821865

Hussain, W., Alkalbani, A.M., Gao, H.: Forecasting with machine learning techniques. Forecasting **3**(4), 868-869 (2021)

Hussain, W., Gao, H., Raza, M.R., Rabhi, F.A., Merigo, J.M.: Assessing cloud QoS predictions using OWA in neural network methods. Neural Comput. Appl., 1–18 (2022)

Hussain, W., Hussain, F.K., Hussain, O.K.: Towards soft computing approaches for formulating viable service level agreements in cloud. In: Arik, S., Huang, T., Lai, W.K., Liu, Q. (eds.) ICONIP 2015. LNCS, vol. 9492, pp. 639–646. Springer, Cham (2015). https://doi.org/10.1007/978-3-319-26561-2_75

Hussain, W., Hussain, F.K., Saberi, M., Hussain, O.K., Chang, E.: Comparing time series with machine learning-based prediction approaches for violation management in cloud SLAs. Futur. Gener. Comput. Syst. **89**, 464–477 (2018)

Hussain, W., Merigo, J.M., Gao, H., Alkalbani, A.M., Rabhi, F.A.: Integrated AHP-IOWA, POWA framework for ideal cloud provider selection and optimum resource management. IEEE Trans. Serv. Comput. (2021a). https://doi.org/10.1109/TSC.2021a.3124885

Hussain, W., Merigó, J. M., Raza, M.R.: Predictive intelligence using ANFIS-induced OWAWA for complex stock market prediction. Int. J. Intell. Syst. (2021b). https://doi.org/10.1002/int.22732

Hussain, W., Merigó, J.M., Raza, M.R., Gao, H.: A new QoS prediction model using hybrid IOWA-ANFIS with fuzzy c-means, subtractive clustering and grid partitioning. Inf. Sci. **584**, 280–300 (2022)

Hussain, W., Sohaib, O.: Analysing cloud QoS prediction approaches and its control parameters: considering overall accuracy and freshness of a dataset. IEEE Access **7**, 82649–82671 (2019). https://doi.org/10.1109/ACCESS.2019.2923706

Schneider, J.: Cross validation (1997)

Landberg, L.: Short-term prediction of the power production from wind farms. J. Wind Eng. Ind. Aerodyn. **80**, 207–220 (1999). https://doi.org/10.1016/S0167-6105(98)00192-5

Mohandes, M.A., Rehman, S., Halawani, T.O.: A neural networks approach for wind speed prediction. Renew. Energy **13**, 345–354 (1998). https://doi.org/10.1016/S0960-1481(98)00001-9

Hosein, S.: Active learning: Curious AI algorithms (2018)

Raza, M.R., Hussain, W., Merigó, J.M.: Cloud sentiment accuracy comparison using RNN, LSTM and GRU. In: 2021 Innovations in Intelligent Systems and Applications Conference (ASYU) (2021)

Soman, S.S., Zareipour, H., Malik, O., Mandal, P.: A review of wind power and wind speed forecasting methods with different time horizons. In: North American Power Symposium 2010, Arlington, TX, USA, pp. 1–8. IEEE (2010)

Joachims, T.: Transductive inference for text classification using support vector machines (1999)

Zhao, Y., Ye, L., Li, Z., Song, X., Lang, Y., Su, J.: A novel bidirectional mechanism based on time series model for wind power forecasting. Appl. Energy **177**, 793–803 (2016). https://doi.org/10.1016/j.apenergy.2016.03.096

Author Index

Printed in the United States
by Baker & Taylor Publisher Services